OFF YOUR ROCKER

ON YOUR ROCKER

OFF YOUR ROCKER

For Mature Travelers on a Budget

NONI GOVE

PARTRIDGE
A Penguin Random House Company

To order additional copies of this book, contact
Toll Free 800 101 2657 (Singapore)
Toll Free 1 800 81 7340 (Malaysia)
orders.singapore@partridgepublishing.com

www.partridgepublishing.com/singapore

CONTENTS

How It Began.. 11

First-time Travellers... 16

What to Take and What to Leave Behind............................. 19

Australia's Most Adventurous Senior 23

Fitness First... 25

General Guidelines... 28

First Big Trip.. 32

Affordability 36

Early Arrival in Tunisia... 39

Solo in India 44

Jumping Out of Your Comfort Zone................................... 57

Joys of Calcutta 60

Meeting the Locals.. 65

Happy New Year Thailand... 67

Energise 75

Horses of Hortabagy Hungary... 78

Buffalo Horn Massage Malaysia.. 81

Koh Samet Thailand...84

Journal Your Journey 92

Lost On a Chinese Misty Mountain 94

De-stress the Gentle Way 96

Skinny-dipping in Canada 98

Keeping Healthy 101

Beautiful Bhutan 104

Hawaii Hostel: *The People You Meet* 107

Gondola or Gandora Morocco 109

Solo Travel 121

Lessons in Tibet 125

Coping with Doubters 129

Mountain Village Life, South Korea 131

Medicine, Supplements and Food 140

Rudi's Pub, New York 142

Talk in Tunis 145

Women on Their Own 146

Komodos and Kuta Indonesia 149

Hurting Hotel Malaysia 153

Loneliness – Homesickness 156

Sailing the Adriatic Croatia 158

Trip Home Birch Lake 162

Letting Go of the Fear Factor 165

Teaching English in Thailand 168

Farming Family Bhutan 174

Hammams 177

Buddhist Pilgrimage.. 179

Hazards.. 186

The Gorged Tiger China.. 189

Five Days with Madonna 191

Birdsville Rodeo Australia.. 197

Roughing it in Burma.. 199

Funeral Parlour Café...202

My Tibetan Twins...204

Peace and Love Paris 208

Laughter.. 210

Penang and Langkawi Malaysia 213

First Time in Hawaii.. 219

Repairs on the Run All Over..................................... 221

Massage Around the World.......................................224

Noni's 10 Best Massages Around the World................228

Ranati a Child of India..230

Travelling Without the Language............................... 231

Bus to Wat Tam Wua...234

Local Transport..236

Yunnan China...240

In a Four Berther on the Pacific Ocean......................246

Cruising...248

Horses Races Saigon..250

Chasing Hobbies...253

Koh Samet Capers...256

Calgary Stampede Canada 259

Mang Madly British Thailand 262

Tearaway Mule Tigers Nest Bhutan 264

Floods and Fun in Southern Thailand 267

Hekou China 270

Mystery Tour Canada 273

Thai Massage Course Thailand 276

Anecdotes 2005 China 279

Quick Promotion 282

Mighty Mice India 285

Trail Riding Whistler 287

Trekking in Nepal 289

Attitude and Dreams 293

Trojan Horses Dali China 295

Sacred Stubborn Bovine India 298

Wild Life in Canada 300

Hello Dogs Thailand 303

Hawaiian Fish Tail USA: Fish *tail* with a difference. 305

Family Travel 306

Travelling With Disabilities: *Set small and gentle goals
and meet them.* Julia Cameron 310

T-shirt Seller's Home Indonesia 312

Forest Monastery Mae Hong Son 315

DEDICATION

This book is dedicated to Betsy Broughton who was, as a small child, one of four survivors of the Boyd Incident in New Zealand in 1809, in which her mother was killed. After a perilous journey, via Peru she arrived back in Australia two years later. At the age of 17 she married my great-great- grandfather Charles Throsby and they had 17 children. Her spirit lives on in me, she is my inspiration. Her adventures were thrust upon her, mine have been mostly by choice.

HOW IT BEGAN

I wrote my book with the intention of travellers taking it overseas for the advice as well as reading the tales of some of my experiences. I find it is great to have something to read about the countries you are visiting. I believe there are many books out there about people's lives and how they began to travel, what inspired them. This is my story, so far.

I started to travel at the age of fifty-one, a backpacking trip for six months, taking in eighteen countries from UK, Europe, Scandinavia and Asia. This was my first real adventure. I had been on a few cruises around the Pacific Islands in my forties, which I enjoyed very much, but they were hardly adventures in the true sense of the word. I had done a Remedial Massage Course at fifty and had my own busy clinic up and running. I was divorced, my two children had their own lives to live and I had been well and truly bitten by the travel bug. I was earning a good living and I could afford to take off, leaving a locum to look after my business. It was really a form of escape. Getting away from problems at the time and being at the beck and call of my clients.

Running a massage clinic from home had many advantages. I didn't have to get in a car or bus to get to work, there was no rent to pay for rooms or an office. In my breaks I could hang out the washing, do the ironing, sweep the floor, clean the bathroom, cook a meal, weed the garden and mow the lawn. All those mundane chores that come with being a homeowner.

The down side was clients knew I would be home on a Sunday night and they could catch up with me to massage their migraine or aches and pains away. Sometimes after I had played competition tennis all day, I would succumb to massage a painful shoulder or tennis elbow of one of the players. Knowing that my appointment book was full, sometimes for three weeks in advance, I felt I had to see them outside my normal working hours. So in a way my travel was an escape, mind you it was one I loved. I used to say the only way I can have a break is to leave the country. I looked at it not so much as a holiday but a rewarding life experience.

My locums did a very good job while I was away and kept the clinic running but massage is such a personal thing that some clients would wait until I came back, wanting me and only me. While this is great for the ego, it also was taking its toll on me physically and energetically. I was a one-woman band. Massage Therapist and teacher, practice manager, receptionist, secretary, bookkeeper, housekeeper, washerwoman, handy-woman and gardener.

When travelling, I could totally cut off from what was happening at home or in my clinic. I seldom phoned home to check if everything was fine, it always was. I sent postcards and letters but I was rarely contactable as my mode of travel was very seldom structured as far as destination or accommodation was concerned. This was before the days of my learning to send emails. That has now made my travel tales and whereabouts instant to family and friends all over the world.

My travels are more than site seeing. People are astounded to hear I have been to India several times and have not seen the Taj Mahal. I once met a man who had been to Egypt and hadn't seen the pyramids. That made me feel better. I have been on trips to

teach English conversation and pronunciation to a class of forty-two
Novice Buddhist Monks in a Monastery in Thailand for six weeks.
I learned more than I taught in this situation. I slept on a cane mat
on the floor and did not eat after twelve noon. I have studied Thai
Traditional Medical Massage in Bangkok for two weeks, two years
running, done an 18-day Qi Gong Study Tour of China, where I got
lost in a misty mountain and only found my group by sheer luck. I
have stayed in a Zen Monastery in a small village in the mountains
in South Korea and had seen about twenty deadly poisonous snakes
there. I did not want to get too close to count them exactly. I slept
on a bed of rocks at a health resort in South Korea. A five-day silent
retreat of Vipassana Meditation in Burma was a challenge. This
style of meditation is to learn insight into oneself. I travelled down
the Irrawaddy River illegally from Mandalay to Bagan, finding out
later that I could have been deported from the country. Lived with
my adopted Tibetan refugee family in Northern India in a Tibetan
Settlement School. This delightful family is so appreciative of my
small contributions to their education and well being. I shook the
hand of HH the Dalai Lama in the spectacular town of Dharamsala
in India. On my own I did a Buddhist Pilgrimage in Nepal, where
the Buddha was born, ending in Bodh Gaya, India where he found
his enlightenment. I too found inner peace. Trekking in Nepal with
a porter called Dharma, who carried my backpack and massaged my
aching legs. A journey of willpower, strength of mind and body. I
vowed and declared I would not trek in the Himalayas again, but
that went by the board in Bhutan in 2007, I just could not resist
the temptation. I have taken a group to India and Nepal. Some of
them had never been out of Australia before. That was a challenge
for all concerned. I volunteered for a short time at Mother Teresa's
orphanage in Calcutta and went to Bali two months after the
horrific bombing in 2002, to see what I could do for the beautiful

devastated Balinese people. I was saddened by their loss of life and income, but gratified by their courage to move on with life as best they could. Volunteering in Uganda for Soft Power Education was fun, especially painting a school in 40 degree heat.

In 1996 I lived with my son and daughter in Montreal for three months. It was challenging, as we had not all lived in the same house for about ten years. They had become adults with their own working lives and strong personalities. On a trip back from Quebec city they both got tired and asked me to drive. Can you imagine me with such a precious load, driving on the *wrong* side of the road and all the signs in French and my two children asleep as passengers? French was never my strong subject at school, and that was about forty years ago. It was in Montreal that I saw Gregory Peck and Johnnie Cash live. Wow. With my kids I travelled to Ottawa where we saw the Royal Canadian Mounted Police headquarters, Quebec for the magnificent architecture, New York for the night life at Rudi's Pub, Niagara Falls for the spectacular water gushing into Canada on one side and the USA on the other. While on my way to Canada once I went via the Inside Passage to Alaska, took the Klondike train and bus to Whitehorse in the Yukon, down through those marvellous Rockie Mountains. I have seen the remarkable Calgary Stampede. A train journey across Canada from west to east was entertaining.

High altitude sickness, without oxygen is no fun in Tibet. This trip took all the patience I could muster. Being rescued by a police launch in flooded southern Thailand was a bit hairy, testing my trust and courage. Riding a mule at Tiger Leaping Gorge in China is not for the faint hearted, in extremely steep country with a stubborn mount who liked living on the edge, literally. Being on the back of a motorbike in Asian countries is a real adrenaline rush. Just sit back and enjoy the ride, is my theory. Once in Athens I decided to set up a 'milk crate' massage in the Plaka with other sellers of various items.

It was with the purpose of earning money before taking off for the enchanting Greek Islands. Let me tell you it didn't work, but I had heaps of fun, and was given trinkets from the other stallholders, when I massaged them, as they had no spare money.

Through my travels, I have adapted to other cultures, learned about their traditions, religions, morning habits, life styles, languages, culinary tastes, and architecture. I have learned to 'accept what is', this doesn't mean you have to agree with it or go along with it, but first acknowledge the situation and then search out the answer. This is particularly the case in India, where poverty is very in 'your face'. If it overwhelms me, I am of no value in helping anyone. I can't save every beggar or street child, but I can make a small difference to their day or that moment even if it is just giving them a smile and acknowledging their existence. In India, one of the morning rituals of the locals is to scrape their tongues with a metal U shaped implement, then clear their throat and nose with gurgling and hawking sounds and spit, which in our culture would not be acceptable. Who are we to judge?

I come home sometimes tired, dirty, thinner in some cases, mainly from the food disagreeing with my system, but I come home changed in some way. I am more tolerant of differences, less judgmental of how things should or could be done. I have more understanding and acceptance. There is no right or wrong, there just is. At times I find myself slipping back into my old ways of wishing things were different, but life will go on around the world and I count my blessings every day for the free life I have. I have learned to cut back on material things and live a simpler, frugal life, having seen how millions of people in many countries can get by on very little.

The stories that follow will give the reader greater insight and a more rounded description of who I am and where and why I travel the way I do.

First-time Travellers

The riskiest thing in life is not taking risks. Realisations

The first time I travelled out of Australia was with my eldest sister on a Pacific Islands cruise. I was thirty-nine years old. We had a ball, ate far too much, wined, dined and enjoyed the entertainment. We got friendly with a tall dark handsome native Fijian called Paddy. Much to my astonishment, my sister invited him to our cabin for a drink. He arrived in a lap lap and colourful shirt and proceeded to show us his battle scars across his chest. He would have been happy to show us the full extent of his wounds but we declined politely! He was disembarking at Fiji and wanted my home address. My sister being a seasoned traveller said, 'give it to him, you never hear from people who you give your address to when you are travelling'. Guess what. When I got home there was a postcard from Paddy. It took some explaining to my husband!

- What interests you? The country, inhabitants, history, culture, environment, religion, art, architecture, music etc.
- Choose a country you have always wanted to visit, your own or overseas.
- Check out the best season to go, the cheapest flights, visa, and currency exchange, get a passport and off you go.

- Do you want to go with a friend, book in with a group, or be independent and 'go it' alone.
- If you choose to go with a friend, make sure you both understand each other's interests, budget (very important), preferences of where you want to go, style of travel, transport and accommodation.
- Discuss fully all preferences before you go.
- Keep clear communication on the journey.
- It is better that one is the leader and one is the follower, but important for each to have their say.
- Join the YHA (Youth Hostels Australia), they are a full of information and great for networking.
- The Lonely Planet Guide books are a budget traveller's bible. As well as cheap deals, they list up market options also, as well as a whole lot more.
- In some countries tipping is the custom, in others it's not. Your guide book will tell you.
- If you pack lightly enough, you can carry your own bag to the room and save tipping a porter.
- Always take a sweater or jacket for warmth on planes, trains, buses, as sometimes the air conditioning is so cold and the thin blankets they hand out are not enough.
- Get your digestive system acclimatized gradually if possible.
- Keep calm when things don't go as planned. (see chapter on De Stress)
- Learn how to use emails before you leave home.
- Keep in touch with family and friends with group emails and send digital photos. The latest travel trick is sending blogs. Free wifi is all over the place, take an iPad.
- Buy an international phone card for use in any country or SIM card for your mobile phone in the country you are visiting.

- Write notes in a small spiral notebook to jog your memory when emailing and remember those funny things that happened.
- Keep a journal, it is fun to look back on in years to come.
- Don't forget to ask for help when you are not sure about anything. Keep in mind that sometimes you are given incorrect information because people don't understand, or don't like to say they don't know and lose face.
- Get a good map of the city you are in. Bus maps are great and a fun way of meeting the locals and exploring a city on local transport.
- Be aware that if you photograph a street performer or his animal, you may be asked to pay something. Don't be bullied into paying too much.
- Be aware also that sometimes they kill the animal's mother to make money out of the baby being photographed.
- Never count your money in public places.
- Cover your pin code with your hand at ATMs.
- Take a credit card, some cash and travellers' cheques.
- When you get into a rickshaw, tuk tuk etc establish a price before you leave.
- Don't be talked into going on any side trips e.g. a silk or jewellery shop unless of course you want to.
- Be street wise, but not afraid to try out new experiences.

What to Take and What to Leave Behind

Having things in life is wonderful, but needing them is attachment. Dr Wayne Dyer

My first big overseas trip was for six months with a backpack, travelling to eighteen different countries. I had no idea how to 'fit' a backpack and only found out after a month or so that I was carrying it too low on my hips. I found it was good to have no side pouches or pockets, as it made the pack bulky when in a crowded train or bus and is better for security. These days I have a much smaller backpack which is lockable and great for 'rough' travel. I also have a bag with wheels and a handle if I am not going too far off the beaten track. I now take only the bare essentials and have narrowed it all down to basics. It is amazing what you can do without, what you can take and throw away, what you can buy and post home. I enjoy reading travel books on the road of other people's adventures in the country I am in. You can buy up to date travel guides second-hand in most Asian and European cities. Books are heavy, so pass them on, exchange them or sell them along the way. eReaders or iPads are the way to go now.

- Comfortable walking shoes are a must. 'Break' them in at home before you leave.

- Sandals with Velcro straps are great if your feet swell on the plane or from heat, they can be adjusted.
- Purchase airline stockings/socks at a pharmacy before flying.
- Buy a lightweight backpack at a reputable travel store and get them to fit it for your needs. A lockable wire mesh safety net can be placed around your backpack.
- If you choose a 'wheelie' bag, make sure the handle is solid and not too short for your height.
- If you choose a four wheel bag, be aware, they don't travel well over uneven surfaces.
- A day pack is handy as carry-on luggage on the plane and for day trips or weekends.
- A bumbag with compartments for small items, where it is easy to find 'stuff' is handy. Some have a spot to carry your water bottle.
- A combination clock, alarm, calculator, calendar can be bought for a few dollars or a mobile phone with these facilities.
- A Swiss Army knife with lots of different functions. Keep it in your cargo baggage.
- Keep a pen in the case with your reading glasses. Handy for signing credit card dockets.
- Take spare prescription glasses or take your prescription, buy magnifying glasses in an emergency.
- Buy a phone card that you can use overseas or SIM card for the country you are in for your mobile phone. Learn how to Skype on an iPad.
- Eye shades and ear plugs are good if you are a light sleeper.
- When you pack, roll your clothes, they take less space that way.
- Leave space for purchases.

- Take mix and match, quick drying, non iron clothes.
- A pegless clothesline is useful to put up in open windows, between trees or bunks. I have put them up in trains and buses at a pinch.
- Take a small towel or even an ordinary car chamois for when you are on a long train journey, or just want to freshen up, or at a pinch dry your whole body.
- If you are going to a Third World country take some toys and books for the children. Once you hand them out, you make space for souvenirs etc.
- If taking a mobile phone, iPhone, digital or video cameras make sure you have the correct power adaptor to recharge batteries for the countries you will visit.
- Take three or four spare films for older cameras.
- A sarong can be used to lie on at the beach, as a skirt, to wrap around your head on a windy day, used at a sheet, hang by your bunk for privacy, or even as a towel. They dry quickly.
- Pack a small first aid kit of band aids for minor cuts, athletic tape for blisters and support for wrists, knees and ankles. Tea Tree Oil for disinfectant, Rescue Remedy for emergencies, aspirin for pain or headaches and other medicines you may use at home.
- I take a Frisbee for playing on the beach or park with the local kids. Something to do when the bus breaks down, or at a pinch use as a plate.
- A floppy cotton hat is great to keep the sun off your face and can be worn in the water if the sun is really blazing.
- A small photo album of family, friends, pets, native animals, your car, city or home. Even if you can't speak the language, it can be a great 'conversation' starter.

- A journal to write your experiences in, not just of places, but your feelings at the time.

- A small torch to put near your bed if you need to use the bathroom in the night and you are in a dormitory. A head torch is useful for camping.

- If you are worried about film getting damaged at airports, buy a lined pouch especially for that purpose.

- Take cash and travellers' cheques in US currency. It is accepted all over the world. In my experience, Visa Card is more accepted than other credit cards.

- Take extra passport photos with you, they can be handy.

- A silk sleeping sheet can be useful if you are going off the beaten track.

- Bacteria wipes or hand cleaning gel is handy to use before you eat.

- Finally, take loads of patience, tolerance, understanding, acceptance, compassion, flexibility, communication, love and generosity.

See also Solo Travel and Women Travelling Solo.

AUSTRALIA'S MOST ADVENTUROUS SENIOR

It was a fresh crisp morning in the winter of 2005. I was precariously perched on a slab of rock only metres away from the foamy surf between Bronte and Bondi Beach, and six kilometres from the city of Sydney Australia. The photographer was asking me to walk left, then right, look at the camera, face the ocean, balance on unstable rock ledges, jump from rock to rock and don't forget to smile. I hardly had time to look where to put my feet.

There was a lull in the action and Mione, a staff member of the Get Up and Go Magazine, which is a travel magazine for seniors, affiliated with the Senior Card, approached me and told me I was the Winner of the Get Up and Go Award for Australia's Most Adventurous Senior. I started to shake, my eyes glazed over, my legs went to jelly and I laughed nervously. Only the threat of toppling into the Pacific Ocean kept me upright.

There was more filming to be done but my mind was off in outer space. I had trouble comprehending that I had topped the list of one hundred and fifty entrants to win the title and a trip for two to Vietnam, staying in the Sheraton Hotel in Ho Chi Min city.

I immediately thought to ask Bindi, my daughter to share the experience with me. We headed off some months later and had a wonderful time together and as she is a fitness freak, we gave the facilities at the hotel a really good work out. To warm up, not that we needed much in that climate, we took to the tennis court then, while she was pounding her feet on the treadmill in the gym, I took to the swimming pool. By the last day I was suitably worn out from site seeing, trips to the Mekong Delta, perilous rides on the backs of motor bikes to the horse races, early morning fitness routines and nearly walking the soles off our shoes. It was time for a warm stone massage, which I got into trouble for calling a 'hot rocks' massage. It lived up to my expectations. It was just as well we had all this activity as the superb high teas at the hotel were to die for.

We decided to extend our stay and flew to Hoi An for an overnight stay and more site seeing before heading to Hanoi to see the Water Puppets and get in some more walking in case our fitness level happened to take a plunge. Bindi headed home after ten days and I met up with my friend Sue to do some hard travel overland to Yunnan, a province of China for four weeks. That was amazing.

I am forever grateful to my friend Mary for sending me the application form from *Get Up and Go* Magazine, as she thought I should enter the competition. I wrote my story in four hundred words of a travel adventure I had had since turning sixty. I wrote about the twenty or so poisonous snakes I had encountered in South Korea, that got me a 'leg in the door' and after numerous interviews and meetings, that is how I ended up as one of the five finalists and the only one perched on the rocks by the sea. On my way home from the photo shoot, my trusty hiking boots 'blew a sole'. The sole flapped off, only hanging by a thread, they had done good service. I thanked them warmly and put them in the nearest rubbish bin.

FITNESS FIRST

So if you put on a little weight, find you need glasses, get a little pain in your knee, notice a few brown spots on your hands, don't despair. There is a fountain of youth: it is your mind, your talents, the creativity that you bring to your life. Sophie Loren

Getting fit before leaving home is really important. With your body being mobile, flexible and healthy you will stand up better to the rigours of long bus, train and plane trips. Walking around cities is the best way to see them and meet locals, but it can be tiring. All those cobblestones, steps and concrete, can take its toll on your body. The fitter you are the more you will enjoy your journey.

- Join a Seniors Fitness Class about six weeks before your departure. These classes involve warm ups, aerobic exercise, stretches and weights.
- Dance Classes or Line Dancing are a fun ways of getting fit and meeting people.
- Aqua-aerobics is easy on the limbs and muscles.
- Yoga is wonderful for the mind and body.
- Pilates is geared for the individual.

- Cycling is great for the legs, whether out in nature or on an exercise bike.
- Aerobics is excellent for the cardio/vascular system.
- Swimming in a pool or the ocean is beneficial for the lungs.
- Salt water works as a detox.
- Play tennis, golf or any sport.
- Learn Tai Chi or Qi Gong, it gets the life force energy going through your body and can be done anywhere, but outside is best.
- Learn to meditate. It calms the mind and helps you to keep your cool if things happen to go pear shaped.
- See your doctor if you need extra prescription drugs. Keep them in their original packet and keep the prescription with them. Some countries may check on this.
- See your own dentist for a check up before leaving for extended travel.
- See a naturopath to find out if you need supplements.
- See a chiropractor if you have old injuries or aches and pains.
- Have some Remedial Massage and relax.
- Join a Laughter Club. Laughter benefits your immune system, cardio/vascular system, gets the endorphins going, which are the natural pain killers.
- Eat healthy unprocessed food to give you energy.
- Walking is the best exercise of all. Do it with a friend, if possible, for motivation.
- Walk with a loaded backpack if you are going to use one.
- Use steps when possible.
- Get off the bus early or walk to work or shopping when you can.
- Park the car further away and walk.

- Exercise regularly, keep focused on your goal by writing it down and reviewing it from time to time.
- Wear the footwear you are going to use on your travels.
- Buy a pedometer, Fitbit or Jawbone Up an excellent motivator.
- Drink plenty of purified water.
- See a travel doctor to get vaccinations, if required or have homeopathic treatments.

Noni 'training' on Tenzing Norgay's Rock, Darjeeling

GENERAL GUIDELINES

The true mystery of the world is the visible not the invisible. Oscar Wilde

When a group of travellers get together, they love to swap stories and experiences. So much can be learned from others 'on the road'. Places to go or not to go, pitfalls and rip offs to avoid and be aware of. Not to make you fearful but to be alert to situations that can happen. Most travellers are willing to share where they found cheap deals for accommodation, whether you want Five Star hotels or No Star hotels, hostels, guest houses, motels, pensions, home stay, B&B's, shared or single rooms, female only etc. Location is important when travelling.

- Is it near public transport, eating places, shops, laundromats?
- Do you want to be near the sea, surf beach, lake, mountains, or forest, walking/cycling trails, off the beaten track or right in the heart of things?
- What about security, is there a safe in the hotel or room that you can leave your valuables in when you go hiking or boating?
- Is there a travel agent nearby, if you want to book tours or ongoing flights?

- Is there an agent at your accommodation?
- Is there a safe place to store your main luggage if you go off to an island or hiking for a few days?
- Do you need a kitchen to cook/store food/eat in?
- Is there an email facility or wi fi? Is there mobile phone reception?
- Do you need a swimming pool, 24 hour reception or an elevator?
- Is the accommodation near an airport and do they have a shuttle bus service?
- Some airports have day rooms where you can grab some sleep, take a shower, freshen up or just get horizontal.
- Some airports have free email. Volunteer staff at most airports are only too willing to help.
- Arrive early at the airport. Planes can get overbooked and late arriving passengers can get bumped off. If this does happen, remain calm, read a book or just people watch.
- Buy airline stockings from a pharmacy and put them on before flying. Wear them in bed if your legs are tired from long walks or concrete jungles.
- Keep a small notebook handy to write down names and addresses of those special people you want to keep in touch with who you meet along the way.
- Write down names of places or situations to jog your memory, so you can write it into an email or your journal.
- Keep a pen in the case with your reading glasses.
- Keep a journal with details of dates and years of where you have been, what you saw and how you felt about it. Write snippets of conversations, quotable quotes, things that made you laugh or cry.

- Don't let one or two unfortunate experiences taint your view. With travel your enjoyment so much depends on who you meet, the weather at the time, what you see, where you stay, the coincidences that took place that can amaze you, and the experiences that you have.

- If you are travelling with a friend, swap copies of passports, next of kin etc with them.

- Take a USB with you include all your details of your medical history insurance etc some photos of home are great to show overseas.

- If going to several countries, take extra passport photos. They can be needed.

- On long distance bus/train trips it is cheaper and mostly better to take some food with you. Take food that travels well like apples, pears, dried fruit, nuts, snack bars, trail mixes, biscuits and some bottled water.

- If two or more people are travelling together, a rented car can be a cheaper option than public transport, and you have the added advantage of being independent.

- Make sure the driver has an International Drivers License in countries where it is required. Be alert to driving on the opposite side of the road especially turning into another street or turning out of a gas station, car park or whatever.

- Check local road rules and have an up to date map or GPS.

- If you are concerned about the cleanliness of the pillow, put one of your clean T shirts over it.

- If you have no pillow, pack your T shirt with soft clothes.

- Leave copies of your passport, visa number, credit card details, insurance policy, and traveller's cheque numbers with a trusted friend at home.

- Your passport must be valid for six months beyond your travel period.
- With travel insurance, make sure you are covered for the country you will visit. Some banks offer cheap insurance with Platinum credit cards.
- Shop around for best prices, read the fine print and check claims, look for exclusions, age limits etc.
- Elder House has branches in many countries and has inexpensive packages for over 60's. These can be educational and usually accommodation is in dormitories with courses, meals and transports included.

FIRST BIG TRIP

I had wanted to travel in my late teens and nearly made it once, with my sister and a friend of hers, but it did not happen. Then marriage and kids came along and we lived in the bush with animals and land to attend to, so my travel plans went out the window for a few years. The kids grew up and left home, the wheels fell off the marriage, I had a new career as a remedial massage therapist with my own clinic and, being the boss, I could arrange a locum and take off when I wanted to.

I bought a backpack, which was way too big and ill fitting. It took me a couple of months to realise it was too low on my hips, but with the help of some fellow backpackers and adjustments it was much more comfortable. Now I have a much smaller one, as I realised I can manage with much less stuff.

I was going to take off on my own, but a friend, Joy, said she wanted to come for two months, so we sat down and mapped out where we wanted to go and where we wanted to stay – it was all very exciting. We had a few nights in Hong Kong before flying to England. We saw the sights of London and stayed in a university dorm. We then hired a car and stayed with wonderful life time friends of mine in Surrey. We saw Prince Charles playing polo at Smiths Field with his parents and Kerry (Australia's richest man) and Ros Packer in the Royal Enclosure. We drove to Land's End and driving through Wales and all the way to the top of Scotland to John O'Groats and on to the Orkney Islands. This friend and I separated at Dover and went our own ways.

I met up with another friend, Mac, in Paris and we travelled for a further two months. We took a ferry across to Ireland. We had purchased Eurail tickets in Australia, which were invaluable. We really got our money's worth out of them, as they took us on ferries, buses and boats as well as a free bottle of Glenfiddick whiskey in Scotland. From Ireland we came back to France and as the ferry ran very late we did not get into Paris until 1am. It was too late to get a hotel, so we camped on the street, with other backpackers, outside the North Train Station for the rest of the night and in the morning took a train to Holland. We stayed in a hostel right in the Red Light area of Amsterdam. That was interesting but we needed to see more of the country, so ended up on the island of Texel, in the North Sea. We rented bikes and as my friend had not ridden a bike for 30 years you can imagine how her body ached after a full day of cycling. I also ended up with my first attack of bed bugs, from Amsterdam. Not nice let me tell you.

From Holland to Denmark and to Sweden to stay with friends, who gave us a right royal time, train to Norway and on the glorious fiord to Flam and then to Bergen. Back to Stockholm, Sweden where we stayed in a hostel that was an old jail. In Germany, we went on the Rhine by boat and down the Romantic Road by coach to Frankfurt and Munich. Train to Austria and the magic of Vienna and ended up at Klagenfurt for some rest, relaxation and much needed massage. Our next stop was Venice, how enchanting those buildings and gondolas are.

Using our Eurail ticket to Switzerland and on to Interlaken where we boated on the lakes and climbed some of the Swiss Mountains. Train to Barcelona, and then back to the French Riviera were we basked in the glory of the rich and famous and then went to our humble room. After a quick look at Monaco and the Leaning Tower of Pisa in Italy we headed to Rome. Mac left from there and I was on my own. It felt really strange and quite daunting but by now I felt I knew the ropes and thought I was street wise. What a greenhorn I was. By train from Rome to Brindisi with other backpackers and slept on deck on the ferry to Corfu. I found I fitted in well with the young group, even though I was twice their age, in most cases. I went to five Greek Islands, thus beginning my love affair with islands. It was here that I met a middle aged America man backpacking around the world. He told me he used to travel first class and stay in expensive hotels and go on tours, but he noticed the backpackers were having much more fun and freedom. He gave his two suitcases away and bought a small backpack and even smaller daypack and he joined International Hostels. Whenever I saw him he had a group of young people around him, telling them of his wonderful travels, but more importantly he listened deeply to their stories. He cooked and shared his meals with them, went to the pub with them and showed genuine interest in them. He was having a ball. I learned a lesson from this fellow traveller. While here I heard about an island in Thailand called Koh Samet, I headed straight there when I got to Bangkok and have been there about thirty times now.

Since that first trip, when I was fifty one, I have been to over sixty countries and I have many more on my wish list.

Getting out of your comfort zone is a challenge but once you have taken those first steps, you are empowered to do more. I try to think positively and not let fear get in the way. It is best not to look back or start doubting yourself. Go with your 'gut feeling' or intuition. I trust people and mostly have not been disappointed. I have always grasped opportunities and run with them. I have travelled alone, with friends, families, and groups and led groups to India, Nepal and Thailand. I am happy with my own company and like my own space but it's nice sometimes to have someone to share a joke or experience with. Travelling alone gives you the freedom to change your mind, not book ahead, join up with others for short stints and I find that others are more likely to start a conversation if you are on your own. I have found that becoming more flexible helps when things do not go as planned. The main thing I have learned from travel is acceptance, understanding, tolerance and patience of different cultures, traditions and religions. My travels have created a thirst for knowledge and insight into the human experience. I have been inspired to help others less fortunate than me and count my blessings every day that I live in this wonderful country of ours, Australia. I have made lifelong friends with fellow travellers and stayed in their homes and gained insight into other cultures and traditions that I would not have access to otherwise.

Remember, at some point you have to lose sight of the shore before you can discover new oceans.

Mac Hanna and Noni set off on a big backpacking adventure to Paris, Ireland, Holland, Denmark, Sweden, Norway, Germany, Austria, Switzerland, Spain, Monaco and Italy

Affordability

I'd rather travel than own a car. Noni Gove

If you are serious about travelling and feel you can't afford it, here are some tips to help you save.

- Work out exactly how much you want to save each week before you leave on your travels.
- Be frugal at home; recycle clothes, look through 'op' shops and garage sales for books, bags, clothes, footwear etc.
- Walk or ride a bike rather than using a car or taking public transport.
- Keep eating in restaurants for special occasions only.
- If you smoke – cut it down or better still quit.
- If you drink alcohol, keep it for special celebrations.
- If you gamble – quit.
- Check newspapers for free entertainment, cheap flights, package deals, or check them out on a computer.
- If you are going to Asia, check out the travel agents in Chinatown or Asian suburbs in your city.
- If you intend to travel to a few Asian countries, book your main flights and when you get there arrange on-going flights to other Asian cities. You could be surprised at the savings.

- Agents overseas can mostly get you a visa in a couple of days.
- Check newspapers for special food deals. Buy in bulk when something you use is on special.
- Shop around for cheaper hairdressers, massage therapists, gyms etc
- Take a picnic to the park and throw a Frisbee or ball to help your fitness.
- Take a job delivering local papers to earn some money and get fit at the same time.
- Be creative, make your own greeting cards and handmade gifts, it is much more personal.
- Get your children or grandchildren to paint small pictures for cards, or use photographs.
- Make sure you are aware of the cheapest time to make long distance phone calls. Use a mobile phone only in an emergency.
- Buy a Lonely Planet guide book for the country you are visiting for full information on budget accommodation and much more.
- Travel in the low or shoulder season rather than high season.
- Shop around at Farmers markets and supermarkets for fruit and vegetables.
- See if you can get a tenant for your home when you are away, who will pay you some rent.
- Check out house swapping on the internet.
- Check out Women Travelling the World for free accommodation, on the internet.
- Check out Elders Hostels in Canada and USA on the internet.
- Join the YHA. There is no age limit and members get discounts on travel, insurance, shops, cafes, laundromats etc.

- If you are travelling solo, check out the deals that don't have a single supplement.
- Check low/high/shoulder seasons deals for flights, trains, buses etc.
- Hold a garage sale to get rid of old unwanted clutter. Be really ruthless, going through cupboards, closets, drawers, attics and garages etc.
- Buy fruit or salad vegetables when travelling and make them up yourself.
- Check if a return ticket is cheaper than two singles.
- Check if daily, weekly or monthly tickets are cheaper.
- When staying in hostels or backpackers, swap addresses with fellow travellers, you never know when you may be in their country and need information or even a bed.
- Share a car ride. Put notices up on boards in hostels if you need a lift or have space in a car.
- Share a taxi from the airport. Ask around to see if someone is going to the same area.
- In some airports that are close to a main road, it is cheaper to take a taxi from the road rather than the airport.
- Buses are generally cheaper than trains.
- Ask for seniors discounts. Some hostels will give you a free night's board for a couple of hours work.
- Except for duty free, don't leave your shopping till you get to the airport.
- Email is free at some airports and libraries.
- Buy a city map and walk to see the sights. You get the feel of the city and its people this way.
- Check out metro deals for daily, weekly tickets.

EARLY ARRIVAL IN TUNISIA

I arrived at Tunis, the capital of Tunisia, at 12.30am one morning; not a brilliant time to arrive in any country but I had no option. To change money into Dinah, Tunisian currency, I had to go right out of the airport, so I could pay for a visa. By the time I collected by bag and went through customs and passport clearance it was 1.30am. The taxi to the city dropped me off two kilometres away from the hotel I wanted to stay at. Another taxi and about an hour later I managed to wake the night manager of my hotel and get a room. At 4am the cocks started crowing, at 5am a loud speaker blurted out the call to prayers and I finally got up at 7am to start exploring the city. I had an omelette, which was more like a pancake and a cappuccino in a glass, drinking it through a straw! When in Rome.

After a look around the incredible *souks*, market place, where I experienced the sights, sounds and smells of spices, hides, *hookahs*, bubble pipes, mosaics and much more, I travelled to Madhia. It took all day in several *louages*, nine passenger minibuses. Madhia is a beautiful coastal town, off the beaten track. I had a swim in the rough sea, only about two other tourists ventured in but I couldn't resist it, it was wonderful. On leaving Madhia, the first *louage* took me an hour and a half west to El Jem to see the most brilliant colosseum, built in about AD 230 by the Romans, for the gladiators and wild African animals to devour the Christians. It is very well preserved, even better than the one in Rome, I think. They carted the stone from thirty kilometres away and their aqueduct system came from the hills fifteen kilometres away. Then I took another *louage* to Sfax and a wait for another one to Jerba. You have to wait for a full load of passengers before they take off.

The country leaving Madhia was flat and barren, except for the acres of olive trees ringed by prickly pear and large spiky cactus. After El Jem it was more rolling plains of scrub. I wonder how animals and man can exist here but you see small flocks of sheep and goats being minded by a small girl, woman or man in their colourful striped full length Berber shawls. Coming through the villages I saw three of four sheep tied up outside a shop, Close to the road, hanging above them a carcass or two of one of their friends, ready to be chopped up and put onto their version of a charcoal BBQ. Beside the carcass will be a skin drying, ready to be tanned. A man on our *louage* bought one and brought it onto the minibus in a plastic bag. Some men still wear the Fez. I saw my first real live camel, which makes for a change from the hundreds of stuffed ones in the market. A few donkeys pulling carts, I saw one parked beside a Mercedes … quite a contrast.

We are pulled up by a police check about every forty kilometres, I have to take my passport out and the locals have to show their ID cards. The roads are narrow but the surface well maintained. Our driver is speedy but cautious. Drivers give each other signals if it is safe to pass and if a police check is coming up. We came on a ferry to the charming island of Jerba and then drove about sixteen kilometres to Houmt Souq the capital of the island in the Mediterranean Sea south east of Tunis.

It is a mix of Greek Island, Mediterranean village with an Italian Piazza thrown in. I am staying in a lovely small hotel in Houmt Souq, basically the market place away from the resort tourist area. My room has a circular beautifully tiled shower recess and basin, the loo is outside. The blue shuttered windows open onto the lane below. I have a reading light and comfortable bed, a chair and the obligatory ashtray. I slept underground in a hotel at a place called Zammour, west of Jerba. You will not find it on a map or even on the planet I feel. I ventured out from Jerba via Medenine trying to get to Beni Kaddache and Kzar Hallouf to view some ancient Berber *ghorfas,* blocks of cell like structures originally used to store grain.

The first hotel my taxi dropped me off at was closed but I managed to get to Zammour and found Mr Othman aged about seventy who tootles around on a Vespa, in a Fez and one of those overgrown shirts that men wear which come down to their ankles. He also has glasses as thick as the bottom of Coke bottles. He speaks no English. I paid him twenty five dollars to cover the room and three meals. The lunch consisted of fresh salad, dinner of tomato and couscous soup, followed by couscous with lamb, broad beans, pumpkin and potato, delicious, then apricots and a peach with tea. Breakfast was fresh bread, jam, butter and a hardboiled egg. The underground cell room is barrel like with a candle in a hollowed out area of the wall and a hurricane light with about a twenty watt globe on another wall and the *douches are* across the courtyard twenty metres away. Funnily enough, I am the only guest.

I got chatting with three young girls whose father is the director and teacher of the school. Their English is quite good and we laugh trying to comprehend it all.

Everyone has a mobile phone. The locals greet each other by kissing four or fives times on alternate cheeks. Yesterday I saw one couple give three kisses on the one cheek. The man sitting next to me on the *louage* wore a fez with a straw hat on top of it.

The driver who Mr Othman organised to take me to Beni Kaddache wore a hooded camel hair full length coat with baubles on it similar to Chinese knots. This and his car had seen better days. The steering wheel did not correspond to the steering arm and tyres and with the early sun in our eyes, it was a miracle we made the journey on a windy road.

I got to Gabes then a train to Tunis for six hours. I hope to catch up on some sleep after the thin mattress over slats in the cell. Right across the aisle was a diabolically spoilt brat of a young boy. He demanded attention from everyone in the near vicinity, screeched and screamed, drummed on the tray of the seat in front of him, yelled, clapped and pulled faces, especially when I gave him a withering scowl to try to shut him up. His mother ignored the whole thing, so no one got any peace.

On arrival back in Tunis I got the metro system to Tunis Marine and changed to TGM train to Sidi Bou Said a heavily touristy beach area, walked down to the sea front to stay for three nights in a very run down four star hotel for a change, which I thought had a swimming pool. Well it does but there is no water in it. The beach is grotty with seaweed and plastic, so it took some courage to get into the water. None the less it was well away from the tourist masses being belched out of buses into the old town fifteen minutes walk up a steep hill.

I visited a private home which is open for inspection. It was fascinating with its intricate mosaic tiles, courtyard with a huge traditional globe bird cage, woven rugs on the wall, myriad of steps and stairs. The whole area is like a Greek village on an island, with blue and white walls, windows, bright bougainvillea, hibiscus and geraniums. In Carthage an area of ancient Roman ruins, there are the most beautiful homes of the rich and famous Tunisians and especially the President's residence. Ben Ali has been in power since 1989 and has more police and body guards around than Fort Knox. I was asked to walk on the other side of the road by a gun toting gentleman all in black with white gauntlet gloves a snazzy peaked cap, braid everywhere and a baton just in case I didn't do as I was told. Ha! I am not stupid!

One night I went to dinner in an up-market restaurant right on the waterfront. Fabulous position but two of the waiters were smoking and as one went to remove the dishes from one of the tables he threw his cigarette down on the floor. UGH!

Back in the city of Tunis and while looking for a cheap hotel I was directed to a large door with no sign outside. I pressed the button not knowing what to expect and a nun answered the door. She soon found another nun who could speak English and before I knew it, I was in the new lift going up to the second floor to a large air conditioned apartment complete with comfy bed, desk, bathroom, fluffy new towels soap, drinking water and a fully equipped kitchen. All this for $25 and breakfast thrown in. I could not help laughing at such a find. In fact I got quite hysterical after all the dives I have been in.

Solo in India

At the age of 64 I backpacked around India alone for seven weeks. After my one and only plane flight from Calcutta to Chennai (Madras) I took local overland transport, sleeping in cheap hotels, rented rooms, ashrams, a Tibetan Refugee Settlement School, Thai Buddhist Monasteries, over night trains and buses. I never booked accommodation ahead, just enquired when I got to my destination, even if it was the middle of the night.

While getting off a bus in Tiruvanamili, after the three and a half hour trip from Chennai, my pants caught on a bolt which caused a large rip and exposed flesh. Not the most propitious way to land in a holy city. I found the Arunuchala Hotel for AUD$8 a night. It was excellent, with a ceiling fan, hot water in the bathroom, TV and a phone. I had a nice lunch of rice, dhal, vegetables and pappadams near the hotel for $1.30. I walked the two kilometres to the Sri Romana Marhrishi Temple, away from the chaotic traffic to the peace of the ashram.

A few days later I took a bus to Whitefields, near Bangalore. For nearly six hours the driver blasted the horn, it was one of those shrill types that permeate every cell of your being. After an overnight stay in a guest house, I took off by car to Puttapathi with friends, who just happened to be in the same area. I stayed in Sai Baba's ashram in a dormitory with eight others for $1 a night. I got a locker for my valuables and walked to the shops for food. After two nights it was back to Whitefields, as Sai Baba was giving a talk there. When I was in Whitefield, near Bangalore, I got friendly with Gita, a lady who did my laundry. She wanted me to give her 5000 rupees (about $200) for the private school fees for her five-year-old son. I told her it was not possible. She tried hard to persuade me. Finally, one day she showed me a certificate to prove how well her son was doing at school. A very formal document, but when I read it, it was for first prize in a Fancy Dress Competition! It was all I could do to hold back the laughter.

The Vasco Express train from Bangalore to Margoa took fourteen hours, an overnight journey and with a 20% seniors discount the cost was $8. In Margoa in the morning I took a motorbike taxi, riding pillion, to the bus station to get the bus to Chaudi. A maniac driver on a narrow road is not a pleasant journey, but all passengers managed to survive. For my next transport I climbed aboard a rickshaw for my destination of Palolem. South of Goa on the west coast.

I found a nice room for $4 a night with two Buddhas painted on the wall, a ceiling fan and outside bathroom, just a short walk to the beach. I had a shower and slept for three hours. Had my washing done for $1.40, lunch of basmati rice and stuffed tomatoes for $3, sent some emails and postcards home, walked and swam, as it is very hot. The Holi Festival was taking place and everyone got covered in vibrant paint, no one escapes. I was invited to my Hindu neighbour's home to celebrate the Festival. Lena, the 18-year-old daughter was washing these wonderful 'plates' made out of palm leaves sewn together in a circular shape. They were put on the earthen floor, then a dollop of rice in the middle, then around the outside all manner of dishes…crumbed fish, mussels in their shells, dhal, vegetables and a type of tapioca with corn and lentils in it. Delicious. Young men from the village ambled in, sat on the ground, and ate their fill. The plates and left over food was then thrown out and a new lot put on the plate on the ground. Several women rushed in and out of the small kitchen feeding the masses. One young boy was responsible for keeping the steel mugs full of water. It was all fascinating to watch and be part of. I felt very honoured to be included in this family celebration. Lena was the only one who could speak English and was so beautiful and hospitable, finding me a chair, instead of having to sit on the ground. Through this wonderful scene at one stage came a hen, running for her life, closely followed by a magnificent rooster, head down, and comb upstanding in hot pursuit! No amount of shushing would put him off his mission. At another time an intrepid half grown chicken rushed in and grabbed a mouthful of rice off the palm leaf plate and bolted out again. I was invited back at night for the dancing (men only) and drumming, letting off crackers and general merriment. Lena insisted on walking me home. How sweet.

Visiting the famous Anjuna Markets was a challenge, taking three different buses and a rickshaw to get there and three more to get back. I met up with a young Greek artist who lives in New York, we were both pleased for the company. The markets cover a huge area and you have to bargain hard to get a decent price. They are near a beach, so we had a swim also. There were many Western style hippies, with green and red tattoos covering their bodies, heavy metal protruding from every lip and lobe, dreadlocks on their dreadlocks. I dread to think what is on the scalp!

After a week in Palolem I boarded the Nizamuddin Express from Goa bound for Delhi, in a second class sleeper for forty one hours, with a seniors discount once again the cost was so cheap, $14.45, unbelievable value. Food sellers go by with everything from Chai (tea) coffee, biscuits, chips, fruit, packaged meals and bottled water. I learned a lot about the habits of Indian people. One lady,

Shalini is a lecturer at Agra University, very nice, but a total control freak. She ordered me to... put your feet up, eat these grapes, lie down and rest, don't eat your food yet, I am not going to let you sleep till 10pm... And so it went on until she got off at Pune at 4am. She very sweetly left me a packet of biscuits near my head. They were called... Good Day. A beggar boy crawled through the train on his bottom dragging his assumed paralysed legs, sweeping the rubbish from under our feet. He looked very disabled, collecting one rupee from everyone. 15 minutes later he WALKED back counting his money, looking very able bodied! We came through some interesting and varied country, from massive waterfalls to tropical jungle, to farmland and arid land, stands of eucalypts, oxen pulling ploughs, numerous goats, pigs, roosters, water buffalo, which I love, Brahmin cattle and a few donkeys. No horses.

Now in case any of you get a strong desire to take a 41 hour train trip in India, here are a few tips. Wash your hands frequently. Get off at every stop to stretch your legs on the platform and do some stretching and exercises, especially Qi Gong. The locals are going to stare at you anyway, so why not give them something to stare AT. Watch the morning ritual of the locals brushing their teeth. Some are 'scrubbers' a total no no. Tongue cleaning with a metal U shaped implement. Gets that fuzzy feeling off. Clearing the throat and nose... noises too horrendous to describe. One man crushed something in the palm of his hand and ate it, or maybe chewed it, could have been chewing tobacco. Read the Lonely Planet Guide for India from cover to cover. Amazing what you will learn about the culture, history and traditions. Gaze out the window and watch in awe as these wiry people survive on little food, hard work and carrying heavy loads. Bring out your small photo album from home and give them the history of your family and lifestyle etc. They will ask lots of personal questions. Wash your hands. Get your Interdens out and massage your gums. Your dental floss creates a few laughs as well. Use your Tiger Balm jar on your back against the seat on your acupressure points, for your aching back. Offer to give your fellow passengers a head, neck and shoulder massage. Buy some food for fellow passengers. Explain foot and hand reflexology. Wash your hands. Snatch a sleep if you can. Bring out your mouth organ and give them a rendition of Waltzing Matilda. Bring a sleeping sheet, very handy for keeping valuables in while you sleep and you don't have to have them round your waist, only near your waist. Bring a padlock and chain to secure your locked bag to the seat. I spent one night in a hotel for $20 near Delhi station, ready to head further north the next day to Dera Dun. I treated myself to a first class ticket for the five hour trip for $15; it is clean and comfortable with air conditioning, soap and toilet paper in the toilets, a newspaper to read and free bottled water.

I read the Hindustan News. Big headlines… OSAMA BIN LADEN CAPTURED ON NEW DELHI TRAIN STATION. SUNDAY NIGHT. Of course I nearly died, thinking I had missed the action by only a few hours! On reading further I realised it was an April Fool's Day joke being the 1st of April. Phew! I actually had a proposal of marriage on this train, but did not accept it, causing a great deal of mirth from fellow passengers. I feel I am in a time warp and I do miss the vendors selling their goods through the open window, the smell of spices and the odours of the sub continent.

On arrival at Dera Dun I took a bus to Paonta Sahib, where I stayed with my adopted Tibetan Refugee family in a Tibetan settlement. My friend Dorjee is a librarian at the school. It was a wonderful experience, one that I treasure; I am Momo (grandmother) to his twins. Dorjee took me to a Sikh Gurdwar (Temple) where we had lunch sitting on the ground with hundreds of Sikhs. The rice was so plentiful that it had to be picked up with a builder's size shovel, we ate it with the right hand of course. Three nights later I was on a deluxe overnight bus to Dharamsala. It may be deluxe by Indian standards but it is rough, grotty and with shocking shock absorbers, the only time I get to sleep is when the driver stops for a meal. I found two Queensland Aussie girls up the back of the bus and we became instant friends and still are. I stayed in a really nice room at McLeod Gang for $6 a night with a fabulous view of the snow capped Himalayas. The first night I slept for nearly ten hours, it is great for recharging the batteries. One evening I was on the verandah enjoying a salad of tomatoes, cucumbers, shallots, capsicum with a squeeze of lime, and brown homemade bread with cheese spread, when over the balcony came this rather large and very fierce male monkey, baring his three inch fangs and grunting in a very threatening manner. I leapt up flailing my arms around and shouting. After about three lunges towards me, he decided it wasn't worth the hassle of fighting me for my dinner. Yesterday I saw a Western Tibetan nun wearing riding boots. Wonder if she was an Aussie? I also met an Aussie man who grew up in Yass and spent a lot of time in the Northern Territory, before ordaining as a Tibetan monk, three years ago. I went to visit an English Tibetan monk, who is a friend of a friend. He lives in a building that is being demolished or rebuilt, not sure which. I navigated my way up the improvised steps, across a concrete floor with holes large enough for me to fall through, passed steel girders, which were handy to hang on to. I finally found Tenzin Josh.

My Saturday night entertainment was to go to the local movie hall and for less than $2 I saw two documentaries. The first was about the seventeenth Kamapa, a reincarnation of a famous rinpoche (monk). Kamapa escaped from Tibet some years ago. The second documentary was Doing Time, Doing Vipassana. I have wanted to see this for years. It is about Vipassana meditation being introduced in the large jail in Delhi, with a very positive outcome. It is also being trialled in Taiwan and USA with excellent results. Yesterday I walked the 1km to the Church of St John in the Wilderness. The pastor greeted me warmly and apologised for not recognising me from when I was last there. That was six years before for Princess Diana's memorial service. He offers me chai (tea) and presented me with a cross very hospitable. He has taken my address and is going to write to me. The church was built in 1852 by the British, when Dharamsala was a hill station. The cemetery is full of very sad graves of babies and young children. A plaque in the church is dedicated to John Knowles, who died in 1889, when a bear attacked him. Another plaque is to an Andrew Rose from Melbourne, who died in 1974 aged 26.

Meeting up with a Tibetan monk, the venerable Bhagdro, who was a prisoner in Tibet for some years before escaping to India was a sad story. He has written a book called *Hell On Earth* which is really horrendous. What he lived through and how he escaped is beyond belief. He was in hospital in Paris for eight months recovering from his wounds of torture. All expenses were paid for by former President Mitterrand's wife. He has been sponsored on trips all around the world to tell people what is happening in Tibet to this day. He hopes to get to Australia soon. He has a wicked sense of humour. I invited him to dinner last night and he said Thank you, I won't have breakfast or lunch or that day! He presented me with a Karta (scarf) as a blessing. My usual breakfast of fruit, muesli and curd (yoghurt) with honey is really delicious. One night I had garlicky mushrooms on Tibetan toast, followed by banana toffees and honey. Yum. Food is very cheap here. A three course meal costs about $3, without alcohol of course. I have met such interesting people from all over the world, Israelis, Americans, Canadians, Australians, Irish, British, Koreans, Taiwanese, Nepalese, French, Germans, Italians, just to name a few.

The highlight of the trip was meeting and shaking hands with HH the Dalai Lama. After hours of standing in a queue for registration, handing over my bum bag full of all my valuables and my bottle of water, for security reasons, waiting with the newly arrived refugees from Tibet, the moment comes. I hand HH the *karta* white scarf and he puts it round my neck and smiles a blessing. I thank him in the few words of Tibetan that I know and he smiles. I am in awe, I don't want to speak for hours.

It is so beautiful here that I want to stay forever, but the journey must go on. After a week I took a bus to Pathankot. It was a steep and windy road and the inevitable happened. A girl leaned across me and vomited out the window. Then the boy beside me was not so lucky. He vomited all over himself and those around him. I offered him a paper towel to clean himself up. A few hundred yards down the track, the driver stopped the bus near a village pump. The ticket collector jumped out and snatched two buckets of water from a poor unsuspecting boy who had just hand pumped them. The water was used to flush out the curried vegetables and rice, which had been regurgitated all over the seat and floor of the bus. In Australia we call it a technicolour yodel. I can assure you it was colourful.

I board the Sealdah Express train for the overnight trip to Varanasi for $11. I did not get a wink of sleep out of the fourteen hours on the train. A family of four moved a tin trunk 5foot by 2 foot in between the lower bunks, with an older couple on the other bunk, which meant there were seven people where there should have been two. The train from Pathankot to Varanasi originates in Jammu Kashmir and was already full of Kashmiri's. I was the only westerner on the train. It had a 'Pantry Car', which means that the food sellers go up and down, pushing their way past bags and bodies. The man beside me had an ear cavity the shape of a tortoise. The reason I noticed this phenomena was because his head was only a foot away from mine. They were all very friendly and spoke no English, but we had a lot of laughs. One young girl of about eight started to cut her finger nails with an open razor blade. I was horrified on this rough train that she would slice her hand or fingers off. I offered her my nail scissors but she politely refused. The tin trunk does not leave any space to put my legs down. I indicate that I cannot sit on the seat with my legs folded for hours. They move the trunk slightly so that I can squeeze both legs into the space, but after a while the circulation in my legs is just about cut off. The older couple has bought their own food with them and when they have finished eating they rinse the bowl with some water and throw it out the window. It is immediately hurled in through my open window and all over me. They are so apologetic and offer their best hanky for me to mop up. The older man took out a small silver canister, about the size of a matchbox or a bit bigger. From one end he scooped out some white paste and rubbed it in the palm of his right hand, then from the other end he shook out some dried tobacco leaves, about the size of caraway seeds. He mixed the lot up, taking out the bigger hard pieces. After mulling it around, he threw the lot in his mouth ready for chewing, Yuk. Later spitting out the window. His wife wore three or four silver toe rings and two silver anklets, a gold nose stud the size of her nostril, with earrings to match, several rings and a bindii (red dot) on her forehead.

I also met up with a Tibetan monk, the venerable Bhagdro, who was a prisoner in Tibet for some years and escaped to India. He has written a book called *Hell On Earth*, it is really horrendous. What he lived through and how he escaped is beyond belief. He was in hospital in Paris for eight months recovering from his wounds of torture. All expenses were paid for by former President Mitterrand's wife. He has been sponsored on trips all around the world to tell people what is happening in Tibet to this day. He hopes to get to

Australia soon. He has a wicked sense of humour. I invited him to dinner one night and he said Thank you, I won't have breakfast or lunch or that day! He presented me with a Karta (scarf) as a blessing. My usual breakfast of fruit, muesli and curd (yoghurt) with honey is really delicious. One night I had garlicky mushrooms on Tibetan toast, followed by banana toffees and honey. Yum. Food is very cheap here. A three course meal costs about $3, without alcohol of course. I have met such interesting people from all over the world, Israelis, Americans, Canadians, Australians, Irish, British, Koreans, Taiwanese, Nepalese, French, Germans, Italians, just to name a few.

I got to Varanasi at 1.30am. Not a good time to arrive, but no other option. Was immediately pounced on by an auto rickshaw driver. We wended our way through hundreds of prone bodies, not only on the platform, but all over the walkways and even outside the station, bumper to bumper people and baggage. Seething masses of humanity everywhere you looked. I chose a hotel close to the station. The rickshaw driver charged me 40 rupees (about $1.60) went round the block, pulled up wanting to take me to 'his' hotel. I was tired and in no mood to be hassled. I had to come down heavily on him and threaten to get a policeman, after which time he took me to 'my' hotel. Only to find out next day it was within site of the train station! It was clean and mainly for wealthy Indians, so was quite expensive.

After three nights in Varanasi, staying right on the Sacred Ganges River, beside the second largest burning ghat, in fact I am so close that the ashes and unburnt straw from the pyre floats up past my window and some lands on my porch. I see numerous corpses arrive carried on a stretcher or top of a jeep mainly. On the menu at the hotel, under the heading of Curd really nice yoghurt) was the following... Plain Turd... Honey Turd... Mixed Fruit Turd... Banana and Honey Turd. Then further down came Garlic Stiffed Tomatoes... Mineral Water (not Ganges Water)... Scramble Eggs...

Butter & Jam of Money Toast… and Freng Toast! In my wanderings I got talked into seeing a famous guru and palmist Lali Baba. I think he is a cousin of Ali Baba and the 40 thieves! He charged a lot but boy was he spot on with my passed history and looks as if the future is going to be good too. He prepared some Ayruvedic oil for my knee, did some numerology and checked my palm with a torch. (There was a blackout at the time) Went on with some hocus pocus and we haggled over how much I should pay him. I got up early one morning to go in a boat on the sacred Ganges. The first thing I saw was a very dead bloated dog. Further along two very dead and bloated human bodies. I can't believe that people are actually swimming, praying, fishing, bathing and doing their washing only metres away from the ghats. I went back to the hotel for a massage from Asok. I read his testimonials and thought I would give it a go. He took to me with what I can only describe as a rolling pin. Up and down my back and ribs he kneaded the flesh. Making it quite painful for a few days. Then on the soles of my feet he used a wire brush. I drew the line at that. It was agony. When he just used his hands he was really good.

Having seen enough dead bodies to last a lifetime, I decided to head east for Bodh Gaya. The train takes me as far as Gaya arriving in the early hours of the morning. It was clean and comfortable with a reading light, crisp white sheets and pillow cases. My fellow passenger in the cabin was an Indian man who spoke perfect English. At Gaya I spent a few hours in a cheap hotel before a hair-raising ride to Bodh Gaya in an auto rickshaw to stay at the Thai Buddhist Monastery for $4.50 a night. It is very close to the Mahabodhi Temple, the temperature rises to forty one degrees Celsius, but there is a fan in my room, there is also a mouse plague, In Bodh Gaya, a sacred Buddhist site in India, where the Buddha became enlightened. I stayed at a Thai monastery. I was not the only occupant of my humble room. Mice were swarming everywhere. In the forty two degree heat I decided to sit in a plastic tub of water to cool off, as there were no showers or baths in this establishment. This tub was normally used for washing clothes, but I sat in it and poured water over myself. Then I soaked my sarong in water, wrung it out, lay on the bed with the fan on until the sarong dried out, and then went through the whole process again. It was the only way to cope with the heat and get any sleep.

There was a bucket of water in the bathroom to flush the loo. In the middle of the night, nature called and in the dark I went to dipper the water out of the bucket and felt something moving, it was a tiny mouse swimming around in circles. I took pity on it and tipped the water and swimming mouse out into the garden.

At breakfast time we ate at tables just outside the kitchen, unfortunately I had a very good view through the door and window into the kitchen. Mice were running over everything and into bags of rice, flour etc, using the cups and saucers like big dippers in the fair ground.

I saw some kids in the street with a length of string and a mouse tied to the other end. They would let the mouse go and when it was about to take off up some ladies leg or run over her foot, they would yank the string and go into fits of laughter. Great fun for the kids... not so sure about the mouse.

I went to visit a monk at another monastery and was very kindly offered tea and biscuits. It arrived on a tray complete with mouse droppings. It was very difficult to concentrate on the conversation and not keep looking at the mouse's calling card.

Luckily my immune system has become accustomed to foreign lands and there were no ill effects.

I got talking to a fellow called Mohammed, who wants to take me on his motor bike to see a mountain. You know the old saying if the mountain won't come to Mohammed, then Mohammed will have to go to the mountain... We shall see. While I was sitting outside the temple, another man complained about his bad knee. I massaged it for him and before long I had a queue of customers, with everything from bad backs to headaches to stiff necks. You name it, they had it. I told them I was taking appointments for tomorrow and appointed Mohammed as my receptionist. He said the only problem is that they won't pay you. So much for my business venture!

My stay in Bodh Gaya lasted one week after which the monks drove me back to Gaya to get the overnight train to Calcutta. This time I have a bunk to myself. In the morning I get a taxi from Howrah station to a Buddhist Hostel, where I catch up with my Anglo Indian friends, who live nearby.

In India the cows rummage through the rubbish bins and eat everything possible, including plastic bags, which would kill Australian cows and cardboard cartons. I wonder do they know about the experiment that was done with rats. They fed one group of rats on cornflakes and one group on the carton. The group eating the cornflakes died, while the group eating the carton thrived!

I travelled with a small backpack, a day pack and a bum bag for the two months.

The total land cost including food, transport and accommodation worked out at approximately AUD$30 a day.

JUMPING OUT OF YOUR COMFORT ZONE

Man cannot discover new oceans unless he has courage to lose sight of the shore. Anonymous

Whether this means a gigantic leap of faith, as in bungy jumping, or a minor chat over the fence to the neighbour who you have never spoken to before, it can be daunting. Your comfort zone is where you feel secure, protected, and happy with your lot in life. Getting out of it is a challenge. You will learn new lessons, become more adventurous with every small step. It is empowering and each time you do it, it gets easier. Soon you are showing others the way and being encouraged to test yourself a little further next time. Those old familiar and comfortable patterns in your life become a thing of the past and are replaced by new ideas, new parameters and new perimeters. Not to make it sound easy, sometimes it is beyond your imagination but rewards are many and the experiences can be life changing.

- Write a list of outrageous things you would like to do and places you have longed to see. Be as creative as you like.
- Narrow the list to five top favourites, write the pros and cons for each.

- Focus on one or two; be guided by your 'gut feeling' or intuition.
- Visualize yourself in this favourite place, making it as real as possible.
- Read books on positive thinking.
- Letting go of past experiences of failure, changing old patterns is a challenge. You can change your thinking and change your life.
- At some point we have to lose sight of the shore to discover new oceans.
- Be enthusiastic about a new project, this adds energy to the end result.
- Seize every opportunity.
- Live life to the full and be grateful for small blessings … and large ones.
- If you cling to the past, you lose sight of the potential joy of the present.
- The riskiest thing in life is not to take risks.
- Do not doubt every new idea without first testing its validity.
- Unless you do something about it, it isn't going to happen. Be prepared to be vulnerable but trust your instincts.
- Peace of mind will help you to overcome your fear of the unknown.
- Fulfil your desires; it gives you the courage to travel further.
- Travel is the best way to trigger your creativity.
- Practice talking to strangers.
- When you start planning a trip, if everything falls into place easily that's fine, if there are too many obstacles, re think it or try a different approach.
- Never give up hope, keep focused on your goal.

- Develop a clear goal, do whatever it takes to achieve it. Choose to enjoy it.
- You are part of the problem unless you are part of the solution.
- Ask, believe, and receive.

Noni buying dried yak cheese in Sikkim, Northern India

JOYS OF CALCUTTA

In the street in Calcutta there was a family group huddled around one young lady who was having her eyebrows plucked. Her friend was twisting two threads of cotton over the hairs, then, with a quick wrench, out they came. Extremely painful, I would imagine, but she did not flinch. I could not help but stare in awe. They beckoned me over for a clearer view. We got chatting and then exchanged names.

Marion was the oldest in the group, she has two sons, John and Ryan, and they have an English great grandfather and a Hong Kong Chinese grandmother, with some Indian blood also. They are known as Anglo Indians. I met Dionne, a 13-year-old cousin who was put in charge of showing me the way to a Chinese Restaurant, but when we got there it was closed. She did not know what to do with me, so we came back to Marion's humble rooms, which she shares with her husband John, and her father in law also John, her brother in law Reg, her sons and umpteen birds plus a dog. The birds are stacked one on top of the other in cages.

Marion invites me to share their lunch, within minutes there is a huge plate of rice, mince, vegetables, and mustard leaf soup, with lemon juice to drink. Such generosity is overwhelming. The men chat away and want to know all about Australia. They are astonished that I don't follow the cricket. They know all the names of the Australian players. I am taken on a guided tour of the tiny backyard to see pouter pigeons, love birds and cockatiels. I met the pet Pomeranian and the neighbour's German Shepherd.

They enjoy looking at the photos in my small album which I carry around the world, for just such occasions. In it are photos of my family, home, animals, etc and I also have a book of the Southern Highlands of New South Wales. They are keen to learn and ask many questions. When I am about to leave for my hostel around the corner where I am staying, they say, no you can't leave, we are taking you to a fair.

We all pile into a taxi and pass the new cricket stadium; it is lit up like daylight and holds 100,000 people. Past the colourful Musical Fountain and the gracious Victoria Building and finally to the St Thomas School Fair, where I throw balls at targets and tin cans, eat ice cream, drink a sweet fizzy drink, listen to very loud jangly music, until a fight breaks out. The family quickly gathers everyone up and we head for the nearest exit with a speedy retreat.

The Chinese Restaurant is now open. I only want chicken and corn soup but they insist I have more. We have fun and I really like this family, not only for their generosity but their total acceptance of me, a complete stranger from a strange land. They insist on walking me to the gate of my hostel to make sure I am safely home and with a firm invitation for breakfast the next day. I insist that I have fruit in my room and will catch up later in the day.

In the afternoon I walk with Marion to pick up young John from school. He is in a foul mood and is being obnoxious. He throws his school bag at his mother; the teacher takes him in hand and pulls him into line. Marion again cooks up a feast of Chinese pork sausages, scrambled eggs, rice and more soup.

I find out it is Dionne's birthday in a few days and I ask her what she would like. She says "Oh Aunty, I have only just met you, I don't like to say". No amount of pressure from me will get an answer from her. Dionne leaves but comes back shortly with a business card for me from Daryl, the stall holder in the street. It is for a hotel in Darjeeling with a hand written note to say "Take care of Aunty, our friend". How sweet that is, Daryl has heard on the grapevine that I am going to Darjeeling. I thought I was not going to enjoy Calcutta but these people have made my stay so special with their kindness and compassion. They have won my heart. They don't want anything in return.

Walking with Marion, I see the most huge garbage dump in the street and opposite there are street dwellers living under plastic, canvas, bags and bricks, with rope as walls. They cook, sleep and live their entire lives in squalor and hopelessness and yet they are happy. There are people lying on the roadway covered by a bag or rug, it just looks as if a sack has fallen off a cart, then there is movement and you realize there is a human body under the covering. It leaves a deep sinking feeling in the pit of my stomach.

The rickshaw pullers look so tired, some sleep in their rickshaws others perch precariously on the handle bars and seat. They hang around for endless hours in lines, as there is not much work for them. I feel to use a human drawn rickshaw is so inhumane but not to is to deprive them of a living. I really don't know what the answer is. We are so blessed and protected in Australia. It is hard to describe the stench, the smog, the poverty, the pain, the utter desperation of this hand to mouth existence. The child labour is painful to watch. The young seem to do things so willingly. Outbursts of anger and violence erupt everywhere, in the streets, on the railway platforms, in the markets or shops.

Marion showed me the remains of a building which is now a hole in the ground where a bomb blast killed thousands of people, only a few months ago and only a street away. I leave for Darjeeling, by train for a week. Before the train has departed my fellow English passenger has had his bag stolen from above our heads in the carriage.

On my return, Marion takes over my life again and gives a bag of my dirty clothes to her sister to wash. She does an excellent job for a few dollars. There is a party at Marion's mothers place, it is small too and houses many people. I sit on the bed as there are no chairs and the kids crowd around me. Whitney Houston is belting out loud music from the tape recorder. I am handed an Indian gin and lemon, a very potent brew but before long I am up dancing and singing and carrying on, making them laugh like crazy. I hand out presents for the family members that I bought in Darjeeling. They want to know every detail about my trip north.

The next day they take me to the zoo, I am sad to see tigers have been crossed with lions and they are all in concrete pens. We see all the other zoo animals but John and Ryan are bored and don't seem interested, they are reprimanded but take no notice. Later we go shopping and I manage to buy the boys some pants. Marion buys a plate and jug and says it is for herself, but later she gets John to present it to me. Reg presents me with a red rose, he is so quiet and shy, and it must have taken great courage. I am honoured to receive it. He took me to a Burmese Buddhist Temple to meet a monk and a nun, then to a Sri Lankan Temple full of ancient Buddhas.

One night a family friend tells me there is only one thing wrong with Calcutta – the roads – they are always digging them up and leaving holes for people to fall into. I am glad he sees that as the only problem! The contrasts in Calcutta are amazing, there are no street lights or head lights on cars or buses at night but there is the stadium shining brightly. No running water in places means people have to wash dishes in water in the gutter or hole in the footpath, yet the Musical Water Fountain flows day and night.

Marion and John's home is in G Block, it consists of about three rooms, there are many photos and a shrine lit up of Christ and in the window is a Buddha. There is nowhere for the children to play because the whole back yard is taken up with bird cages, there are even some in the kitchen. There are children in English style school uniforms and then there are those in Hessian bags. In a land where thousands are starving, a woman on the third floor is throwing wheat onto the street for the pigeons. Marion's mother told me that one day she had a sleep in the afternoon and when she woke up there was no one in the room. She felt awful and started calling out "where are you all?" They are so used to living on top of one another. I saw a man in the street injecting himself with what I presume was heroin; it made my blood run cold. There is a man living under the stairs near Marion's front door.

Yet another party in the main room at Marion's sisters place, they eat, cook sleep and live in this room. We sit on the bed and drink beer and lemon fizz. For a non drinker…I am not doing badly. We dance and sing, eat kebabs and steamed fish wrapped in pastry. I gave Dionne a pendant on a chain; she wears it proudly to church. She tells her mother that she loves me, I love her too.

After corresponding with Marion for nine years I surprise the family by just turning up unexpectedly. Marion and John are at work, Reg invites me in to show me his new pride and joy, two beautiful Pug dogs, Perry and Masey, and they are gorgeous and love lots of attention. They get so excited they will not do their tricks. When Marion arrives home she insists on taking my washing again. John and Ryan are now very pleasant young men who love playing football and proudly show me there trophies. Marion's father- in-law has died. I really enjoyed his company on my first visit. I stayed for a delicious meal and wished them farewell. We correspond at Christmas time and I hope we always will.

MEETING THE LOCALS

Peace begins with a smile. Mother Teresa

You can't really get to know a country without getting to know its inhabitants. By travelling on local transport you get to know their habits and idiosyncrasies. By opening up a conversation I have learned so much and been treated to invitations to homes, temples, restaurants, walks in national parks, cups of tea, coffee etc. I have become Momo (grandmother) to Tibetan Twins, fairy godmother to an Indonesian family, teacher, to Buddhist Novice Monks and Laughter Leader to South Korean Novice Catholic Nuns. I was remembered by a Greek, non-English speaking, taverna owner on the island of Koffonisia from ten years ago, because I swept the taverna for her. She remembered the room I was in and gave me the same one again at a discount. My address book is full of international addresses of people who I have met in my travels and have become my friends. The people you meet will determine whether or not you had a great time in that country. Reach out and be the first to say hello.

- In third world countries take children's books on Australian native animals to give to youngsters along the way.
- Take small lapel pins of Australian native animals to give to adults who have shown you kindness.

- Visit a local hospital and ask if there is anyone who doesn't have many visitors. In some countries you can visit your own countrymen/women in gaol.

- In Asia, monks don't touch women and vice versa. Men don't touch nuns and vice versa. When in a temple in Asia, remove your shoes, leave a donation and don't point the soles of your feet towards the deity or monks. Dress respectfully. In Asia don't step over another person's body. If you must touch someone on the head, ask first. Be aware of not showing too much affection to the opposite sex in public places. Holding hands is fine.

- If eating food with the fingers in Asia, eat with the right hand only. If passed food accept it with the right hand. If you don't remember all this, Asians are very forgiving of our ignorance of their ways and culture.

- When the opportunity presents itself, try the local food and wine, beer, spirits. It is polite to try even a little.

- Learn the 'Greeting' and 'thank you' in the language of the country you are visiting, the locals will appreciate it. At least make an attempt. If you see a need, lend a hand. Volunteer at an orphanage or soup kitchen.

- Accept that in some remote areas you will feel like an exhibition on display. People will stare, ask personal questions, touch your skin, and hold your hand. Smile and answer as honestly as you can. You may have been brought up to believe that to stare is rude. You may feel uncomfortable; realise not everyone is brought up the same way. Show tolerance.

- Always ask if is alright to take photos of temples, shrines, sacred places, naked babies, local people etc.

- If invited into homes, take a small gift.

HAPPY NEW YEAR THAILAND

Sawadee Pee Mai Kar

A few years ago I celebrated New Years Eve with Thai friends, Chit and Rune, at a small village in the Surin District, east of Bangkok, named Ban Somrong in Thailand.

In 1962 I celebrated New Years Eve by announcing my engagement in a small town in Australia at a private party, held by close friends. That was a night to remember as well. That night I only had to drive 15 minutes.

In Thailand it took eleven hours to get to our destination, half an hour on the ferry from Koh Samet, an island in the Gulf of Thailand, to Ban Phe, a town on the main land. A wait of one hour before the Disco Bus picked us up to drive through the night. Never having been on a disco bus before, I had no idea what to expect. The aisle and small space at the back of the bus was soon packed by young and old disco dancers! With two cassette players pumping out two different songs at eardrum shattering volumes with a beat that sent the natives into a frenzy for the full journey. The two rotating lights and flashing coloured lights either side, in the bus, finished off the atmosphere of a full blown disco bar.

Smoking and drinking patrons combined delicate Thai hand movements with gyrating western hip thrusts that sent the whole bus into a pounding rhythm. I prayed the shock absorbers and axle would stand the strain.

We had numerous pit stops along the way, to allow fluid in and fluid out! Food was eaten on and off the bus. As the hours wore on and sleep escaped me, I remembered I had some earplugs in my bum bag, they did help to block out some of the harsher rasping sounds and I was able to snatch a short but much needed sleep.

At 6.30am we arrived at Buriram for a final pit stop and look around the markets. The locals seemed amazed to see a *farang*, foreigner, at that hour of the morning in their midst. Just when I was enjoying the sight of the unusual fruits and vegetables that we never see in Australia, there was a large dish of freshly killed and plucked rats, slit down the front of the body, innards intact, ready for cooking! My main thought was: Will they be on the menu tonight? Luckily Rune assured me that she did not like them. Phew!

We drove past small lakes with beautiful lotus blooming, fields of rice stubble and stacks of hay packed up high around the trees. The dusty black water buffalo, chewing on their cud, had an inquisitive stance as we drove by. The calves frolicking at their mother's feet, or cooling off in the muddy ponds.

Finally the Thai and temple flags appeared as we came into the village of Ban Somrong. The main part of the celebration was to take place this day for the completion of the new temple.

We settled into Chits home, in the village, close to the temple. Chit and Rune both massage on the beach at Koh Samet, to pay off their home. They can be justly proud of their efforts. It is neat and tidy, spacious and clean, easily the best home in the village. Chit's eight-year-old son by a previous marriage greets me with hands together in a *wai*, bowing politely. "Sawadee Kup" (the male Thai greeting) he says without any prompting. He has the normal haircut for Thai boys; head shaved to within a few inches of the crown and the crown a little longer shave. He is friendly and well mannered, speaks no English, but we 'communicate' and I show him my family photo album and let him play my mouth organ.

On the short walk to the temple we pass a house with a water buffalo and her calf in the front yard, skinny roosters scratch in the dust for any tasty morsel. Across the road in front of the house is a large lake, where Chit collects two buckets of water on a wooden pole slung over his shoulder. He makes several trips, so that we can have a *mandy*. Bucket shower. At the temple we see a band playing traditional musical instruments.

A long line of Buddha images are for sale. For twenty baht (one Australian dollar) you can buy a hundred and eight small coins, to be put in the hundred and eight small bowls, to bring good merit. Further along there is a carousel with six 'dummy' monks going around carrying their alms bowls. Another twenty baht buys more small coins to place in the bowls.

Then there is a mechanical device carrying tiles to the top of the roof of the temple. These tiles are also purchased for twenty baht. A small Buddha image is included with each tile for you to keep. Across the way is a lottery. Something like our chocolate wheel that one sees at fetes and carnivals. Here you can win anything from a toothbrush to an electric fan or bottle of wine. There are the usual 'money trees', where you tie money to lines strung up to the branches of a small tree, which is placed in a plastic bucket of sand, to hold it upright. They are decorated with fringed paper and sometimes have monks requisites such as soap, toothpaste, razors and small towels attached to the tree. All money donated goes to the building fund and the disciples certainly have fun, reaching into their pockets for *dana* donations.

A huge marquee has been set up to feed the masses out of the scorching sun, and we have some noodle soup. Chit makes sure my every need is met. He is the perfect host; his generosity is typical of Thai people. So giving, it is overwhelming. Beside the marquee is a truck decorated with ribbons, flowers, rosettes, draped red white and blue material, the colours of the Thai flag. On top is a conical shaped wooden object covered in gold leaf. The gold leaf is purchased to bring good merit. This carries the final tile to the top of the temple, but first it must do the rounds of the local villages. I have no idea when we set off with a crowd of villagers that I will be involved in Thai dancing for fifteen kilometres, which will take four hours in the heat of the day.

Thirty odd years ago the dancing was to a fourteen piece orchestra wearing tails that had been flown from Melbourne to Sydney for the occasion in a private mansion.

This year the three Thai bands performed nonstop while we gathered dancers along the way. Some people chose to partake in the procession in trucks, utilities and cars, even tractors, until about two thousand people twirled their way along the dusty roads, through tiny villages and rice fields. Water was handed out at front gates to either drink or throw over our parched bodies.

We were propelled by the excitement and hype of it all and barely noticed the kilometres passing by. Finally the gates of the temple were in sight, but no, we took a side track to yet more small villages.

After this I must confess I accepted a lift in a car with a Spanish man who is married to a Thai girl. He has seen all this before, so he came prepared. The last few kilometres were enjoyed in the luxury of his air conditioned Toyota car.

Always time for more food before a short walk through the village with Chits son Bee, who reluctantly accepts some chips, colouring pens and a book. He writes his name beautifully with much mindfulness.

The other New Years Eve we had a sumptuous banquet with glazed ham, roast turkey, sides of beef, carved by chefs in tall white hats, followed by Bomb Alaska in full flame.

At sunset a performance by the school children began, the stage was lit up like fairy land. The band, after a few false starts get their act together and the young dancers start their routine. A nervous little singer steps forward with a microphone. The master of ceremonies must be all of ten years old. He refers to his notes from time to time but mostly ad libs, next an umbrella dance with vibrant colours blending as they twirl, sometimes getting caught up with each other, as the stage is rather small. People walk up to the stage to interrupt performers to donate money. The kids have trouble getting back in step again, but it is all for a good cause and no one minds.

We have time for a *mandy* and change of clothes. I wear a simple cotton skirt and top, I purchased in Nepal.

The night I got engaged at that party all those years ago, I wore a long formal evening gown and the men wore Black Tie dinner suits

A screen was erected in the paddock with loud speakers and projector, showing Thai *soapies*. On a large stage nearby the main entertainment started at a couple of hours before midnight. We put our cane mat on the ground ready for the big show, Cabaret Style. The MC made announcements in Thai, which I didn't understand. Then on came the dancing girls. Well actually one or two were 'lady/boys'. A Thai man who dresses in women's clothes. Their revealing costumes were too much for some of the girls to handle, so they wore different coloured underpants and bras to conceal more of their bodies, beneath silver lama costumes.

They had many quick changes and danced while others sang, it was nonstop all night. I mean literally till dawn the next morning. Then the whole stage, sound system, banners and scaffolding was dismantled within an hour. Leaving no sign of life, except for a heap of plastic bags, bamboo clamps, which held barbecued chicken, the odd burst balloon, water and beer bottles, wrappers and chip bags, all lying in the dust. Sorry to say I didn't last the distance. Sleep overcame me and it was back to Chits house for a few hours rest.

In Australia that night we danced on cloud nine, celebrating till nearly daylight and falling into bed at my mother's home, which had been my family home where I grew up. It was a New Years Eve never to be forgotten.

New Years Day dawned hazy. The Buddha year 2540, the Western year of 1997 had begun. The sun shone on the temple, ceremonies started again. The loud music had become softer, or was it the fact I had become accustomed to it?

By now my many Thai friends all wanted me to sit with them and join in the chanting inside the temple. I made my bows to the Buddha and took five precepts, sitting beside Chit's sister. She was quite astonished that I knew the protocol and Pali words of the ceremony. She pats my leg to show her approval.

The important moment of sending the final tiles to the temple roof had arrived. Followers put the last garlands on the cone to bless and make safe the temple, so as to carry on the *dhamma*, the Buddha's teachings. White string was strung out among the crowd to be touched by everyone, so that each person can send their blessing. Afterwards, this string is broken or cut into pieces to put around your neck or wrist for good luck.

A pulley system takes the tiles to the highest peak of the roof, where a makeshift scaffold of rough timber sits precariously with two men to work the ropes. A cheer goes up, crackers go off with a loud bang and the ceremony is complete.

I suppose in a way my engagement ring is a good luck charm and form of commitment too. At the Australian party I wore my mother's engagement ring, a glistening green emerald, surrounded by diamonds.

We were having a replica made and it was not finished in time for the gala night.

When all is quiet I take a final walk through the village of Ban Somrong, by now everyone is my friend. I am welcomed to their homes; they are taken to my heart. As I pass by each home, I am invited in and offered food and drink. Unfortunately I must refuse. I have eaten beyond my capacity and I explain 'I only drink *nam*' water.

A drunken man falls down in the dust; he is legless and attempts to stand up without success. As I go to help him up, I see his cigarette has landed on his chest and started to burn a hole in his shirt. I quickly remove it. He is beyond getting vertical and puts his hands together to thank me, as he rolls onto his side. A Thai man nearby indicates to leave him. *'Mai pen lai'* never mind, he says. I walk away reluctantly. About half an hour later I see my drunken friend being wheeled away on a trolley, by a slightly less drunk mate. The blind leading the blind!

Chit told me the bus was to leave at 5pm, so I stroll down back alleys and along the lake, passing the bus stop at 11.30am. I see people preparing to get on the bus. When I ask what time it is leaving, I am told, to my astonishment, in half an hour! I rush to Chits house to alert him and start frantic packing up, cleaning the house and we all make it to the bus with only nine minutes to spare. Chit loads two bags of rice in the baggage space underneath.

It is not long before the disco bus swings into action. This time I figure, if you can't beat 'em, join 'em. So this tired and worn out *farang* gets up in the aisle with the Thai ladies, who are very merry on Mekong Whiskey, and discos in to the night as we make our weary way back to Ban Phe. We have the usual stops and Chit buys fruit, noodles and water for me. He is thoughtful beyond words.

The bus driver is excellent, unlike some I have experienced in Thailand. He drives the eleven hours without a relief driver and doesn't appear to need sleep. He is cautious on the steep downhill runs, changing in to lower gears to save the brakes and allowing traffic behind to pass.

Our weary group wakes the ferry driver at Ban Phe to take us to Koh Samet. We walk to Chits rented shed, where he and Rune live on the island. He carries one bag of rice nearly a kilometre, and then goes back for the other one on his motor bike. He then insists on taking me back to my bungalow on the motor bike to Pudsa Beach. Everything is closed down and shut up, as it is after midnight, I choose to sleep the rest of the night on the beach in a deck chair. I only have my sarong as a sheet to put over me, but the night is balmy and I love to sleep under the stars in paradise.

You ask me which was the most memorable New Years Eve…
Comparisons are odious, as they say.

In a small village in Southern Thailand, Noni
celebrates the opening of a Buddhist Monastery,
in street dancing with the locals

ENERGISE

There is vitality, a life force, energy, a quickening,
that is translated through you into action, and because
there is only one of you in all time, this expression is
unique. And if you block it, it will never exist through
any other medium and will be lost. Martha Graham

If travelling with one person it is best to have a leader and a follower. The leader checks out the options, gives the follower a chance to discuss those options and if it suits both that's fine. If it does not suit both parties it is best to go your separate ways and perhaps meet up at a future place and time. Everyone needs their own space and nothing will drain you quicker than friction and lack of communication. If you are travelling with a friend; make sure you have clear guide lines as to your needs *before* you leave. Do you have a similar budget? Do you both want to stay in the same level of accommodation? Are your preferences for buses, trains, taxis, tours? Are you both good walkers? Do you like similar eating establishments? It is much better to clarify these things before you decide to go travelling with someone. I have travelled with one friend, two or more friends, relations, groups of unknown and known people and as an independent traveller. All these situations have their advantages and disadvantages it is a very individual thing.

- Arrange a lay day or some down time every so often to catch your breath.
- Take a tip from the locals in tropical climates and have a siesta mid day.
- If it is really hot, wet a sarong; lie under it with no clothes on, preferably under a ceiling fan.
- Power naps are good pick-me-ups.
- Get to bed early if you can. It is important to get enough sleep.
- Use eye shades and/or ear plugs for a better night's sleep.
- A few drops of lavender oil on your pillow makes for a restful night.
- If the mattress is too soft, sleep on it on the floor.
- If the mattress is too hard, put a doona or blankets under the sheet.
- Eat healthy unprocessed food for energy. Wash fruit and vegetables in bottled water.
- If your energy is failing or you are climbing a mountain and need an extra boost, 'thump' your thymus. The area just above your breast bone.
- Beware of negative people draining your energy.
- Gently direct negativity in a positive direction, or at worst just walk away.
- Give of your own energy where it is valued and returned.
- Lack of sensitivity and consideration to others feelings can lead to exhaustion of both parties.
- If we spend our time and energy wisely the journey will be smoother.
- Tiresome people can drain your energy and wear you out.

- Get rid of clutter in your life, it can weigh you down physically and mentally. Not just material clutter but mind clutter also.
- Write the situation down on paper to diminish stress.
- Write down positive affirmations and things you are grateful for.
- Drink plenty of clean filtered water.

HORSES OF HORTABAGY HUNGARY

It was cold and raining heavily when I arrived by train in Debrecen in the eastern grasslands of Hungary. None of the staff can speak English and I am the only guest at the Hotel Italia. There is no heating in the room and the bathroom is a long way down the hall. As I have not prebooked any accommodation, I do the usual cupped hands to my tilted head eyes shut. It is the universal language for a bed.

I stood at the nearest bus stop in my raincoat, not having a clue which direction to take to get to the city. A young girl and I used sign language and somehow I got to the city centre, then another bus to the Tourist Information Centre. I wondered why it was the only place open and the city was so devoid of people. It is a public holiday, someone shows me in a dictionary that it is Wild Monday. That accounts for the weather. The tourist officer, Balaza, gives me information I need and arranges a trip for me for the next day to Hortabagy. This is the reason I have travelled across Hungary nearly to the Romanian border. I have heard about the famous performing horses and riders of Hortabagy and come hell or high water I am going to see them.

I ask Balaza if he knows where I can use an internet to send emails. No problem, he says use ours and doesn't charge me. I could stay in the office all day, it is so warm and the staff friendly and helpful. I finally drag myself away and on to a trolley going to the railway, as that is the only place a café is open and by now I need sustenance. I would love some Hungarian Goulash but unfortunately I can only get Pizza.

I make myself understood to get the right bus back to the hotel as by now it is cold, wet and windy in the streets and walking is out of the question. The next day the rain has stopped and I now know my way to the Tourist Centre, so I choose to walk, you see so much more that way. I picked up my tickets for the tour of the National Park and performance by the horses. I bought some cakes for the staff to thank them for their help. They are very modest and say "we are only doing our duty".

I walked to the train station and took the 50 minute ride to the small village of Hortabagy. I started to follow the people from the train going into the village and thought I had better ask where the horses are. I was directed through a boggy paddock, then a corn field, past some bales of hay and over a footbridge. There was not another soul in sight. Then I saw the Epona Hotel and the stables. For one and a half hours I was taken in a carriage drawn by two beautiful bay draught horses, with a visiting German family who could speak a little English, through the National Park.

We first saw an ancient breed of sheep, then some grey cattle contentedly chewing their cuds. We climbed down from the carriage to see a spectacular performance by riders and horses. One rider was standing on one horse while holding the reins of five others; they galloped around us in a circle. There was nothing to hold the five together to stop them going their separate ways, but they were well trained and stayed close to each other.

Three horsemen came from nowhere cracking stock whips and racing each other to see who could go the fastest. They then stopped in front of us and the horses sat on their hind quarters with their front legs stiffly out in front of them. To my astonishment they just lifted off the saddles, there were no girths. I took a closer inspection to make sure what I had seen. I indicated 'where are the girths'. They laughed and waved their hands in the air, meaning 'no girths'. After a few more tricks they rode off in the distance, it was surreal. We were in the middle of a flat grassed area as far as the eye could see.

Back in the carriage, the German kids laughed heartily at the pigs and piglets wallowing in mud. We saw mobs of warm-blood horses and back at the stables I was allowed to pat some of the beautiful dressage horses. One of them was called Noni.

A trolley ride to the Thermal Hotel Baths found me wallowing in the warm mineral water in bright sunshine. I walked in the forest and watched frogs, birds and bees lazing by the pond. I swapped a massage at the hotel and finally got my meal of Hungarian Goulash, it was up to expectations. The next day I took the train back to Budapest. What a wonderful journey.

The Horses of Hortabagy, Hungary

BUFFALO HORN
MASSAGE MALAYSIA

Fear not, the buffalo is not attached to the horn at the time of the massage, but it might as well be!

Penang, Malaysia leaped out at me from an advertisement in a Sydney newspaper. It was a good package deal, so it did not take much for me to make my mind up while visiting a Cabramatta Travel Agent with a friend. I went off to an ATM, withdrew enough cash for a deposit and a couple of weeks later I was on my way.

While staying at a hotel in Georgetown, the capital, I went out exploring the local area. Called in to a shop looking for a small jar of honey and ended up making a plan to massage the owner, Mr Deh at 5.30 pm. A price was established, which incidentally paid for more than one night's accommodation at the hotel. I gave him a combination of Swedish and Thai massage – he went away happy.

Then I went to a beach area at Batu Feringhii, half an hour away on the local bus for the day. Got off at the police station and walked to the beach. No swimming because of the dangerous red jelly fish, read the sign, so I strolled along under the palm trees and there was Mr Anthony, Chinese/Malay, ready to pounce on the next passerby. Trade was slow that day. He advertised neck and shoulder massage for twenty ringgit about AUD$7.50 for twenty minutes. He learned to massage from his brother, who learned from a Taiwanese man.

His strong massage concluded with a scraping of my neck, shoulders, back and arms, with a beautifully carved buffalo horn. It was shaped like a razor and only a couple of degrees off being as sharp.

He did not miss an inch of the area. I could feel the heat it generated. Then coming down my arms to my wrist he suddenly thrust the horn in between the web of my first and second finger and pressed like hell. Wow! Just as well I have a high pain tolerance. Then he put some Chinese herbs on two acupuncture points on my shoulders and said 'This will burn, let me know when you can't stand it any longer?' He was right. It burned OK and I finally said enough. I said my goodbyes and walked away feeling fantastic. I had the best night's sleep I had had in weeks.

A few days later I booked into an apartment, Sri Sayang, on the twenty-sixth floor overlooking the beach at Batu Feringhii. I once again took a stroll along the beach past large and luxurious resorts. On the beach under shaded umbrellas were many massage and reflexology treatments taking place. I chose an older Chinese/Malay man, Mr Foo, for a foot reflexology and leg massage. Mr Foo is fifty-two years old and been massaging since he was five. He cured his father's hip problem at the age of eleven. He massages seven days a week and still loves doing it. He can't understand why I am semi retired. 'Keep going' he says.

He starts with foot reflexology. His diagnosis is spot on, even to the fact that I only need glasses for reading. He says my blood pressure is fine, lungs okay, brain very good, also hearing no problem. My left neck and right shoulder and lower back all problems – dead right. Knees running out of 'grease' – absolutely. Heart a little weak, kidneys fine. 'Last night,' he says 'you woke only once or twice'. *True*. Now how did he know that? 'You should drink five litres of water a day while you are in Malaysia'. Well I have been going well on three but he was right about everything else, so why not this?

He wishes me well and tells his next client, an English lady, that I am a massage therapist from Australia. I tell her he was accurate with his reflexology. She doesn't want to know, she says she has too many things wrong, he would find out that every organ in her body has a problem.

A few days later I had another massage with Mr Anthony, at the northern end of the beach. The buffalo horn man. This time I got him to work on my lower back, which had been objecting very strongly to the board like mattress for the last three nights at the Sri Sayang Apartments. He finishes again with the scraping of the buffalo horn and puts the burning Chinese herbs on my lower back. The burning sensation is strong but I am determined to 'sweat it out', till he removes the cotton wool, which carries the burning lotion.

When he is finished I thank him very much and stretch out on the coarse sandy beach, listening to a full brass band practicing in a nearby building. My back is so much better. My body has had a marathon workout. I feel I have been running with the bulls in Spain. I succumb to sleep.

KOH SAMET THAILAND

A day in my life on a small island in the Gulf of Thailand.

My early morning meditation starts at 6am on the beach in front of my bungalow. It is easier on the beach to dig my ankles into the sand whilst sitting cross-legged. The sun is coming up over the horizon on the water. A gentle breeze dusts my face. The negative ions coming off the waves help me to breathe more clearly and deeply. The distant sound of the generator fades as I focus on my breath.

Half an hour later the meditation is complete. I open my eyes to find two local dogs have joined me. They do this every morning, it takes me a few seconds to see them, as they blend in so well with the sandy rocks. They lie so still, not a flinch of an ear, not a flicker of an eye. I thank them for their company.

Just before seven my young sixteen-year-old friend Stick (so named because of his tall thin body, like a stick insect) arrives with his plastic bags full of fresh vegetables, rice, and water for the old monk on his alms round.

Stick sells fruit from two baskets up and down the beach during the day. His English is very good. I give him a small gift, he seems surprised. "For me?" he says, "Yes" I reply. "To keep" he says. "Yes for you" I say. He places his hands together in a *wai* and bows slightly. Then he shakes my hand. So both cultures are covered. He is so polite and uncomplicated. The gift is a pair of groovy sunglasses, the young people all wear them in Thailand. I found them washed up on the beach. He looks at himself in a mirror and is delighted. The old monk appears on his alms round, his faithful dogs preceding him. He and I have been friends for many years. He speaks no English except to say "Hello" to attract my attention to the fact that he is going to give me something from his bowl. Usually food or a drink. I offer him bananas; Stick places his offering in the monks bowl also. We squat down while the monk chants his blessing for us.

Today the monk has given me two strands of yellow cord, to tie on my wrist, to keep me safe. Stick ties them on for me, as monks don't touch women and vice versa. Stick translates for me. I tell him I am teaching English at a temple school in Rayong, on the mainland for six weeks. I will come to Koh Samet every weekend. I will return next Friday for two more days in Paradise. The old monk grins in the sun, with the odd stump of a decaying tooth behind the smile.

Stick says his farewells and again thanks me for the sunglasses. I see him later selling green mangoes, sticky rice in banana leaves, coconuts, pineapples and bananas. He hasn't any ripe mangoes and the green ones, I find really sour. The locals dip them in a mix of salt, sugar and chilli.

After reading on my porch for an hour, listening to the clink of the beautiful shells, which Sala has given me to make into wind chimes, with old fishing line and bamboo sticks. Some I made from coral, bones and cuttlefish. As a joke I made one from rubbish I found on the shore, a green plastic toothbrush, white plastic flowers, plastic spoon, orange float and green spool. It gives me pleasure to listen to them and watch the faces of passersby.

For breakfast I decided to go to Samed Villa, the next group of bungalows along the beach, for yoghurt and porridge with banana.

It is yummy but when I get to the last mouthful, I discover a fly has decided to commit suicide in the rolled oats. I push it aside saying "Mai pen lai kar" Never mind.

As I walk from the restaurant I notice one of the ever present dogs has decided to leave its *calling card* right where everyone walks in and out. I point it out to my sweet young waitress friend Amak. She says "mess" and sits down….doing nothing about it! Oh well I tried. I didn't tell her about the fly in my porridge. What would have been the point?

Time for a dip at Pudsa Beach. It is less crowded now, because a pile of rocks has been dumped in the middle of the beach, as a landing for the trucks and backhoes that take material from a barge to the site, where they are building a dam. At present there is no fresh water on the island, it has to be pumped each day from boats from the mainland, through a large blue hose to every group of bungalows.

My friend Jack has had to move his windsurfers for hire further north to Jep's Beach, as it is too dangerous at present at Pudsa. The wind surfers could come hurtling into the rock pile. His inner tubes are still here to rent. His mother Nom has a small hut with a bench and seats beside the Pudsa Café, where she makes the best *tom viteo gai*, chicken noodle soup on the island. I have my lunch there every day. For 20 baht (less than an Australian dollar) who could ask for better.

At 10am Sala comes to cut my finger and toe nails. He does it with so much care and mindfulness. He files the rough edges of each one with loving strokes, and then finishes off by kissing my hand. I ask you; where else in the world could you get such treatment, in such beautiful surroundings for 50 baht.

Kathryn from San Francisco calls by. Her friend Victoria is sick and they are leaving the island. I had dinner with them last night.

Two very interesting women. Not surprising really, I am always meeting fascinating people on Koh Samet. I call on Victoria to assure her she hasn't got malaria and see if there is anything I can do to help.

The German fellow in the next bungalow, who is married to a Burmese lady, is playing dominoes with her. They look thoroughly bored. Jack introduced me to them last night and when the German asked me if I had been to Koh Samet before, Jack answered" Yes! Mama is a Samet person". That gave me a warm feeling of acceptance.

Later as Jack went by he laid his hands on my shoulders saying "Hi Mum, how are you?" Jack is gorgeous, unlike most Thais; he doesn't give a toot about his skin going dark in the sun. Most of them are so worried; they perpetually lighten their skin with powder and stay out of the sun. Such a contrast to us *farangs*, (foreigners) who are all, trying to get darker. Maybe one day we will strike a happy medium. Jack is almost hyperactive. He always has to be doing something, whether it is windsurfing, turning cartwheels on the beach, playing Frisbee, soccer or teaching me the Diablo. He even enjoys throwing a tennis ball with me on the edge of the water. Not for Jack, this sitting around playing cards, drinking and smoking.

Da owns the small shop on Pudsa Beach; she is always well groomed and has good English. Her husband Tuang doesn't do much at all except complain about the lack of money.

The big chestnut dog who rules the canine world at Pudsa lies under the shade of Jeffrey's boat. He snaps at flies with little success. I have noticed this dog over the years as he referees smaller dog fights on the beach. He wears a red woven collar, which gives him high status in the pecking order. He is by far the best kept and healthiest dog on the island.

Jeffrey's speed boat sits on the trailer under the trees, with a new coat of paint, proudly displaying the name Jeffrey-The Islander. He seldom has it in the water and doesn't promote his business, aside from a faded board stating that he takes trips to Ban Phe, on the mainland or around the island to coral reefs off outer uninhabited islands. Jeffrey speaks very good English and is married to a lovely girl called Mow, who works at Ao Phao (Alpine) Bungalows, a few hundred metres up the beach. She is recovering from a kidney operation at present. Jeffrey's passion is cards, which he plays with Da, Tuang, Somsak and Jow, the owners of Pudsa Bungalows.

A very hairy *farang* is *cooking* himself on the beach, no umbrella, no shade. Many *farangs* are having Thai massage on the beach under the shade of the coconut trees. One hour…150 baht, really good value. Young girls and fellas have their hair plaited in fine braids finished off with coloured beads. It is a work of art and cost 150-250 baht.

At 1pm sharp my friend Sala turns up to give me a massage. He now knows where my sore spots are and puts extra work in on them. He greets friends as they walk by, but he is still very focused on this work. Just the way he picks up your limbs and puts them down, shows such care. His wife Sai also massages and plaits hair. They are a popular pair and make a good living out of working very hard seven days a week.

My other massage friend Chit has gone to Surin, in the northeast of Thailand to plant rice on his family farm. Last New Year's Eve, I went with Chit and his wife Rune to their village to celebrate the completion of a new temple. It was quite an experience.

There are three young Thai children clinging to an inner tube in the shallow water. They smile and say 'hello'. Most Thai women swim in T-shirts and shorts, unless they are very liberated. The more Westernised ones are usually Patpong girls who come from girlie bars in Patpong Road, in Bangkok. They are with foreign men, usually European who have *bought* the girls for a weekend beach holiday.

Some couples seem to be enjoying the experience, others are not so happy. It is interesting to sit and watch the body language and relationships on the island.

Jow is always asking me to massage her shoulders as I walk past her while she is sitting for a well earned rest. As she gives me a good discount on the bungalows it is the least I can do.

Unfortunately most Thai people have not been educated about rubbish and pollution. I find the younger generation, as a rule are more likely to look for a bin. Then of course it is someone else's responsibility to empty that bin in a proper place. It doesn't always work out that way. I always enjoy cleaning up around my bungalow.

Foreigners pay an entrance fee to the island, as it is a National Park. This doesn't stop the locals from shooting the birds and eating them.

Jet Ski boats are only allowed in two areas. This rule is not always adhered to. If the young Thai drivers can see there is money to be made, they will come into any beach, disturbing the peace and quiet. The same with the Banana Boats. The long banana shaped plastic blow up seat for four of five people sitting astride. They get towed through the water at break neck speed. They wear life jackets, so that when they are thrown unceremoniously into the water, when turning too fast, or a large wave capsizes them, at least they will float until they are picked up again.

Jeffrey's Banana Boat has deflated like a dead snake, on a bench under a tree. Its lifeless body seems to have accepted its fate. I once saw him make a half hearted effort to pump it up.

The odd job man sits drinking his Mae Kong Whisky from early morning till late. His eyes get redder and his body folds over more as the day progresses. He indicates he would like his shoulders massaged. Then he massages mine. He is quite strong all things considered. A group of young Thais, probably university students, sit on the cane chairs at Pudsa Café One is strumming a guitar others sing softly. A group of older men sit watching Thai Boxing on the TV. They are so enthusiastic about the game, they could be right there in the ring. They cheer and shout, jump up from their chairs as an opponent lands a foot on the others waist, or a left hook finds its target.

A *sangtaew*, local taxi, arrives with more Thai and *farang* tourists. A *sangtaew* is a utility truck with seats either side in the back. The road is rough and windy, with great washed out areas and shaky bridges. There are bars for you to hold on to so you don't get speared out.

I walk along the beach past Samed Villa, Silver Sands, Sea Breeze, Ao Phao, and Jeps Little Hut to Naga. Naga is the seven-headed snake that is said to have protected the Buddha as he was meditating. The new stairs to Naga bungalows have just been decorated with huge concrete snakes painted vivid green, bright yellow and flaming red. My friend Sue Wild is there to greet me. She and her Thai husband Toss have owned Naga for many years. Sue came originally from England. They have three children, who attend an international school on the mainland. Sue and the children only get to Koh Samet on the weekends they run the Post Office and a very good bakery on the island, as well as renting out bungalows. Their baguettes are legendary. Chocolate brownies, Danish pastry and Lime Pie are delicious too. They provide a snooker table and tennis table for guests.

Back at Pudsa, Wuan provides a post box, overseas call service, money exchange and travel bookings. He is very obliging and speaks good English. You can make phone calls on your visa card, which is convenient, but expensive.

My front row bungalow costs me 200 Baht a night. For other tourists it is 250-300 Baht. It has a squat loo, shower, 24 hour water, electricity from 6pm to 6am. There is no mains electricity on the island, only generators. A good thick mattress on the floor, clean sheet and two pillows, two blankets, two cane chairs and a table on the porch. Clothes line at the side for drying sarongs and bathers. A mosquito net and coil. It is perfectly adequate and the view is worth a fortune.

The geckos have a feast every night catching insects around the light. They are like greased lightning, snapping onto their prey with dexterity and agility. They will tackle moths much bigger than themselves and have to take several gulps to devour them!

My mandy shower (throwing dishes of water over your body from a trough) is cool and refreshing. I wash my hair too. Put on clean clothes before going to dinner. Dinner at night is always at Samed Villa, my favourite restaurant. It is owned by a Swiss man, Joseph and his Thai wife. He runs a very good business, clean bungalows with western loos, hand basins and shower in a fully tiled bathroom. Water and electricity 24 hours a day, a speed boat service to Ban Phe or the outer islands for lunch and snorkelling. His banana fritters and ice cream are a real treat. The music in the restaurant is soft and gentle in the background. No video belting out murder and mayhem, as in some restaurants. The menu caters for Thai and *farang*. The food is excellent.

The walk back to my bungalow at night is safe and pleasant. Sometimes I walk further along the beach to Tub Tim to catch the cool night air. I buy some bananas at Pudsa to offer to the monks in the morning on their alms round.

The final meditation for the day is taken in a sarong, in the dark on my porch, listening to the gentle waves lapping the shore. I count my blessings and soak up the beauty and peace that surrounds me.

I am blessed beyond words.

JOURNAL YOUR JOURNEY

The words that enlighten the soul are more precious than jewels. Hazrat Inayat Khan

Never in my wildest dreams did I think that when I wrote about my travels in a journal, that it would result in a book. Apart from reliving the experiences and bringing back forgotten memories, it stimulates your desire to want to do it again. So many names and places fade over the years but here you have a perfect record to refer to forever, to re – live your amazing experiences.

- Make sure you write the day, month, year and country at the top of each page, for easy reference.
- As well as writing about people and places, include your feelings at the time, whether you were happy, sad, angry, joyful, irritated etc.
- If you wish, paste in tickets, menus, maps, flyers or brochures etc.
- If you are able to draw, enliven your journal with sketches.
- Make it a work of art or a scribbled masterpiece that speaks to you.
- In the back of your journal keep a record of your passport number, dates it is valid for, where it was issued and any visa numbers.

- Record travellers cheque numbers and date and places they were cashed.
- The company you are insured with and the number to ring in an emergency.
- Names and addresses of people at home you want to send postcards to.
- Who you sent postcards to.
- Names, addresses and phone numbers of contacts in the country you are going to.
- What medication, supplements you are taking and the prescription for glasses.
- What helped and what didn't.
- Write down helpful information from fellow travellers of places to see and stay and people to meet.
- Funny spelling on signs and menus.
- Quotable quotes from people you meet.
- The price of meals, accommodation, taxis, buses, trains for future reference.
- Record airport departure tax for countries you will be leaving from, if it is not included in your ticket. Keep that exact amount in your passport in the currency it is to be paid in.
- The names and addresses of people you meet overseas and want to keep in touch with, plus their email address.
- If you want to keep a record of where you took photos and who was in the picture.
- Record interesting coincidences.
- In the back of your journal write the words for 'hello/ greeting' and 'thank you" in the language of the country you are visiting.

LOST ON A CHINESE
MISTY MOUNTAIN

Climbing Ching Chendu Green City Mountain in China with a group of eighteen other Australians was quite a challenge. I am getting used to being the oldest in the group. Our purpose of travelling was to study Tai Chi Qi Gong.

As we got off the bus we were told there was only one way up the mountain. I decided to set off promptly, so I would not hold them up. There was a lovely light mist as I prepared my wonky knee for the long steep climb. My focus was on getting up and down the mountain without resorting to being carried in a sedan chair by two Chinese men. The ancient forest trees along the way caught my gaze, as did the little timber rest structures, but I pressed on until I came to a delightful lake. There was a beautiful ornate timber ferry weaving its way across the water to the other side where there was a chair lift operating. I decided to wait till the group caught up with me, as I had been so speedy that they were nowhere in sight. I waited…I waited and I waited. There was no sign of them at all. What had happened to them?

There was not a soul around who spoke any English, so I took some photos and enjoyed the peace and tranquillity of this serene scene. I kept thinking, they will turn up soon, I can't have been that fast. But they didn't. Finally an English couple appeared on the horizon with a Chinese Guide who had a map and I found there were two ways up the mountain. I had to back track and by this time the mist had turned to soaking rain. I trudged on, lifting one weary leg after the other.

Up, up I went not having a clue where my group was or how far they had climbed. I finally came to a substantial building and a Chinese man sitting outside beckoned me in through an ancient wooden door. There inside was my group listening to a lecture from the Master Taoist Monk. Relief was written on faces all round, especially mine!

DE-STRESS THE GENTLE WAY

Stress and humour are two emotions that simply cannot occur in the human body at the same time.
Segel and LaCroix

There can be stressful moments when travelling. You can misplace your passport at a crucial moment. In the customs queue, you wonder nervously if you will get through with that wonderful wooden artefact you bought. You may have too many bottles of alcohol etc. You can have an altercation with authorities, be late for a bus or train, be given incorrect information and be sent off in the wrong direction. You can have a difference of opinion with your travel companion; get bugged by their behaviour or irritating habits. The heat and humidity can start to take its toll. You can get sick and tired of waiting another minute for broken down transport or get ripped off by some sharp wheeler dealers. Can't fend off another biting insects or get attacked by a mob of mangy dogs walking innocently down the street can ruin a day. Having a bad dose of altitude sickness or diarrhoea on a bus without a loo is very stressful. Enjoying a lassi (fruit, yogurt, milk drink) in Nepal when you see a snotty nosed cow drinking the dish washing up water. Eating a Toblerone chocolate in Greece and you find a wriggling weevil in it. Nearly treading on a poisonous snake in South Korea or hearing a bull elephant trumpeting loudly beside your tent in Africa can raise your stress levels.

What can you do?

- Take three deep breaths.
- Have a relaxing massage as soon as possible.
- Meditate watching your breath.
- See a funny movie.
- Relax in a bath with essential oils.
- Write down what has stressed you (see chapter Letting Go of the Fear Factor)
- Go into nature, really looking deeply at trees, leaves, trunks, bark, dew drops, ants, waves, shells, sunsets, flowers or petals.
- Take some Rescue Remedy, just a few drops under your tongue or on your wrist.
- Laugh (see chapter on Laughter)
- Massage your feet after soaking them in warm water.
- Pat a friendly dog, cat or horse.
- Offer to help someone less fortunate than you.
- Go for a swim or snorkel in calm waters.
- Doodle with a pen or draw a picture.
- Build a mandala with available material.
- Make a wind chime from shells and fishing line.
- Throw a Frisbee or ball.
- Do Tai Chi Qi Gong or yoga. Massage a friend; it can be a two way healing.
- If you are at the beach, build a sand castle.
- Read a self help book or any book that absorbs you.
- Listen to gentle calming music, dance and sing.
- Count your blessings.

SKINNY-DIPPING IN CANADA

Who would have thought that three women in their sixties would be brave enough to get their gear off and jump into an icy mountain stream on Vancouver Island? Of course it was easy for the other two because they do it all the time. For me, the newcomer, it took some courage, believe me. We were close enough to hear the odd car on the road above the ravine and had seen other cyclists in the area. Oh well! What the hell, when in Rome…and all that.

I met Gerta in Amsterdam and here I was fourteen years later staying with her and her family in their beautiful home on Loch Glen not far from Victoria, British Columbia, on Vancouver Island, Canada. Gerta is married to an Australian and they have lived in Canada for many years. Gerta and I met at The Shelter, a hostel right in the heart of the red light district. She is an avid cyclist and was waiting for her bike to turn up, so she could take off for a long ride to her native Austria. She thought nothing of such a daunting task. Meanwhile Gerta and I took off with my travelling companion Mac to Texel Island. Mac had not ridden a bike for thirty years, so it was a challenge to circle the island in one day by bicycles. The locals all greeted us as we passed by, we stopped off at lovely cobblestone villages for sustenance, watched horse-drawn vehicles in the fields, checked out the lighthouse and were nicely tired by the end of the day. Gerta and I kept in touch over the years and visited each other in our own lands of Canada and Australia.

Back in Vancouver Island we started this day with yummy waffles for breakfast to sustain us on the six-kilometre bike ride to the Galloping Grove. Another friend Margaret came too, they are great adventurers, who love to get out into nature, rain, hail, snow, shine nothing deters them.

We parked our bikes near the road and clambered down into a ravine. At the bottom of the escarpment was the mountain stream, I'm sure it came straight from melting snow. We left our clothes on the rocks and slowly, slipping and sliding on the slimy rocks we slid into the 'pot holes'. The water was icy; taking our breath away by gasps, it was invigorating, refreshing and skinny dipping is fun.

Gerta had packed a delicious lunch and hot toddy in a thermos. We lay on the warm rocks and soaked up the sunshine heating up our bodies inside and out.

On our bike ride home we chatted about the books we had read, only to find out that Margaret and I had read so many of the same books. We sang songs, as we pedalled along the dirt road. We marvelled at nature and felt at peace in this wonderful country of snow capped mountain peaks, alpine trees, tumultuous rivers, mountain streams and lakes, forbidding wild life and friendly people.

When we got to Gerta's home on the lake we dived into the lake, this time in swimming costumes, for a much milder experience in the water. Neighbours came over for drinks and after a delicious meal we played Scrabble. We all got absolutely hysterical over the fact that I had all the letters for BORDEAUX and a place to put it on the board but one of the neighbours took my spot. I was mortified and ranted and raved, chuckled and wheezed in devastation. We will never forget that Scrabble game. It is etched on our minds and the skinny dip is pretty well scratched there too.

Noni skinny dipping in Germany

KEEPING HEALTHY

To keep the body in good health is a duty...Otherwise
we shall not be able to keep our mind strong and clear.
Buddha

Eat organic food if possible. Fresh unprocessed food gives you energy. Cut down on sugar and alcohol and drink plenty of purified water. Avoid ice in your drinks overseas. If you are going on a long journey, have a dental check up before you go. Eat where the locals eat. Pub meals are great in the UK, Asian street stalls are fine if you can see the food being cooked just before you eat it. If it has been sitting around a while, give it a miss. Let your digestive system come to terms with different food gradually if possible. (See chapter on food as medicine)

- Bless the road ahead of you. A Burmese Buddhist Monk gave me this advice years ago: Do it every day and before you take off on a plane, train, boat or whatever.
- Positive thoughts. It has been scientifically proven that positive thoughts enhance your immune system and negative thoughts diminish it.
- Toe wiggling and Body stretching. When you wake up, stretch your arms, legs, back, and feet in any order. Rest a

little then wiggle your big toes back and forth about twelve times. By this movement you are stimulating all the nervous system. Pay close attention to the movement.

- Body Scanning. Start by becoming aware of your toes and take your awareness up through the whole body to the top of your head. Visualising the bones muscles, tendons, circulation, nerves, organs etc. This boosts your immune system.

- Thumping your thymus. Like Tarzan, thump the area at the top of your breast bone, where the thymus is. This helps to activate the immune system.

- Raising on the toes. Stand with your feet shoulder width apart, point your toes slightly inwards, raise yourself onto your toes slowly. Lower yourself slowly. This exercise benefits the liver, gall bladder, nerves and heart.

- Arm flapping. Stand with your feet shoulder width apart, toes slightly pointing inwards, eyes closed. Let your arms hang and move with your body as you turn flap them from right to left. Let your head turn also. Keep the swing easy and natural. This helps your balance.

- Laughter. The benefits of laughter are well documented. Laughter activates the endorphins, which are the body's natural pain killers. Even fake laughter works. The mind does not know the difference and fake laughter usually turns into real laughter.

- Learn Tai Chi or Qi Gong. These ancient forms of moving meditation can be done inside, but it is much better outside near a lake, river, beach, mountain, forest, anywhere in nature. Wonderful to boost your energy.

- Solar plexus exercise. This can be done sitting, standing or lying down.

- Place both hands on your stomach just under your rib cage. Inhale feeling your stomach expand.

- Exhale using your hands to push up and into your stomach, turning the upper torso and head slowly to your left as far as possible, as you twist your pelvis to the right.

- Inhale bringing your entire body back to face the front. Letting your hands release slowly.

- Exhale again as you turn your upper torso to the right, look right, while pushing your stomach up and in as you twist your pelvis to the left.

- Inhale bringing your body back to the front.

- Repeat this exercise 4 to 36 times starting with small repetitions and gradually building up. When you do this exercise be aware of the solar plexus which is located under the heart, behind your stomach.

- This exercise is good for diarrhoea, constipation, neck and shoulder stiffness, lower back problems, headaches, jet lag, confusion and so much more. Used every day it works as a preventative.

BEAUTIFUL BHUTAN

Being in Bhutan is a dream come true. It is everything I expected and more. In fact I never expected to get to Bhutan with the hefty tariff to pay and then a tour group to contend with. But here I was on my way, due to the generosity of Megan, a friend of my daughter's who is working here and has allowed me to be one of her three guests a year.

On the flight from Bangkok via Kolkata I had the best window seat to see a clear view of Everest and the Himalayas. It never fails to take my breath away. On landing in Paro, Megan arranged for Kinzang to pick me up in her new car. Even the airport building is built in traditional style and a quick trip through passport check, visa check and customs saw me on my way. The fifty three kilometre drive to the capital Thimphu was fascinating, if rough and windy. In fact the road dictates that you cannot go faster than thirty kilometres an hour. The road work is done by male and female Indians with babies being restrained in sawn off forty four gallon drums, or sitting on a hessian mat or playing with witches hats on the road. Breaking up rocks, shovelling gravel and dirt, digging solid ground is back breaking work, especially in the heat of the day. Kinzang has all the windows up and a woolly jacket on while I am melting and suffocating! At times I can have the window down, that is when there is no dust blowing around and Kinzang is not freezing. By about five o'clock in the evening the weather turns quite cold and I am pleased to have a warm top.

The rapidly flowing Paro River is spectacular and hydroelectricity is one of Bhutan's main exports.

Megan's housekeeper, Beena, has prepared a delicious lunch, I then head into Thimphu for the afternoon to explore the shops. The Bhutanese men in their traditional *ghos* woven garments with long socks, large white cuffs on their shirts look so dignified and their manners are those that I have not experienced in a very long time.

Megan's sixteen month old half Bhutanese son Norbu is just divine. He is not a bit shy of me and loves a cuddle. He enjoyed the striped socks I knitted him. I also have a bag full of hand knitted scarves and socks to give away as gifts for those cold winter months.

This morning I did a tour of the Traditional Herbal Medicine Institute. An amazing display of all the native plants and how they extract the herbal juices from them.

Climbing two mountains in one day was not on my agenda; in fact I had firmly convinced myself I would NOT be trekking in Bhutan. However I found the opportunity too good to miss. Having seen the Cheri Monastery high on a mountain top after crossing the ancient foot bridge over the Wang River festooned with Tibetan prayer flags, I could not resist the temptation.

With my twenty two-year-old female guide Kinley we climbed and clambered for one and a half hours over solid rock, loose stones, muddy water courses, tree roots, gravel, dust and dirt with many rest stops for me to regain some semblance of breath. The high altitude and steep incline of the zigzagging track had me huffing and puffing but I was determined to make it to the top.

The rewards were spectacular, the views of the adjacent mountains, valleys, the forest aged trees covered in moss and ferns, the autumn colours of the leaves, the unusual pines and undergrowth, the small streams of icy water and then the crowning glory of the nearly 400-year-old famous Cheri Monastery at the summit.

It is a training college for learning Buddhist scriptures at a high level. Fifty of the more senior monks are in silent retreat, some for three years, three months, three weeks, three days, three hours and three minutes – what dedication. Leaving twenty monks to greet the visitors and show them around this magnificent building and into shrine rooms with altars of Buddha and famous deities.

It took half an hour to get down with the muscles in my legs seizing up. After a short drive we got to the Tango (meaning horse head) Monastery, to go through the same procedure. (Being a tiger for punishment) As we neared the top a group of about fifty monks were descending at a rattling pace, making quite a spectacle in their maroon robes, wending their way down the switchback trail.

We later saw them coming up carrying heavy steel frames and bags of sand at a much slower pace. This monastery is built on the side of a precipice in timber and stone with no nails, once again in the 16th century, how on earth did they do it? They must have had supernatural powers!!

HAWAII HOSTEL

The People You Meet

This heavily tattooed lady burst into our dorm at the International Hostel in Waikiki in a rush to shower and go out for dinner with her fiancé.

She had never stayed in a hostel before and wanted to know all the ins and outs, as she unzipped numerous bags. It seems she is a police officer from California in the US of A and she met her fiancé one year ago to the day and it is also her 40th birthday, so there is a double celebration. Her fiancé is 28. He is attending a conference here and is staying in a hotel, as his company is paying for the hotel room and he is sharing it with a male colleague, she had to stay elsewhere, in case his boss found out.

She had a tattoo covering her calf and shin on one leg with the names of her sons, a smaller one above her left breast, which she regretted as it was showing because of her new Hawaiian sundress, but the *piece de resistance* was the huge modern art crab, her Cancerian star sign, in black and red on her back. Its hind claws grabbed her sacrum, the upper ones spread from hip to hip and its eyes were focused about L1 L2 on her spine.

Her fiancé rang three times, once while she was in the shower, once while she was blow drying her hair and once while she was slathering her legs with lotion. It seems he is pretty darn keen. She sprayed some clear liquid on her arms and massaged it in, used her cigarette lighter to burn the tip of her eye liner, covered her face with makeup and blusher, rolled her eyelashes with mascara, smeared her lips with gloss, and smothered herself in perfume. She pinned up her multi coloured brownish, reddish, blondish hair with a clasp after tossing it back and forth several times. Why all this could not have been done in the bathroom beats me. She packed her stiletto black heeled shoes in a bag and wore her 'comfortable', platform sandals, for the street. She showed me a card she had bought for her loved one which played romantic music and said sweet words disclosing her undying love for Mr Right forever. When I asked her if she had planned a wedding date she said 'Oh I probably won't marry him, he drinks too much and we fight nonstop'.

She finally left, getting the OK from me and our bemused Japanese roommate. In the morning her bunk had not been slept in, I am assuming they threw caution to the wind and forgot what his boss may say about her sharing the hotel room.

After I came back from my early morning swim, her bunk was stripped of its sheets and bags gone. Oh well she did have a nice shower, wonder if the dinner was up to her expectations? She wanted sushi and cheesecake at the Cheese Cake Factory; he probably wanted something different… cause for further disagreements. I could see wedding plans drifting into oblivion.

GONDOLA OR GANDORA MOROCCO

On the Road to Morocco, Bing Crosby and Bob Hope would be proud of me!

I arrived in Casablanca with only the clothes I wore, at a very pleasant International Hostel. I got there close to midnight, having been either in airports or in the air for twenty-five hours. Quite a marathon. My bag however did not make it. I spent ten hours at Madrid airport on a stopover, as the flight I was going to Morocco on was cancelled and they had failed to tell me, despite the fact I had reconfirmed it all from Tunisia the day before. Hence my bag had nowhere to go. I must have walked miles being instructed to go to Terminal 1, then Terminal 2 then back again. I felt like a human ping pong ball. I ended up leaving from Terminal 4, a brand spanking new satellite airport in Madrid. Well maybe the exercise would do me good! I finally got put on a later flight with a different airline and had to keep chasing them up to find and deliver my bag.

The internet is free at the International Hostel, so I am like a kid in a candy store. It is well situated in the medina or market and close to the business area of the city. I went out and about trying to orient myself and keeping my mind off the fact that I had no other clothes except those on my back. I believe in travelling light... but this is ridiculous! Luckily I bought a pair of red quick dry undies in the market *souk* in Tunis and was wearing them when I ventured out of that country. There is no shortage of belly dancing sparkle and spangles about but I chose to purchase a traditional caftan. The name of it in Arabic sounds something like *gondola*, so I hope I don't suddenly start drifting down a canal. I had some fun buying it and a small wool and silk traditional Berber hand woven carpet. The salesman and I ended up singing Bob Marley, Cat Stevens and Beatles songs. *Imagine*? The caftan will be handy for a nightie on the warm summer evenings and during the day it can be worn over the top of everything with your bum bag underneath, I blended in nicely with the locals, although I think I should have covered my grey hair with a scarf.

The Moroccans are much more traditional than the Tunisians and not nearly so pushy in trying to get you to buy things. They are not nearly as westernised.

I called on a tour office to see if they could arrange to fit me in with a group on a bus, as I figured without my Lonely Planet Guide book it would be very difficult to find out how to get around and I would be better off using a tour company. They were not too helpful in that regard. I think all that sort of thing is arranged outside the country.

After three days my bag turned up at the airport. I was overjoyed to see it again. I had some much needed help from a very nice Moroccan gentleman at the Hostel; Bel Mustapha was a lifesaver.

Yesterday I thought I had found heaven when I arrived at the Youth Hostel in Fez on the four and a half hour train journey from Casablanca. It has three peaceful courtyards decorated with beautiful ceramic urns and bowls, hand-woven mats on the wall, a garden with a fountain which little birds dive in and out of as I do my early morning Qi Gong and meditation. A few tortoises slowly inch their way between the rocks and foliage seeking the early sunlight. Beautifully tiled areas with brass kettles, pots and pans, hookahs, colourful cushions and shade cloth surround the buildings.

One fellow passenger on the train was a gorgeous little boy, Karim, about three years old, so well behaved and delightful. I played tickling games with him and he nearly lost his thick glasses, poor little mite.

One night I went to the Kasbah and had a traditional meal of salad, tagine, consisting of delicious stewed vegetables and grilled chicken, slices of orange with nutmeg sprinkled on them, fresh orange juice and mint tea. The glass was so full of mint there was hardly any room for the green tea and copious amounts of sugar. The whole lot cost just over ten dollars. I sat opposite a lovely two storey restaurant called Le Kasbah des Fez. I took some video of the mass of people, mostly locals going by and there in the thick of it came a mule, laden with bags of goodness knows what overflowing it's harness.

I had a wonderful day trip to Meknes in a Grand Taxi, Mercedes, with four of us sitting on the back seat, very squeezy for over an hour. We passed many different crops other than olive trees, the soil is fertile. I saw beef hanging uncovered in open stalls beside the road; obviously they don't have blow flies like we do. Also the sheep have long tails, so how come they don't get fly blown? No cruel mulesing needed here.

On my last day in Fez I ate the most fantastic fruit salad. The bowl was piled high with banana, peach, apple, melon, orange, strawberry, walnuts, sultanas and topped with mashed avocado, all for A\$2.

The foul smell of the tannery is something best forgotten. Poor unfortunate men waist deep in filthy water washing the hides, what a terrible job. I saw orange hides drying in the sun coloured by saffron. The wool from 'dead' sheep (from the hides) is made into carpets, while the wool from 'live' sheep (shorn) is made into blankets. At the Medersa Bou Aninia, a fourteenth-century theological college I was in awe of the most intricate wood and stone carving, a very quiet place inside the bustling medina. I decided to have my picnic lunch in the peaceful surroundings. I saw two people carried out of the medina on stretchers. The forty degree heat may have had something to do with it! I saw the most beautiful pottery and African drums made from goat, camel, mule, sheep and fish skins. Saw inside the small Synagogue in the Jewish sector and the Royal Palace, where the King Mohammed VI resides on eighty acres. No one allowed beyond the gates, which are very ornate and splendiferous.

I had a young lad of about ten showing me around and everyone we bumped into or owned a shop was his brother! He informed me that he eats the snails that we saw climbing out of tubs in the market! He kissed me on alternate cheeks when I paid him. How sweet.

In the market I met Abdoul, a Berber man who can speak seven languages. He went into hysterics when I told him I had bought a traditional garment, a *gondola* and informed me it is a *gandora*. Oh well, I was close. He showed me photos of his family in the desert. What an amazing life they lead in what appears to be such a barren waste land.

I think part of the reason for me to be here this life time is to help others not having as good a time as me. I was the only one in the dorm the last night in Fez and I woke at about 1.30am to find the light in the bathroom across the hall on. I went to turn it off and there was a girl on a towel, with a pillow, lying on the floor of the loo, shaking and shivering. I said are you OK? She said she had been vomiting and had diarrhoea and her dorm was too far away from the bathroom, so she had taken up residence closer! I said come into my dorm and lie on a bed, which she did. I ended up giving her some Stemitil, my bottle of water, my roll of loo paper and a blanket to put over her. Real mothering stuff. Neither of us got much sleep, as she leapt up and down all night, poor girl. I know from experience how awful that situation is. Her name is Moira and she comes from Georgia USA and her travel girlfriend had just about wiped her hands of her. Most unhelpful in the morning when I went at 7am to knock on her door to tell her about Moira. She reluctantly went out and bought some of the essentials but forgot some of the most important ones, like loo paper.

While spending hours in the lost and found departments at Madrid airport, I handed out tissues to a girl who just lost it (and her bag also) she was in floods of tears. I gave her a hug and she got her self back together. Then a guy from New Zealand went ballistic, swearing and cursing because he had missed a presentation he was meant to give. I gave him my place in the queue and patted him on the shoulder and told him to calm down.

I must say some people have been very good to me too. What goes around comes around, as they say.

You may think that nine and a half hours is a long time to spend on a bus but I loved every minute of getting from Fez to Marrakech. The one driver drove all the way with only a short break after about seven hours into the trip. He was excellent.

On the outskirts of Fez we passed the Royal Fez Golf Club. The delightful, manicured green lawns with curved rows of the ever present olive trees were tendered and cared for even in the heat of the day. We drove through the Middle Atlas and part of the High Atlas Mountains. What a contrast to the rest of the country, forests and fields scattered with bright red poppies amid orange rhododendrons, pines and eucalypts and others I had no idea what they were. On the lower areas men were tossing freshly baled hay with pitch forks on to high trucks to be stacked and transported. It is hard work in the heat of the day.

We weaved our way around the steep roads and stopped at a few small towns and one quite large University City that could have won the Tidy Towns Award. It was superb with new dwellings tastefully built in modern architecture yet blending in with ancient Moroccan style. Some four storeys high with lovely gardens full of shady trees.

The small villages were quite poor and as we crossed one river I saw many women doing the back breaking work of washing clothes. Some of the more remote Berber villages looked as if their 'houses' had grown out of the earth. In one of the larger villages it must have been stock market day (as in animals). While waiting in the bus station I saw sheep being handed up into a truck, being grabbed by a man up top and levered over the edge. Why the poor things didn't break their legs I have no idea. Mostly they landed spread eagle on their fellow flock or got trampled under them. No RSPCA here.

One man came into the bus station dragging a sheep backwards on three legs, using the other hind leg like a lead. Three other sheep followed, as they do. The luggage compartment under the bus was opened and they were all thrown in. I saw horses, mules and donkeys being carted in what we would call a tip truck. I wondered if, when they were unloaded at their destination, by being tipped out. In a van I saw calves in side with sheep on the roof rack.

I saw small donkey and mule carts along the way with some being ridden by old men and women who had obviously been doing it all their lives. I saw some camels, but not real desert here.

One cafe we passed was called Cafe Frank Furte!

I have had snakes draped around my neck in Thailand, Malaysia and now Morocco. It was hard to escape the black cobras, pythons and numerous others of the snake family at the evening markets in the large Square of Djemma el Fna in Marrakech. The snake charmers are rousing their slithery performers into rearing up with bent necks and glazed eyes, mesmerized by the sound of the flute, drums and chanting. There must be about fifteen groups of them all vying for attention. The onlookers only have to show the slightest interest or want to take a photo and the next thing you know you have been draped with a moving necklace and fifteen dirham (about $A2.50) has been extracted from your pocket. Well it is all part of the journey and I got some good video footage as well.

The souk or markets are a real test of your senses. The constant beating of drums, jangling of sharp castanets, stringed instruments all just feet from the next group doing variations of the same thing can get a little tiresome. Amid all this are motorbikes going at breakneck speed, cyclists, push carts, donkey carts, mule trailers, carriages drawn by two stallions, petit taxis, food sellers, stalls of souvenirs, wood carvings, pottery, clothes, brass ware, you name it.

In contrast, sitting quietly on the ground are the medicine men and witch doctors with all their potions around them.

Porcupine quills, ostrich eggs and feathers, dried lizards, deer antlers still on the heads, chunks of what looks like coal, powders of all colours, charms to remove evil spirits or to cast a spell on your enemy.

I was looking through an album of designs for henna tattoos for the feet and hands and before I knew it I had a brown stripe of henna on my ankle. We had not agreed on a price or design, or even the fact that I desired one. The girl artist got very angry when I asked her to wait a minute and intentionally smudged part of what she had done already. I ended up giving her twenty dirham just to get out of her clutches!

I then headed to the food stalls, the appetizers where a bowl of common or garden snails in sauce, picked out of the shells with a tooth pick. NO thanks. Then fish, prawns, scampi, squid with chips. NO thanks, too far from the sea. Sheep's heads or hearts. NOT interested. Grilled eggplant, tomatoes, capsicum, olives, and onions in a salad. YUM. Hard boiled eggs cut up and placed in a pocket of bread roll, pita style, with sauces squeezed on to the egg. YUM. Delicious fresh orange, lemon and grapefruit juices.

Groups of four or five old men jig up and down, beat tambourines and sing to entertain you while you have your meal. After a while you pay them, just so they will move on to the next table. Poor unfortunate monkeys looking terrified are dragged around on a lead to be photographed with tourists.

There are men doing magic tricks, acrobats leaping and somersaulting in mid air, men walking around with conical red and green hats and coats with baubles dangling off them. They carry a bagpipe which is the hide of some black hairy animal presumably a goat.

There are men whirling ropes around their heads on the top of their hats, something like the hammer throwers at the Olympics only smaller and it stays intact. They also beat drums, bash cymbals and dance. The frenetic noise level sends me off to my quiet room. Must be showing my age!!!

The drive from Marrakech to the coastal town of Essaouira by bus took three hours. I sat beside a dapper Frenchman and with limited English he told me he spends nine months in Morocco and three months in Paris. I also ran into him on the promenade in the afternoon and he passed by my table at night while I was having a nice fish meal of sole, scampi and squid. He stopped to say he would probably see me in his dreams that night.

The bus was comfortable and the sights exciting. I saw goats up trees, eating the leaves, dry stone wall fences with a spiky dead bush on top of them, held down by stones. Not sure if it was to keep animals in or intruders out. Many acres of orange trees, grapevines and the local Argane trees, found only in this part of Morocco and nowhere else in the world. The oil from them is very good for your skin and very expensive.

There were hay stacks the shape of an up turned boat beside the Berber homes, with what looked like a sheet of concrete draped over them to stop it blowing away in the wind. In one town I saw hundreds of donkeys at a market and many people riding or leading them by the side of the road, some of them laden with bags or bundles of bushes or dry feed. Saw only a few camels. At one stage we went for miles with eucalyptus trees either side of the road, which is called Eucalyptus Street. Of course.

I found a nice clean apartment in the medina at Essaouira for 100 dirham a night (A$15), only five minutes from the beach. After lunch I ventured to the beach to be greeted by the ever present washed up plastic but the waves were good and the water chilly so I dived in. The local lads are playful and try to copy me floating on my back. A French woman looked after my bag while I swam and vice versa, all done by sign language. Essaouira is much cooler than Marrakech about twenty degrees but pleasant. I lay on the sand, dozed and did some people watching for about four hours. What bliss.

The second day I rented a bike for the full day. Having been critical of the locals riding through the souks, I found myself doing the same except I was going at snail's pace and there were a lot less people here. I rode along the beach promenade and into the countryside for four or five kilometres, and then I found the camels and horses on the beach. I checked out the horses and one black stallion called Atlas took my fancy. That figures, seeing I am doing my best to work my way round the world. I will ride him when I haven't got a bike, and had another swim padlocking my bag to the bike on the beach. Met up with a Russian man Vladimir in the surf, he has two Australians working for him on a documentary he is making in Marrakech. His daughter ran from the water after putting her toe in saying (translated) 'that poor woman (me) the water is freezing'. Loved it.

The next day I got up early walked about two km along the beach but no Atlas, so I decided to have a two hour camel ride instead. I chose Cappuccino, milk coffee coloured one humped with a frothy mane. Abdul ran behind until we took to the sand dunes and then a rocky area. I took pity on Abdul's feet and indicated did he want to sit behind me. In a flash he made a running jump at the back end of Cappuccino, who was moving at the time and landed neatly behind me. He grasped me in some very private places, so I gave him the sign language to desist forthwith. There is no room for hanky panky on a camel, thank you. I was so high up, I felt like I was on top of the world, the view was spectacular looking back at the walled city and medina and up to the distant hills with the surf of the Atlantic Ocean lapping the fine sand. We came upon the ruins of a large decaying and crumbling building, we passed a mob of female camels with calves and Cappuccino got very excited, his pink tongue gurgling in and out of his mouth, while making the sound of a boiling kettle. He is aptly named. A policeman rode up behind us on a horse, checking that the tourists are OK. For me I was more than OK… I was marvellous.

We stopped for a rest in the dunes and Abdul took the blanket off the natural wood 'saddle' and put it on the sand for me to sit on. He arched his back as if in pain. I ended up giving him a short Thai massage and he gave me a Moroccan one. He was good too with a few well placed instructions.

I walked back to the medina one happy little Vegemite.

After my four days in Essaouira I was refreshed and ready to go again. I had an excellent massage on the last night from a Moroccan girl trained in Swedish, aromatherapy and Thai massage. It is a wonderful place and it did not take me long to get orientated. The local boys tried to drag me into their shops and one Yassar got quite aggressive when I would not go upstairs to see his carpets. That's a different angle to the etchings. Near my apartment they all know I am from Australia, having seen me on the bike and in the surf, they think I am very 'sportive'. The old fort is spectacular with at least twenty canons along one wall. The sea is rough and bursts from the rocks as seagulls squeal and leap for their lives. Some fishermen go out in a blown up inner tractor tube with a very open net wrapped round one side to hold all their fishing gear. What a feat.

I also saw many tourists on crutches with bandaged or plastered arms, legs or heads. I speculate... did they fall down a hole in the footpath, or maybe run over in the medina by a motorbike or even fall off a camel?

I arrived at the bus station at 6.30am in the morning ready for the seven hour trip to Casablanca. There are two buses a day and would you believe, getting on to the same bus was a very aggressive Frenchwoman who had been on the same bus from Marrakech. On that occasion she had insisted that I was in her seat. I insisted I was in the right one; it was at the front of the bus with a great view. I stood my ground and finally she moved up the back. She did not speak any English. On today's bus we sort of played a 'Mexican standoff' game pretending we had never seen each other before. I nearly gave myself whiplash looking from one side of the road to the other. On her seat over the aisle I could see her reading the Lonely Planet Guide (in French) from cover to cover for the whole seven hours. She honestly did not look out the window once. At the short stops she did not eat or drink anything, just walked around chain smoking. Poor dear, she is missing so much in life.

I am astounded at the number of gum trees on either side of the road. They have been pruned so severely and have come back bushy and beautiful with their painted white trunks. We passed a mosque where the storks had built a magnificent nest on the tower. The usual donkeys, goats and sheep with large acres of crops and ploughed land, people doing their washing at wells were all so fascinating.

At El Jadida a distinguished looking man in a grey suit with a camel hair fez got on the bus. It was obviously too cold for him, so over the top of this he put his grey *gandora*.

The night before I left Casablanca, an American girl and I decided to have a 'slap up' meal in a classy restaurant just a short walk from the hostel. Sqala is set in the old fort with a delightful garden, live music, efficient service and beautiful food. The ambience was superb and a really nice way to say farewell to Morocco.

SOLO TRAVEL

*When we are in alignment with ourselves there is a
kind of magic that happens in everything we do. To be
in alignment with ourselves we have to love ourselves.*
Behran Gista

Travelling alone has many benefits, as does travelling with a
companion. Either option will not suit everyone. Solo travel creates
a lot of flexibility and for those who need their own space at times,
it is excellent. I have travelled alone thirty nine times to twenty
different countries. I prefer to go to remote areas and avoid the well
trodden tourist tracks. I like to meet the local people, learn about
their customs, traditions, culture and religion. I have made lifelong
friends with people I have met along the way. When you travel
alone, people are more likely to talk to you and you too will be more
likely to approach others. When you don't want to join a group and
just want to travel independently, this leaves you with a lot more
flexibility. I don't normally book ahead but find great discount deals
on arrival. I landed in Los Angeles once and looked at a notice board
of accommodation. Rang the number of a guest house, gathered
up two other backpackers and we were picked up and returned to
the airport the next day, I had a complimentary drink on arrival,
a continental breakfast and a free bus trip to Venice Beach all for

US$12. There was also a swimming pool and a restaurant. In China I met a 91-year-old Danish lady travelling on her own.

- Start conversations by offering a snack to someone sitting next to you.
- Ask for information on a map. Just a pleasant hello, where are you going?
- If saying hello to strangers is too hard, just start with a smile.
- Thank the bus driver, taxi driver, shop assistant, offer a word of praise.
- Don't be surprised in Asia if you are asked your name, age, and marital status, what you do for a living or your religion.
- Become a good listener; speak up if you don't understand what is said.
- Swap travel tales.
- Keep a pen in your reading glasses case.
- Always look back after you leave an area to make sure you haven't left anything behind.
- Take a small chain and padlock for the times you must leave your bag unattended, for instance going to the loo. A dog choker chain is good as it has a ring at each end.
- This chain is handy for buses and trains also.
- Offer a helping hand when you see a need.
- If you want to stay a while in a certain area, check out volunteer work. They sometimes provide cheap accommodation.
- Keep your money, passport and valuables close to your body but don't become paranoid about it being stolen, better to put energy into it being safe.
- Team up with another person for a few days if you are heading in the same direction. Cheap hotels sometimes charge by the room, not the number of people in it.

- If you feel comfortable about not booking accommodation ahead, it gives you more flexibility, if other options turn up.
- If you don't feel comfortable not having everything prearranged, booking ahead is fine but remember you can get locked into a situation which may be not as good as the one you heard about on the road.
- Many older people travel alone around the world. You will find them in cheap hotels, hostels, backpackers, guest houses, tents, campervans, caravans etc.
- Keep your wits about you. Be aware, alert and friendly and make the best of every situation.
- Learn how to email and Skype. Family and friends like to know you are OK.
- Learn the words for 'greeting' and 'thank you' in the language of the country you are going to. The locals will appreciate it.
- Most importantly, buy yourself an up to date travel guide for the country you are about to visit.
- Round the world tickets are a great option if you have time and want to see a variety of countries.
- A Eurail pass or Busabout is good value when travelling in Europe.
- Ecotourism is popular. Many countries offer farm stay where you can join in activities
- Research when local festivals are taking place.
- So much can be learned about a place and discount travel, when you are on the spot.
- You do need to have a faith and trust that all is going as planned.
- If your plans don't work out, be open to other options and don't dwell on what didn't happen.
- Check out the internet for special deals for singles.

Waiting for a bus, Noni plays her harmonica to fill in the time

LESSONS IN TIBET

Miracles do happen and I live to tell the tale. The highlight of this trip was to see the Potala in Lhasa but I could barely put one foot after the other on flat ground.

The journey by local bus from Kathmandu in Nepal to Lhasa in Tibet is quite a challenge. It tests your patience, compassion, endurance, stamina, energy, acceptance and many other emotions. On the bus were sixteen people, a girl from Australia, a French Canadian woman, with very little English, two Austrian professors, a young Swiss couple, he is a doctor, some Germans, Japanese, Americans and me.

At the border of Nepal and China (Tibet) at Kodari, we were herded off the bus and into a truck. The French Canadian lady and I sit in front with the driver, as we are the elders of the group, the rest pile in the back for the eight kilometres of a sort of demilitarized zone area between the two countries. It is a no man's land, with no road maintenance. At Zhang mu, the Chinese border, they are reluctant to let me through, because I have just come from Darjeeling and Sikkim, where there has been a plague scare. I talked my way on to the next bus which took us on a rough, winding road up to 3500 metres to our first nights stop at the Snow Lion Hotel. The room was very homely with orange and pink bedspreads and heavily embroidered pillow cases. The loo is down the stairs, out the front door, down an unlit passageway and into a 'long drop'. The Tibetan people are friendly and helpful, with no English language. The night was freezing cold and no hope of sleeping, even with a sleeping bag, doona, tracksuit and beanie to stave off the chilly air.

We set off early for Xigaze, 3900 metres up. We had wonderful views of Mount Everest and other peaks but by now the high altitude was affecting my senses. Thick heads and tiredness were experienced by everyone on the bus. The dusty road seemed never ending; I wore a cotton mask and had no appetite for food which is most unusual for me. We pass donkeys, ponies pulling and carrying heavy loads, yaks decorated with colourful harness, mobs of sheep, goats, people threshing barley and children wanting handouts. I really felt too awful to appreciate it and did not have enough energy to get out of the bus to take a photograph.

The second sleepless night left me with black circles under my eyes and thumping headaches, which I don't normally get. My back is aching from the unforgiving hard seat in the bus and the surface of the road. My nose bleeds, I take some homeopathic medicine, which helps a little, but I have nothing for high altitude sickness. We walked to a Tibetan Buddhist Monastery and a carpet factory. I can barely drag myself around, I am still not hungry and no way to sleep soundly. By the third day when we arrive in Gyantse, I am running a temperature, others in the group are ill with coughing, vomiting and diarrhoea. We walked to another monastery and I hitched a ride back on a pony cart, much to the amusement of the locals. The next day we stopped at a small village for lunch with only a couple of buildings, no one could eat except the driver, morale was really low. Some local boys were playing snooker on a table outside, I took out my mouthorgan and played *Waltzing Matilda* for the Australian girl, *Wooden Heart* for the Austrians and Germans, *Do Re Me* for the Swiss couple, *Frere Jacques* for the French Canadian,

When the Saints Go Marching In for the Americans and *Sukiyaki* for the Japanese, the small crowd clapped and a happier group got back on the bus with more energy and communication. We went over high peaks of 5500 metres.

As we drove into Lhasa, the capital of Tibet, to the Friendship Hotel, we got our first view of the magnificent Grand Potala Palace, the main monastery of the Dalai Lama, before he went into exile in India in 1959.

When we booked the bus in Kathmandu, we paid for our flight to return from Lhasa to Kathmandu. We were given vouchers and told to see Mr. Chen or Miss Olga at the Holiday Inn Lhasa for our tickets. The Austrians and I spent hours waiting, discussing and cajoling these people for our tickets. The Austrians rang the travel agent in Kathmandu from a public phone, with great difficulty and he said he could see what he could do. We managed to see the Norbulingka Summer Palace of the Dalai Lama and the Sera Monastery. By this time I too had diarrhoea and with no public toilets around, it was pretty woeful. I felt dead beat and just wanting to get to lower ground. At last I am issued with a ticket but they won't confirm a seat. What to do...what to do. Mr. Chen wishes me a 'Blessing from God and good luck'. I am going to need it. I am not coping well without food or sleep and the obstacles in my way. The Potala is all steps, after three steps I am out of breath and this was to be the highlight of my trip. Good lesson in not having expectations.

On to the Jokhang Temple were pilgrims are doing full prostrations, as they have for centuries. I need to rest frequently. Our guide confides in me that the Austrian professor and I are the pacifiers of the group. Nerves are frayed and bodies are heavy and crying out in pain, minds and emotions are stretched to the limit. On the day that the flight leaves, I get a bus at 3.30am to the airport, two hours away. Most of our group is convinced they will not get on the plane and have booked on a local bus for their return to Kathmandu. I could not face that journey again in my present state. There is no guarantee I will get on the plane, because my ticket is not reconfirmed. I refuse to let a negative thought enter my mind.

We go through the security check and pay departure tax and join the queue for our boarding pass. When I get to the counter, my backpack is unceremoniously thrown off the conveyor belt and I am told I have not had my ticket reconfirmed. I quietly explain that for three days I have been trying to do just that, I am ill and need to get to Kathmandu the quickest possible way. The Swiss doctor explains that I am his patient and he wants me on that plane. They take no notice but I thank him for trying. I stand patiently with determination until all the boarding passes have been used up. An official comes to talk to me; I tell him my tale of woe. He says 'follow me'. I am taken over the conveyor belt, down a dark corridor to his office. He demands I pay thirty yuan. I only have a fifty yuan note, I tell him to keep the change. He stamps my ticket; I get back to the boarding pass area and can't find my backpack. I am told I will get it in Kathmandu. Miracle of miracle it does arrive and I have a seat on the right side of the plane to get the full view of Mount Everest above the clouds for the second time. There are several empty seats on the plane. No one has lost face.

COPING WITH DOUBTERS

The people who matter don't mind and the people who mind don't matter. Bernard Baruch

There is always someone who says to you 'Are you mad? I wouldn't do that for all the tea in China'. Just smile sweetly and say 'just as well we are all different'. Some people can be a little envious that they haven't got the courage to do what you are doing. In 2002, two months after the Sari Club and Paddys were bombed, I went to Bali. The Australian Government was saying don't go and many planes had been cancelled. The only seat I could get was on a flight that left on Friday 13th. Was that an auspicious date? I could only get a flight home one month later – I took it. The airfare was double the normal rate but I was intent on going to see how I could help the beautiful Balinese people, if only by boosting the economy a little. I met only four other Australians which was most unusual. The experience was very enriching despite the obstacles. Some friends said I was crazy, others said, go for it. I'm glad I did.

- Set your goals and set your boundaries.
- Once you have made up your mind that you are going, tell family and friends your plans. When you are going, where you are going and when you are coming back.

- Tell them you have heard and read of others doing what you are doing and you can do it too.
- Make positive statements. Try to put their minds at rest by telling them you have done your research and intend to have a wonderful time.
- If you like, give them copies of your itinerary and contact points if possible.
- Tell them you will send group emails and would love to hear from them in return.
- You will find the biggest doubters are the ones who have never travelled. Those that have been bitten by the travel bug will encourage you.
- Don't let a few doubters put you off. Go with your gut feeling.
- If you start doubting yourself that gives others an opening to give you more doubt.
- Bite the bullet and go for it.

MOUNTAIN VILLAGE LIFE, SOUTH KOREA

Hye Won and Moon Su Ji live in a beautiful, isolated area about five hours away from Seoul. Hye Won is a Zen Buddhist Monk of some renown, having been a lecturer at university on Buddhism. Moon Su Ji is his attendant and chief cook and bottle washer. She has a bright, sunny disposition, always cheerful, even when she doesn't understand when we speak English too quickly. She is helpful, generous and a wonderful cook and hostess.

I first met this couple when they came to stay with me at Bondi Beach in Australia for two nights and stayed two weeks. I felt blessed to have such a fine teacher and master on a one to one basis. We had lengthy discussions, dharma talks on the Buddha's teachings, Qi Gong lessons a form of Tai Chi, enchanting tea ceremonies, we laughed, we played, we sang, we walked in nature and did exercises in local parks, much to the amazement and amusement of the passersby. Hye Won is a tall, good looking man and wears his robe of grey long cotton jacket and grey pants with a band at the ankle with style. He sometimes wears a large brimmed straw hat on his freshly shaved head.

One day Hye Won dived into the surf and kept going. I was convinced that he was going to end up in New Zealand. To watch him do his own form of Qi Gong was breath taking, his actions and

mind totally focused, poetry in motion. I wished his time with me
and my friends would never end, but in Buddhism we know that
everything changes, nothing is permanent.

Six months after Hye Won and Moon Su Ji's visit I went to
South Korea with my friend Dennis to visit them. Hye Won met
us at the splendid Seoul airport in Madonna, his twin cab truck,
and after a short tour of the city we were invited to a very stylish
Japanese Restaurant by a disciple of Hye Wons. After the long flight
I enjoyed sitting with my legs in the pit under the table and my back
against the wall, where I promptly went to sleep, after the meal. No
one seemed to mind.

After a long drive to the Saebacsan National Park with a few
stops for shopping and sightseeing we arrived at Hye Won's beautiful
retreat monastery about seven hours later. We bounced around for
the final miles on a dirt road and then up a rocky overgrown track.
We had our own rooms in the guest house and as we were being
shown around Hye Won removed a spider from inside my mosquito
net while being told to be careful not to tread on any snakes. As
Dennis has a phobia about snakes, this came as not such good news.
As time would tell, we had plenty of occasions for him to overcome
his fears.

We ate dinner off a low table, sitting on the floor, this was to
become the norm for every meal and our Western legs and backs
suffered greatly. I took a mandy shower throwing buckets of water
over myself. Dennis decided to bathe in the waterfall pond about
fifty metres away. Later in our stay we encountered a poisonous
snake sliding through the rocks, just below this pool. Just as well
Dennis didn't see it that first night while doing his ablutions; I think
he would have been airborne.

The next morning we walked over the mountain stream and up
the rough track to where Hye Won is building a pyramid house of

Perspex and timber. The second storey is his sleeping quarters with a large window opening out onto a magnificent view of the other side of the mountain with the valley down below. It was in this space that he gave us a talk on the five elements, water, earth, fire, metal and wood. Hye Won's philosophy is a mixture of Zen Buddhism and Taoism. His English is excellent and very understandable. In this pyramid he will grow vegetables under the slanted Perspex sides. He intends spending five months in winter, here in retreat with no electricity or heating device and only eating raw food. It is hard to believe that it snows here in winter, as everything looks so tropical and grows so profusely.

We were about to gather flowers in the forest to make into juice, when visitors arrived, Father Paul, a Jesuit Priest, and Mr. and Mrs. Thak from Seoul. Mr. Thak spent eight months here last year on retreat after an extensive bowel and liver cancer operation. He is now totally recovered.

For breakfast we had five grains ground to a powder with powered pine leaves and pepitas and nuts. You must chew this concoction for at least five minutes in silence before you swallow it. To be honest it is like trying to swallow a spoonful of Johnson's Baby Powder and just about as tasty, I imagine. I don't care how good it is for me, I am not going to attempt it again. I did not wish to breathe my last breath choking on a beautiful mountain in South Korea... sorry. Luckily we had other choices of food, large juicy peaches, yellow Kiwi fruit, bananas and almonds. For lunch we had grain bread, peanut butter, jam, croissants and grapes, which the visitors brought with them. We also tried some fermented wines made from pears, quite delicious.

While Dennis, Hye Won and Mr. Thak went for a dip in the waterfall pool, I did some hand washing. Another visitor arrives, a neighbour with hot steamed cobs of corn, there after he is called

Mr. Corn on the Cob, we later find out his real name, Mr. Chin and his wife is Mrs. Moon. We are invited to their farm, just down the hill. They are a retired couple whose son has gone to the city to further his career, as have many young men, leaving his elderly parents to run their family home and vegetable farm. Then two older very serious black suited men arrive; they leave their black shiny car down the road, as the last part of the drive is rough. Dennis and I are intrigued as to their business, but it really is none of our business, so we are left in the dark.

After another dip in the pool Dennis and I walk to the small village of Namdaeri about a kilometre away and at the local store the lady owner invites us to have a can of iced coffee, which was very pleasant. She feels the material of my pants, my T shirt, my magnetic bracelet and we chat away in sign language. Further on we walk past some road construction workers and get invited into their temporary building for food and drinks. Everyone is so friendly and not a word of English is spoken.

For dinner we had tofu and vegetable soup, Chinese noodles with vegetables, pickled garlic, which I became addicted to, and the root of some unknown vegetable. Father Paul and Mr. and Mrs. Thak are staying the night. The three men slept in the pyramid house. When I wake each morning my back and neck are stiff and my legs ache from all the sitting on the floor. I must immediately stretch and do some Qi Gong.

I then sit on the porch and watch the morning mist rising off the mountain like dry ice, clouds billow down the folds in the forest to dissipate into the valley floor. What a pleasant way to start the day. This morning for breakfast we ate ginseng, carrot, sweet potato and lettuce in kelp before going to see the farm that the Thaks have bought a few kilometres away. We walked over the rough and rocky forested hills and saw fields of beans, growing in profusion.

Dennis and I decided to walk home, calling in on a policeman at his weekender where he makes wonderful timber furniture as a hobby. He has made nearly a hundred stools that are to be presents for the guests at his daughter's wedding. He has given one to Moon Su Ji also. Here we drank red ginseng, for medicine he explained, in his limited English. Along the way we called at the only other store for more iced coffee and were given a delicious apple. We seem to do nothing but eat and drink with these hospitable, friendly and accepting strangers.

When we arrive home there are more visitors bearing gifts chillies and apples. Mr. and Mrs. Im live at the other end of the village and have heard about our visit. They have a beautiful baby and they all smile constantly. Their smiles say it all. That night we are invited by Mr. (Lee) Weightlifter to a party with friends and neighbours. More food is produced out of thin air. This time it is grapes, pineapple, fried chicken, savoury biscuits, chillies, lettuce, the white roots of something and fermented mulberries. They drank wine and spirits, Korean Whisky, like sake and lots of beer. Before long the music, laughter, singing and dancing began. These people really know how to party.

The next day Mr. Chin and Mrs. Moon put on a luncheon banquet for us with lots of really hot chillies. Maybe they think we are getting used to them by now. That's debatable. Her spotless, sparkling home is squeaky clean and before we are finished our meal Mrs. Moon is on her hands and knees polishing the floor. She is a real party animal and when the dancing starts, she is the first one on her feet to shimmy and shake like a teenager. We are joined by Mr. (Lee) Government and Mr. (Lee) Weightlifter and two other men, whom we have not yet tagged, who all join in the frivolity.

To shake some of this abundant living down, we travel in two vehicles to the Punggi Spa Baths, where we spend two hours soaking, showering, scrubbing and skittering from one hot tub to another in temperatures ranging from 26-44 degrees. Then we sit or lie quietly in the dry or wet saunas. Moon Su Ji scrubs my back; it feels wonderful to get all that dead skin removed. Outside we have a really delicious walnut ice cream and then off to dinner at a traditional restaurant. We have dessert back at Mr. Chins of vegetable pancakes, rice cakes and fruit. The after dinner entertainment started with Dennis standing on his head, and then Hye Won and Mr. Chin joined in. Mr. Weightlifter did the splits and then put his head on the ground, Moon Su Ji stood on one leg and tucked the other one to the opposite hip and put both hands out in front. Hye Won did his Qi Gong movements and I sat and watched, too tired and too full to move.

The next morning with renewed energy, Dennis and I walked to the International Monastery a few kilometres away, a beautifully maintained area of lush gardens, mown lawns and well kept buildings. There was a retreat in progress, so we didn't venture in. On the way home we helped a lady take her chillies out of the dehydrator and put them into bags, before carrying them to the drying house, a domed cloth structure down the road.

Back to Mr. Chin and Mrs. Moons for yet another meal where Hye Won danced Tai Chi style rock and roll, Mrs. Moon got in the groove and we all sang and danced and laughed till we were exhausted. The meal consisted of delicious soybeans in sauce, noodles, steamed potatoes, garlic, chilli and chilli sauces. Then we had an exhilarating experience, a Korean Traditional Tea Ceremony. First warming the small drinking bowls, then boiling water is poured onto the tea leaves in a small tea pot, then from the tea pot into the pouring bowl and finally into the drinking bowls. First we must feel the warmth of the bowls on our hands which are both wrapped around them, we then look at the colour of the tea. The first brew is pale and gets stronger until the final third bowl. Next we smell the aroma taking in a deep breath, gently and slowly we take a small sip, savour the taste and finally swallow, following the path of the tea through our bodies we feel our feelings and changes as the tea passes through our digestive system. This whole procedure is done with mindfulness and silence except for slurping the tea to cool it. This is accepted practice. It is really a meditation, being one with the tea. It is invigorating yet at the same time calming and peaceful.

One day we visited a Home Stay owned by friends of Hye Won. Mr. Lee and Mrs. Shin have a daughter Leo, who speaks perfect English and is a very switched on and super bright twelve-year-old, who attends the local school as well as an English Academy in Seoul. The Home Stay is called Wind Sound Water Sound and is set in a tranquil valley with three guesthouses on both sides of a swiftly flowing mountain stream. These mud brick and timber cottages have under floor heating and as we slept on a mat on the floor we nearly got cooked. They have full cooking and bathing facilities and are very pleasant to sleep in. The main house is two stories and built of large timber logs. Beside this house is a long open-style, covered, eating area, at one end there are thousands of chillies drying.

A professional snake catcher arrived to show us his catch for the day, numbering about twenty snakes, seven or eight of which were of the deadly poisonous variety. Mr. Lee said (through his daughter interpreting) 'if one of these bites you, you can kiss your life goodbye'. Dennis and I felt much better when they were all back in their bags, after a romp around the gravel drive. Mrs. Shin cooked a delicious meal and afterwards we played Monopoly, which proved that Hye Won has a good business mind, as well as a wise and spiritual one. The following day I checked my emails and was able to send some on Leo's computer. Her own apartment in the house is wall to wall books, some in Korean but most in English.

Mrs. Shin prepared lunch of fried chicken, chives, turnip, stewed onion, rice tomatoes and corn. The generosity and kindness of these people amazes me.

When we left Wind Sound Water Sound we visited a gallery of ancient art belonging to a friend of Hye Wons. When we finally got home we walked with Mr. Weightlifter, Mr. and Mrs. Corn on the Cob and Moon Su Ji to the next province, where we jumped up onto a man made concrete platform to sing and dance. I was worried that it was the tomb of some famous person, but was assured it was to mark the boundary on the next province. We walked home in the dark a very happy bunch despite the language barrier.

I really enjoyed dipping into the icy waterfall pool several times and experienced a massage from the village healer and massage therapist. He was very good and we had a charming tea ceremony with him as well. On our walk home we found Hye Won and Moon Su Ji at the road construction camp. We were invited in and were happy to find they had chairs to sit on, ah, what bliss, as our legs were still not used to the floor sitting. Here we are plied with tinned coffee, noodles, soup and eggs; all served cold, with pickled garlic and afterwards, watermelon, which was sweet and juicy. Then came the usual singing and dancing.

After half an hour's rest we headed to Mr. Weightlifter's place for a Full Moon party where once again we sang, danced, laughed and ended up sitting on a rock in the middle of nowhere, in silence, looking at the full moon. The next night was more socializing at Mr. Government's house with an overnight stay. Our usual gang turned up and proceeded to build a dining table outdoors, using a ladder on bricks, on top of the rocky ground. Next two wire mesh trays were placed on the ladders with newspaper as a table cloth. This last addition being very useful for Dennis and me as we have not quite mastered chopsticks yet and we tend to splatter our food on our dining companions and the table. We manage to drop food between the serving dishes and our bowls. Moon Su Ji and Mrs Moon cook the feast of raw squid, kim chi (pickled cabbage) pickled garlic, a small melon, which we thought was cucumber, apples and peaches. Mrs. Government does not come here very often, preferring to live in the city, the rustic life is not for her, Mr. Government thrives here and so do the red berries that he grows for some type of natural medicine. During dinner we listen to western music from the 60's, in sharp contrast to Beethoven at breakfast. Moon Su Ji and I share floor space in a bedroom. No one here has beds as far as I can see. We had barley and sesame porridge for breakfast with curried vegetables and rice, followed by a Chocolip, a chocolate-coated biscuit, which is popular in Korea.

Hye Won owns a lovely dog called Jingle. I took him for a walk many times into the village and kept getting invited into homes for refreshments. On our last night Hye Won and Moon Su Ji put on a surprise farewell dinner for us. The gang turned up and the feasting was fabulous. Dennis and I sat on our verandah after the guests had gone home, we gazed at the moon. We marvelled at the wonders of nature. We are in awe of the people we have met. The fulfilling lives we lead, the journeys we have taken, the loving kindness that has been bestowed upon us, often by total strangers, the laughter, the joy and tears, the happy and sad times but mostly just enjoying the present moment.

MEDICINE, SUPPLEMENTS AND FOOD

'Trust that still small voice that says 'This might work and I will try it.' Diane Mariechild

There are travel doctors around who know exactly what vaccinations you should take for which countries. Some vaccinations are compulsory, others are optional. There are also homeopathic doctors who can advise you on what to take. Rescue Remedy is very useful. I have taken homeopathic remedies with great success. At customs, pass them through on a tray rather than let them go through the x-ray machine. It can change their vibration. Parex is good for parasites. If you need to take prescription drugs, take the prescriptions with you. A letter from your doctor is required if for any reason you are carrying hypodermic syringes. Take any supplements you use at home with you, or buy them in most major cities. If you get leg cramps from all that hiking, biking, walking or standing try some calcium, magnesium or potassium. An old remedy is to place a cork mat or cotton bag full of corks out of a bottle in your bed. It works for me. Food can be used as medicine, of course if you are ill or have a fever, see a doctor as soon as possible. The following foods are suggestions only from my own experience.

- Expel worms and parasites with pumpkin seeds.
- For energy eat rolled oats and Kiwi fruit.
- For digestion try pineapple and watermelon.
- To cleanse purify and destroy harmful bacteria eat lemons and horseradish.
- For the heart eat garlic and onions. Garlic wrapped in bread or eating parsley will reduce the odour.
- For diarrhoea eat grated apple with the peel on, let it go brown first. Eat really ripe bananas or take Slippery Elm, charcoal or St Johns Wort..
- If you are low on energy, eat almonds, carrots, beans and figs.
- For colds and flu, drink apple juice with peel included, lemon balm tea, eat onions, garlic, almonds and oranges.
- For motion sickness, avoid eating and drinking too much before the journey. Peppermint or ginger tea will settle your stomach. Plain bread and an apple is also helpful.
- For joint pain, drink celery, carrot and lemon juice with apple cider vinegar.
- For itching bites use aloe vera or lavender oil.
- For sun burn, rub the area with cut cucumber or use Aloe Vera Gel.
- Avocado is a complete food, rich in vitamins and minerals.
- Young coconut juice and flesh is freely available in most Asian countries. It is filling and refreshing.
- Watermelon juice is good for the kidneys. Helps flush them out.

RUDI'S PUB, NEW YORK

We heard about Rudi's from three Australian guys. We met them just after getting off the ferry from The Statue of Liberty. They were dangling a huge albino python around their necks for a photo opportunity when we spotted them.

My son recognised one of the guys as being a friend from Perth. Being Aussies they had sniffed out the cheapest beer in town. Rudi's was the place to go. An Irish pub with lots of atmosphere and a local clientele from all walks of life

A Pakistani named Hyatt offered me his seat at the bar. He was a proper gentleman. His life story was relayed between buying drinks, which took some time as there was only one barman. Hyatt helped to marry off his six sisters before coming to New York. All arranged marriages "Much better" he explained "because it is important to have your family blood line carried by someone you know, from a respectable family, rather than any old person off the street". He was an officer in the army at the youngest possible age of eighteen years. His reason for coming to America was because he was convicted of killing a bloke, but was acquitted. If he stayed in Pakistan he would have 'had the rope', gesturing to his neck! He had a handicap of two in the army polo team. So was no mean player. He proceeded to show me his polo swings, right there in the bar. The nearside backhand shot, the forehand off side swing. All very impressive. I then decided to show him my polocrosse ball catching ability. Not so easy in a crowded bar!

We met two brothers from Montreal. As we were living in that city and had only been there for a few months, we were keen to find out more about it. They thought the fact that I was in the bar with my son and daughter was 'awesome'.

Then there was Woody, a distinguished looking grey haired Afro American. He was missing a few teeth, was neatly dressed in a suit and wanting to buy me more drinks. He had lived in England during the war. Unfortunately as we were sitting next to the loud Jute Box, I only heard half of his story.

Des the barman has a brother living in Adelaide. His brother told him when he found that city, *he thought he had died and gone to heaven.* It was so beautiful.

An Afro American guy came in dressed in drag. He had on a blond wig, green mini skirt and skimpy top. His false boobs looked more like watermelons than the real thing. He went straight into the ladies loo. My son spoke to a blond person for about half an hour and could not work out whether it was male or female!

Another person strutted in with a bouffant hairdo, dripping with jewellery and wearing a very revealing dress, which exposed the side of one breast. He/she hung about in strategic places trying to attract attention. Then pressing through the crowd or propping up a post, waiting for a pick up, but no one took the bait.

There was a little old couple in the corner, looking down and out hunched over their beers. Both wore floppy hats. Looked like real live characters. From time to time the pace got too much for them, so they would nod off, cuddled up as one. Finally they called it a day and wedged their way through the diverse crowd to the door. I was told later they were so wealthy they could buy and sell the whole block. So much for appearances.

Next we met Chan, a tall good looking Asian guy, oozing charm and charisma. Well mannered and 'drop dead gorgeous'. He looked me in the eye and shook hands as he left. I liked his style.

We got a Yellow New York cab back to our accommodation – the Banana Bungalow. Anything less like its name is hard to imagine. It was grotsville backpackers but it did not spoil a night to remember. It was 3.30am, the city was still very much alive and Rudi's will live in our memory for a very long time.

TALK IN TUNIS

Here is something that will make you laugh!

Walking along the street and these two tall young men start chatting to me.

Them: Hello, we just want to speak English.

Me: OK.

Them: We are political students, would you like to sit down and have a coffee and talk.

Me: No thank you, I don't drink coffee at this time of day but I would be pleased to sit while you have one.

Them: Well you see we don't have any money.

Me: Too bad.

One of them: I would like to have sex with you, I need the practise.

Me: Well I *don't*.

Him: You don't want to have sex with me why not?

Me: It would be like having sex with your grandmother.

Much laughter.

Me: Why don't you practise with a Tunisian girl?

Him: I want to try something different. Will you let me kiss you?

Me: *No*.

Them: Well goodbye.

Me: Much laughter.

WOMEN ON THEIR OWN

Remember no one can make you feel inferior without your consent. Eleanor Roosevelt

Nowadays lots of mature women are travelling on their own. I met a mature Australian woman in Cambodia who went on a train ride, not in a seat but on the ROOF of the train. She was pleased she had done it, but didn't need to do it again. I met a mature age Austrian woman in Amsterdam who was waiting for her bike to arrive so she could cycle her way from Holland to Austria. We cycled around the island of Texel and became close friends. Over the last sixteen years I have visited her often on Vancouver Island, where she has lived with her Australian husband for many years. We hike, and bike and skinny dip together. She has also stayed with me in Australia. An older English woman in her seventies was in the next kuti (hut) to mine in a monastery in Thailand. A woman I met briefly on a train in Ireland and I have corresponded for sixteen years. A French Canadian, with hardly any English was on a bus with me from Kathmandu in Nepal to Lhasa in Tibet. We shared a room and both suffered badly from high altitude sickness. A Danish 91-year-old was travelling in China alone, having spent three months painting in Laos. I met a German woman in Austria, who is married to an Italian and they live in Canada. I have visited her family and ridden bikes with her in Quebec All these women were travelling alone.

- Join the YHA (Youth Hostels Australia). There is no age limit and it is a great way to meet hikers, bikers and adventurers, nationally and internationally.
- Talk to young people, sometimes they need a mother figure for advice or even a hug or a shoulder to cry on.
- If you find yourself in a dodgy area, walk with purpose.
- Don't hang around unlit streets at night. Stay where there are lots of people.
- Team up with fellow travellers sometimes. I went from Athens in Greece to Istanbul in Turkey on a train for a few days with a young Australian man who was not brave enough to go alone.
- If you need a companion for short trips, check out the notice board in the hostel, or put your own sign up.
- Leave hair dryers at home. If necessary get your hair cut short, it is easier to manage when travelling.
- Bring a walkman, CD player or iPod and an adaptor to recharge batteries.
- Check out Women Travelling the World on the internet.
- Leave jewellery at home. It can attract the wrong sort of attention.
- Wear simple or no makeup, especially in hot, humid climates.
- Pack underwear that is easy to rinse out and quick to dry.
- Wear your bumbag on the front of your body and make sure the waist band is a snug fit.
- You can buy light pouches to carry spare cash, travellers cheques, passport etc to wear under a blouse or round you waist under pants.

- Don't wear provocative clothing; respect the countries customs, especially in temples.
- If the travel guide book says no topless bathing, respect those wishes, even if you are in a country that has topless bars and sex shows.
- For comfort on a long plane trip, wear a loose bra or none at all.
- Pack mix and match clothes, natural fibres in tropical climates.
- Sandals that you can wear in the water are handy for rocks and shells.
- Sarongs are handy to lie on the beach, wear as a skirt or shawl, wrap around your head or to dry your body. They dry quickly too.
- Don't overload yourself with books and souvenirs too early in your journey. If your pack gets too heavy, post some things home or give them to a local charity.
- Take toys and books to hand out to children in Third World countries, this makes space in your bag.
- Keep a torch near your bed if you have to use the bathroom in the night and you are in a dormitory.
- For jet lag, ground yourself by walking barefoot on damp sand or grass for half an hour.

KOMODOS AND KUTA
INDONESIA

In 2002 the horrendous bombings took place at Kuta on the island of Bali, Indonesia. I decided to go there to see what I could do to assist these beautiful people. The Australian Government had other ideas. They were advising Australians not to travel there and making it almost impossible to do so. I had several travel agents trying to get me on a depleted flight schedule. Finally I was told there was one seat on Friday 13th December. I took it, presuming most people were too superstitious to fly on that day. The only return flight I could get was a month later. I accepted it and started packing my backpack full of toys and books for the local children, who I visited in Denpasar Hospital, where I also donated blood. The hospital was geared to do sixty blood donations a day, but after the bombing they were managing six hundred a day, a valiant effort on a traumatized city. I became friendly with a female doctor and we whirled around the busy traffic of the city on her motorbike, visiting her relations and seeing the local sites. What generous, hospitable people.

To give a small boost to the economy I booked a boat tour of several islands. From the island of Lombok I boarded the Perama Company boat, a twenty two metre sailing vessel with eighteen fellow passengers from England, Scotland, Japan, Canada, Germany and France for five days and nights. I was the only Australian.

Normally this boat takes forty passengers plus seven crew, but it was only two months after the bombing in Kuta and there were hardly any tourists around.

We first stopped at Perama Island for a BBQ of large Tuna fish and entertainment by the crew, it was so special; they sang and played drums and guitars. Guess who was the first passenger up to sing? You guessed it. Yours truly. I sang The Pub with No Beer, with apologies to Slim Dusty. After that I was always expected to start the passenger sing-alongs. We had so much fun and the group got on really well together.

We stopped at a small island called Satonda and swam in a crater lake while watching monkeys frolic in the trees on the bank. It was magic, to think it had once been a volcano! On to the island of Sambawa we snorkelled and swam with luminous rainbow fish. Off to Komodo for a Christmas Day with a difference – no ham, turkey or plum pudding and party hats from bon bons but dragons that are huge and look slow and cumbersome but boy can they move. Something like our Australian crocodiles. As we walked in the heat of the day, which is the best time, as they are a bit drowsy, we saw four dragons tearing a carcass apart, eating the bones and all. They can break a buffalo's leg with a swish of their tail. We sang all the Christmas carols at night on the boat and were given traditional paper horns to blow. We made a terrible noise, I played Silent Night on my harmonica and Clementine went down well too. Rinca Island entailed a five kilometre hike through steep country in over bearing humid conditions, but it was worth it to see the water buffaloes wallowing in mud pools, under the shade of beautiful large trees, hiking through small villages, meeting the locals and numerous dragons.

On the next island, we went to a small village via a dirt road with very fine dust, about six inches deep, covering our legs, our clothes and even our hair, what we in Australia would call bulldust. We were followed, Pied Piper style by the local children, singing and laughing. I taught them nursery rhymes, they particularly liked Humpty Dumpty, with actions. It started to rain, so our guide took us on a *short cut* back to the boat. We went around a sheer cliff face, with the sea below us, now wet and slippery, clambering over volcanic rock, which under normal circumstances would have been very interesting to stop and look at, but it was all I could do to keep upright. We jumped over ravines of turbulent, gurgling water, splashing at our ankles. My sandals were soaked and didn't want to stay on my feet. I tried going barefoot but the rocks were too sharp and painful to stand on. The local kids ran past like mountain goats. One, very helpfully, gave me a stick for support and balance. We finally made it to smooth rocks washed up upon the beach and there to greet us were several dolphins that put on a beautiful aerial water display to sooth our aching bodies. The worst part of the journey was over it only left us a long hike over broken coral and shells back to our boat.

We anchored at some small islands were the brave young passengers jumped from the top of the mast into deep water below. We also went to Flores, a larger island east of Bali. There my sandals totally fell apart and I bought a pair of thongs for a dollar. We headed back to Lombok, stopping at Moyo Island for more snorkelling. I had a cabin to myself on the boat, being the oldest passenger, some of the young people slept on deck. The food was excellent but a bit repetitive, the crew helpful, friendly and happy. We had live chickens on board, so we knew when we ate chicken, that it was fresh. We had pineapple for dinner every night and I drank lots of tea, which I never do at home. The young fellows bought Arak in Flores and partied into the early hours but in my cabin the noise was drowned out by the engine. The engineer wore an orange helmet the whole time, even ashore, we wondered if he slept in it. Our five days were excellent value for money. Perama is a great company and they gave me a ten percent discount because I had used their shuttle bus before the boat trip.

HURTING HOTEL MALAYSIA

Have you ever stayed in a hotel that has a feeling of sadness? I have. In Penang, Malaysia in November 2003 I stayed in one such place. Its name is the Agora, which in Greek means market place. That is where we get the word agoraphobia from – fear of the market place. Well this may once have been an agora, but no longer, I'm afraid.

The staff are pleasant and helpful. I arrived on an evening flight, the porter Sami, a friendly third generation Indian/Malaysian, jumped out of the foyer to greet me and carry my bags from the taxi. He waited patiently while I checked in at reception and was given my breakfast vouchers. My room on the fifth floor is 'tired', the curtains hang listlessly trying to hide the odd hole and stain in the folds. They must have large moths here. The four bedside lights don't function. Sami tries them and one gives a flash but in an instant has crashed with a big bang and a fizz. He leaps back as if shot. He offers to go and find some new globes, checks the bathroom to find I have no towel. He turns the TV on to see if it is working. Bravo, the screen is filled by a Camel Race in the Northern Territory of Australia. It is in English with Bahasa Malay subtitles. What a welcome to Penang.

Soon Sami is back with a towel and light globes and after a lot of tinkering under the bed; he has one of the lights working. In the morning, the handle of the toilet goes kaput. The bed is clean but

153

the mattress is spongy. I will end up putting it on the floor. I have learned this trick a long time ago. For mattresses that are too hard, I sleep on the bed cover or doona or anything else I can get my hands on to soften the rigid board like mattress.

Breakfast is in the dining room on the ground floor. Fried eggs, baked beans, fried rice and white bread toast with margarine and strawberry jam. The waiter is Indian/Malaysian and very helpful. There is only one other family group sharing this scene. They are Malaysian and we chat a little. The dining room tables don't match, nor do the chairs. The fork bends as I place it into the egg to cut it. They don't make 'em like they used to!

I decide to visit the Sauna and Fitness Centre on the twelfth floor. As the lift only goes to the eleventh, I walk up one flight of stairs to see a few doors with heavy padlocks and no sign of life at all. The one sign says "Muslim men are not to be massaged by females". The Disco/Karaoke/Restaurant on the third floor is also in the dark, long since shut down and music turned off. I conjure up scenes in my mind of young virile Asians singing and dancing shyly, but busting to break free of the shackles that bind them. They try to copy Western culture which is sad really, as their own is so beautiful.

In the afternoon I venture to the fourth floor swimming pool. It is outdoors and quite large. I am the only person availing myself of the cool water that is running in constantly from a makeshift pipe at one end. Obviously the original system has gone kaput and it is easier to start a new rather than repair the old. The pool cleaner suction pad has come to a halt in the pool. There are leaves and feathers around the high water mark but the water is quite clean.

I plunge in, or should I say step carefully in at the deep end, down the ladder. The sign says nine feet deep. The water is surprisingly cool, considering the outside temperature of heat and humidity. This area is the saddest of all I feel. It needs kids dive bombing and young people playing, splashing and laughing. It is lifeless. The bar is empty and dusty, the bar stools pointing towards the pool are rusting and the cushions are sitting in an untidy pile with dust and splashes of white paint on their green vinyl. Some of the stitching is worn out exposing the thick sponge rubber in side. The tables need a good scrub. There are drink and glass marks left by revellers from long ago, in happier times. The tiles surrounding the pool have an intricate pattern but they have taken on a new design from grot and grime. They need a polish to bring life to them.

The shade covers over the tables are, or were, of a sleek appearance with shingle roofs and carved wooden struts coming down from a high pitch. There is only one left with a few shingles, the green paint has curled up in places to expose the yellow undercoat. Even the plants lack lustre, some have succumbed totally and are stone dead, brown and shrivelled. No longer can they stand the heat, lack of water and attention. They have curled their leaves and will end up as compost no doubt, fulfilling their role in the big scheme of things. The peeling paint and missing boards surrounding the pool show signs of what was once someone's dream, a vision – how sad to see it all fading into oblivion.

LONELINESS – HOMESICKNESS

There is no connection between loneliness and being alone. Pamela Stephenson

There can be times when you feel lonely travelling, just the same as when you are at home. Homesickness doesn't only affect young travellers, adults too can feel that pull of home and familiarity, especially if you are feeling unwell or everything seems to be going wrong. Music can bring up emotions of long forgotten memories, emotions that were sad or significant. Smells too can trigger emotions. Remember that this too shall pass. Nothing lasts forever, everything changes, nothing is permanent.

- Write down why you think you are feeling lonely or homesick.
- Then write down what you can do to turn it around.
- Write positive affirmations to focus on, rather than dwell on the negative.
- Others can be lonely or homesick too. You are not alone with these feelings.
- Sometimes young people on the road look for a mother or father figure to give them a hug or just be a listening ear.

- Your healing will be faster if you reach out and lend a hand to others.
- Don't sit down and brood. Take a walk, paint a picture or look for a great photo shot.
- Take a series of photos of doors, flowers, trees, temples, funny signs, kids etc.
- Talk to a stranger. Keep communication light.
- Visit a hospital and enquire if any patients haven't had a visitor lately.
- Have a massage, if it brings up tears fine, they can release stress.
- Buy yourself a nice bunch of roses.
- Go for a swim in cool water.
- Visit a jail to see if there are fellow country men or women inmates. Overseas jails are not a bed of roses.
- Take a pencil and paper and doodle.
- Write lists. They can be of anything. How many relations name can you remember, how many countries have you travelled to? Name the islands you have visited? The friends you have sent postcards to etc
- Buy some food and give it to a beggar in the street.

Sailing the Adriatic Croatia

Unfortunately it has done nothing but rain since I arrived in Split, a beautiful city on the Adriatic Sea.

Luckily I have my emergency yellow see through plastic raincoat and with my blue and white striped T shirt underneath, I feel decidedly like a banana in pyjamas! I have wandered the alley ways, malls, old city and waterfront. Wonderful markets with delicious strawberries, lavender in every shape and form, bakeries to tempt the senses (not good for me, who tries to steer clear of bread), loads of shoe stores, flowering window boxes, castle ruins, ancient architecture, wooden shutters and coffee shops, the cappuccino is good and only costs $1.75.

I find the local men rather dignified and the women wearing many variations of the Australian Drizabone rain coats. I even saw a nun in a black version. The constant smoking in cafes, shop assistants, bus drivers etc is very putting off. One tends to forget how bad it used to be in Australia. I also notice a lot of the women have large colourful moles on their noses, cheeks, and foreheads, in fact anywhere from the neck up!

The Split Hostel where I am staying is owned by an Aussie born Croatian and she is very helpful. It is very well situated and squeaky clean. There are quite a few Aussies staying there.

Back in Split after a fantastic seven day cruise of the islands in the Adriatic Sea and some mainland ports I ventured inland. I had the best time on the Dalmatinka, a small sail boat with only sixteen passengers, twelve Aussies, two German and two Poms. We sang, we laughed (I ran a laughter session for them on deck) we swam every day, sometimes from the boat sometimes at a beach. Rode bikes on the island of Miljet National Park around two glorious lakes. One had a monastery on an island in the lake.

I taught a Qi Gong class most mornings and then we would all jump into the chilly water. It was fabulous. I was coerced into playing my mouth organ on two occasions; of course Waltzing Matilda was a favourite. The cook had a bad knee, so I massaged him a couple of times and he is not hobbling as much as he was. He gave me a Dalmatinka T shirt, which I am delighted with. I gave him a big hug and I think he nearly fainted. I bought two striped T shirts with me not knowing that most locals wear red and blue striped ones, so quite often get mistaken for a local. I have had people carry on long conversations with me, only to tell them 'I only speak English'.

My cabin on the Dalmatinka was small but clean and comfortable with a shower and loo, plus two port holes. The cook did an excellent job of over feeding us each breakfast and lunch. We had delicious dinners on a different island each night. One night on the island of Hvar, we sat watching the sun go down eating lamb off a spit with yummy vegetables. A trip to the loo meant walking over a glass topped fish tank with small sharks in it! We have seen a few steel grey dolphins, much bigger than ours and I saw a wondrous jelly fish with fluted tentacles and a body the size of a car tyre.

Dubrovnik lived up to expectations, we walked the wall of the old city and wandered through the quaint alley ways and went into cathedrals. Unfortunately there were hordes of tourists and I actually preferred Hvar which has a beautiful water front and walk up to a fort and the most incredible views of the town and other islands. We saw a huge procession of priests, nuns and Franciscan Monks in their brown robes and hundreds of followers singing hymns. Very moving.

As we left the sail boat I said to Damir, one of the crew, "it was so good I will tell all my friends in Australia and you will have a boat load of Aussies before long" his reply 'Oh! No PLEASE don't do that'!

My new friends, I met on the Dalmatinka, from Manly, near Sydney, and I took a bus to Trogir, an old city about an hour north of Split. We bought food at the local market and had a picnic in a park near the canal. Can't get over how nearly everyone grows their own vegetables with grape vines on the fence and fig and olive trees in rows, as well as beautiful roses, bright red poppies and geraniums. Why don't we do that? The poor things have been invaded by so many countries including the Venetians, Turks, Hungary, Italy, Germany, Bosnia and Yugoslavia. Still they rise from the ashes with new highways and apartment blocks, concrete block homes complete with satellite dishes.

Today I took a bus to Sinj about an hour east and sat in a cafe bar. That is a cafe that serves coffee and alcohol but no food. Had my own picnic in the park and then went horse riding on a beautiful bay show jumper called Korney. He was 17.5 hands high and very well mannered.

Needless to say I had to mount from a rock wall. Saw a snake and had a lovely green grub on my hat but other than that, no wild life, went up a steep rough track through the forest for a magnificent view right to the hills behind Split. It was twenty eight degrees today, so it was hot work for the stable owner, as he walked all the way. He rides race horses and his ambition is to see the Melbourne Cup in real life. He would never make a jockey in Oz he is way taller than me.

My twelve days in Croatia was excellent value for money and I would recommend the whole experience to anyone who is contemplating the journey.

Noni with friends in Croatia, sharing a
picnic on a sarong table cloth

Trip Home Birch Lake

The wedding in Sudbury Ontario was really nice. My daughter-in-law Coline's cousin Jamie married a Chinese girl, who is very Canadian, Her father on the other hand cannot speak a word of English and is a successful businessman from Hong Kong. The only time he smiled was when I greeted him in Mandarin!

My granddaughters Molly and Olivia did an excellent job as flower girls and looked so pretty in their cream organza dresses with burnt orange sash at the waist to match the bridesmaid's dresses of burnt orange flower design. The meal was excellent, the wedding cake (3 actually) was decorated with fresh strawberries, raspberries, blueberries and blackberries and tasted superb.

As my son Will and Coline had imbibed quite a lot of alcohol it was decided that I would drive home. I thought they were joking. Me... Drive that humungous 4WD red monster of a Ford F150 with twin cab and only a month old, on the wrong side of the road on a pitch black night!! No... They were serious. The dash board lit up like the instrument panel of a 747 Jet, the automatic gear stick on the steering wheel was on the wrong side and before we had left the car park, I had put it in neutral, thinking it was the traffic indicator! The hour's journey was not looking brilliant.

One of the guests had said to me as we were leaving "look out for the moose on the road". Well, no self respecting moose would have been out in what was to come. Three minutes out of the car park and with major road construction taking place, no lines to indicate where the road was and black and yellow striped witches' hats in what appeared to be random order, the heavens opened and down poured the rain, absorbing the light from the headlights and everything else in the near vicinity.

Will, the navigator and instrument panel operator got too hot, while on the other hand Coline and I were freezing. Much dial twisting and knob pushing went on to get the temperature just right and vents going to those who needed them with hot or cold air. Meanwhile the windscreen had fogged up and I was grappling with the windscreen wipers, which turned out to be on the left hand side of the steering wheel, which had several speeds and intermittencies. Full bore was the way to go. We negotiated the slalom course and traffic lights (when I could see them) and out onto the Trans Canadian Highway heading west to Goveswood. I finally found the high beam on the lights through trial and error on the windscreen wiper stick. When nearing the small township of Webbwood, about 20 minutes from home the rain cleared and at last I could see the lines on the road, remembering to keep the yellow centre one on my left.

We turned off the highway onto Birch Lake Road, a narrow gravel track and at once we were hit by a dense pea souper of a fog. It blocked out any vestige of vision. Even if there had been guide rails and lines I would not have seen them. We crawled home narrowly missing the Goveswood turnoff and a large ditch while trying to avoid a big pot hole full of water. Will at this stage was giving me hand signals to keep left. Molly was in great doubt as to whether Granma Oz had ever driven before and

Olivia had sensibly passed out on the back seat with Coline running a close second in the sleep stakes.

I managed to deliver the family home safe and sound and in one piece. A much relieved driver and passengers thought "I don't want to do that again". (To quote Olivia after the dress rehearsal for the wedding)

LETTING GO OF THE FEAR FACTOR

We cannot escape fear. We can only transform it into a companion that accompanies us on all our exciting adventures. Take a risk a day – one small or bold stroke that will make you feel great once you have done it.
Susan Jeffers

Bless the road ahead of you in whatever way you feel comfortable with. A Burmese Monk told me this some years ago and I do it every day and every time I get on a plane, boat, bus etc before takeoff.

- Generate positive thoughts. If negative thoughts come into your mind, transform them right away with a positive affirmation. If you hear yourself speaking a negative thought, change it on the spot.
- Make a list of supportive, enthusiastic friends and talk to them about your travel plans.
- Start a Travel bank account, add to it regularly and make sure it earns good interest.
- Create a collage of your destination; put it where you can see it every day.

- Follow your dreams and doors will open. Start with small steps, buy travel magazines to whet your appetite, see a travel agent to check out package deals, discounts flights etc.
- If you are thinking of an overseas trip, get a passport, or if you have an old one, make sure it is valid for six months after you complete your travel.
- If you don't feel comfortable to travel alone, find a companion with similar interests, fitness level and budget.
- If you have a fear of flying, contact the major airlines. They have programmes to overcome that fear.
- If you have a fear of not knowing the language and not being able to read the signs, from my experience the locals are only too willing to help and if they don't understand, they will go out of their way to find someone who can. Don't be afraid to speak to strangers.
- Start travelling closer to home, if an overseas trip is too daunting.
- Writing down your fears helps to diminish them. Write a list of your negative beliefs and opposite each one write a list of positive alternatives.
- Challenges are self empowering, the more you challenge yourself the greater the success.
- Follow your intuition, be creative, allow yourself to think laterally. Visualise your planned trip, see it happening just the way you want it.
- Learn to laugh when things don't go as planned. Forgive yourself for any self doubt you may have.
- Reward yourself in a loving way when you have overcome even a minor fear or make a small break through. Don't spend energy on self doubt.

- Be kind to yourself. Love will help you overcome fear. Be willing to trust your own judgment. Write down why you are procrastinating.
- Find out how others have overcome their fears.
- Rid yourself of clutter in your mind and in your surroundings, this makes room for new experiences.
- Break through limiting thoughts like "I can't travel because... I am too broke, too shy, too scared, too fat, too thin, too old, too busy, too set in my ways, too disorganised, too lazy etc.
- Don't expect everything to be perfect. Perfectionism is based on fear.
- Breathe deeply and often.

Noni and the 62 kg snake, Malaysia

TEACHING ENGLISH
IN THAILAND

One of my favourite sayings is 'never miss an opportunity'. You will find them everywhere, if you are looking. They usually come unexpectedly, so you need to be alert and aware, so you can either run with them or put them on the backburner – but once on the backburner, that is usually where they stay.

As I was coming out of the surf at Koh Samet, an island in Thailand, a Thai man started talking to me in his limited English. We walked along the beach as he told me he was a teacher at a Buddhist Monastery School on the mainland, at Rayong. It was just a ferry and motorbike ride away. He asked me if I would like to visit the school. I took the address and told him that when I left the island I would call in on my way to Bangkok.

A week later I arrived at the school which has 450 high school age novice monks. They come from the poorest areas of Northern Thailand and would otherwise not get an education. I met the abbot who is an enthusiastic, self educated monk with vision. He started the school twelve years before with eighty novices. He was twenty five at the time and had been a monk for five years. He has no university degree and taught himself to speak English.

He proudly showed me into all the classrooms, one was full of computers, where about thirty saffron robed young men were learning skills that would equip them for the future. Chemistry, physics, geography, history maths etc are all taught as well as Buddhist principles and meditation. The boys do not play sport but after school hours they all have their set tasks, which have to be done with mindfulness.

One day a week after school the students have a meeting where a leader or school captain and council are voted in by the students. Their job is to make sure the school runs smoothly and responsibly. I learned that discipline is seldom needed. The abbot places great importance on the students learning English. When he asked me if I would like to come and stay and teach English pronunciation and conversation at the school, I immediately said 'When do you want me to start'? He answered 'What about right now'? I explained I was not a teacher and that I was on my way home as I had a business to run, but as soon as I could organise it, I would let him know when I could be back.

Some months later I found myself back at the school, I presented the abbot with a small bell with a kangaroo for a handle; he placed it on his desk with a laugh. On my first day I was confronted with a class of 40-45 students, given a timetable, my own desk in the teacher's room and told to take the class out into the expansive grounds and 'talk about nature'. Not being a qualified teacher, I could see it was going to be a challenge. One of the boys picked up a feather and asked 'what is this'? Before I could answer, another boy said 'it is the leaf off a bird'. I thought that was lovely.

I was given only four periods a day to teach, which was just as well, as I started to lose my voice and the heat and humidity were exhausting. Late one afternoon I walked to a resort with the teacher, who was responsible for introducing me to the school, he said it was not far. I started to get blisters on my heels from my sandals and ended up walking barefoot and then hitching a ride in the back of a truck. When we arrived home and I told the abbot where we had been, he thought it was a great joke and told me we had walked about twelve kilometres. That night I fell into bed, or should I say, onto my floor mat and slept like a log.

My sleeping quarters were in small bungalow with another teacher in the next room. We shared a bathroom and kitchenette. My 'bed' was a thin cane mat on the floor, a new pillow and doona, which I slept on, rather than over me. Some students arrived with a solid table and chairs for me to eat at in the garden. Every morning the secretary, her sister and I would walk along the beach and I would teach them some English words, we had lots of laughs trying to understand each other.

About five people have been told to look after me and with the generous spirit of the Thai people they do a great job, but each had a differing opinion on what I should do. They keep plying me with food, food and more food. I got hooked on the dried fish which I have never been brave enough to try before.

The students are like boys the world over, some are serious and studious, some are boisterous, some are class clowns, some are shy and some are totally disinterested. I soon realised that there is no way I could keep them all engaged and interested. Some drift off to other parts of the grounds, some sneak a look at a comic, some even doze on a rock wall, but most are enthusiastic and keen to learn.

As part of my teaching I made up word games, the students enjoy competing against one another and form two teams, one called Australia and one Thailand. Competing was probably not strictly within the bounds of monastic life, but at least it held their attention. One day I asked them to make up two words of four letters each. They came up with 'Love Noni'.

Some days I would take out my small photo album with family, friends, pets, etc and explain who everyone was. They really enjoyed this. They loved the nursery rhyme of Humpty Dumpty and did it with actions. Simon Says was another game that got them laughing and they became very good at.

I had my 59th birthday while I was there and the word had got around. The secretary gave me a beautiful bunch of roses and two amulets. A Thai friend turned up with a huge box of delicious biscuits and took me to see a famous monk living in the area.

Each weekend I would take a motorbike taxi to a small village, and then get a *sangteaw,* taxi truck, then ferry to the island of Koh Samet. I have many friends there after eight years of holiday visit. Here I learn to speak Thai from the families who I have got to know over the years. I have a Thai Traditional massage on the beach, which is sheer bliss, for my body is not used to sleeping on such a hard surface. One day a Thai friend arrived with some beautiful shells and with some old fishing line, we made them into wind chimes to hang outside my beach bungalow. I sometimes walk to Nuan, a smaller secluded beach to meditate. It is off the beaten track and really peaceful.

One day a ten-year-old boy was dumped at the monastery, his parents have disappeared. He has a scar on his forehead from where someone had thrown a rock at him. The abbot is so kind to him and tells me he will keep him at the school, so he can get an education. Nut is a lucky boy to have found such a large, loving family.

Each afternoon after school the novice monks help me with learning Thai too. This way they also learn English, in a less formal situation. I love these times with the students and get to learn their names and hear about their families. One day one of them was really sick, the doctor diagnosed appendicitis. The secretary and I took him in the back of a *sangteaw* to the large hospital about half an hour away; he looked so weak and helpless. I felt so sorry for him with no family there for support. I wanted to hug him but of course being a novice monk that is a no-no. His parents could not be informed as they have no phone, nor the money to travel from Northern Thailand to be with him.

As we were walking through the garden of the school one day the boys pointed out a long snake, I jumped aside as it slithered through the branches of a small bush next to me. I think this gave them an idea, because the next day we were sitting in a complete circle on the ground in the garden, I had been looking down at my notes when one of the boys said 'What is this?' I looked up to see a rather large fierce looking lizard. It had obviously been 'planted' there as there is no way it could have got into the circle otherwise. I calmly took a deep breath and said 'It is a lizard'. With that it ran straight towards me, right on cue. I lost my cool calmness rather quickly and let out a shriek, grabbed my notebook and pushed it away. I gathered my wits finally and asked for it to be put outside. By this stage, they were all enjoying the joke and laughing heartily. It could not have come off better and I too could see the funny side to it.

The school captain was such a nice young man, wise beyond his years. He has been home once a year for the past six years to visit his family. He is number thirteen out of fourteen children. He wants to disrobe when he finishes school and do engineering at university. His family are poor and he wants to help them.

While I was teaching at the school for six weeks, an Australian friend Lorraine came to visit and help for a week. It was wonderful to have her support and she related to the students so well. One night the secretary invited us to dinner at a local restaurant. We all piled into the back of an open truck to get there. We had an excellent meal and a lot of laughs.

I massaged quite a few teachers and their relations at the monastery. I was pleased I had done a Traditional Thai massage course in Bangkok some years before.

Just before my six weeks came to an end, the school captain came to me with the news that he had just heard that his sister had contracted AIDS. I was so sad for him, sad at leaving and feeling so helpless. As I climbed into the back of a *sangteaw* for my departure I could not stop my tears from flowing. I had bonded with teachers and students alike and have since been back to visit them all and been greeted so warmly. I still correspond with some of them who are now at university.

I had learned a lot more than I had taught and not only the language. It is an opportunity that I would not have missed for the world.

FARMING FAMILY BHUTAN

To stay with a local farming family is an experience I savour. Bhutan was no exception. My hosts in Thimphu Thinley and Megan arranged a two night stay with a family in Upper Tang in the village of Gamling in Bumthang, central Bhutan. The father of the household Patula is a lay monk, which means he wears robes and is allowed to marry. He is a gorgeous smiling man with a few missing teeth and no English but he and his whole family welcome and spoil me with delicious meals and warm hearts. He shows me his altar with great pride; it was made by his eldest son and is a masterpiece of construction and artwork. The statue of the Buddha takes centre stage with Guru Rinpoche on one side and another important deity on the other. Numerous ornaments, flowers and offerings adorn the many shelves, *thankas,* religious paintings are everywhere, wall hangings and circular colourful hangings of what looks like men's ties hang from the ceiling. The large *chorten,* a type of pagoda, outside the house was built by Pema, his son in law, the only member of the family who speaks a little English. He is so nice and when I leave, I take off my fleece top and give it to him. He is shy in receiving it. It is confusing because his wife's name is Pema too. She has three husbands. Quite legal in Bhutan; the King has four wives, all sisters.

To greet us, on the wall of the large two storey imposing traditional home is a painting of a tiger about to pounce. As I was born in the year of the tiger, I feel right at home. When I tell Patula this through my translator/driver Karchung, it takes him only seconds to work out my age. The home is about 500 meters from the dirt road, through fields of wheat and a small village, over wooden planks and small bridges. It is a two hour drive from Jakar the nearest town. Their main cash crop is potatoes and they have a large veggie garden, milking cow. Healthy chickens run free and lay their eggs in a shed. They make their own butter and cheese; eat the river weed, which the young kids gather from the fast flowing river.

From the day they plant the potato seed for a period of seven months, every night one man and at least three dogs have to guard the paddock from wild boar, which tend to dig up the newly planted potatoes. Small crops of buckwheat, maize and wheat are ground in a wonderful ancient water wheel mill over a stream. Chillies and thin slices of pumpkin are drying on a sheet of corrugated iron. Much to Karchung's amazement I tried out the pumpkin – apparently they only eat it cooked but it was yummy. Colourful cloth is woven in to mats or material on a loom made by the son; he is making a timber bed at the moment. The granddaughter works endlessly in the kitchen churning out delicious meals of cauliflower, choko, beans, cabbage, potato and turnip each in a different sauce or with cheese, the obligatory rice and chillies with every meal. Homemade buckwheat noodles and pancakes are yummy too. I tried the butter tea but not the local arak. Not my favourite drink.

Karchung and I walked for three quarters of hour up a steep winding track to the Ogyen Chholing Palace Museum. The locals do it in fifteen minutes. A fascinating and bountiful selection of ancient local artefacts like gunpowder made from dried yak dung and a dakin dance costume made from bones, large woven baskets to hold grain and much more. The grandson Tshetim goes off to school in his *gho* the traditional garment for males and looks so gorgeous in his knee high socks and black school shoes. On leaving I give him a pair of wraparound sun glasses, He is so excited he races off around the village showing off his new spunky image to his friends.

I am sad to leave this warm and beautiful family who have taken me into their home and shown me such hospitality. How privileged I am to be a small part of their lives for such a short time. They present me with a traditional mat made from yak hair. I will treasure it.. My blessings are with them.

Hammams

I have been scrubbed to within an inch of my life in a *hammam,* a public bathhouse and massage, by a Big Tunisian Momma. She would make three of me!

I first sat in a steam room with other ladies and one small boy, with my feet in a bucket of hot water. After about half an hour I lay down, as indicated by BTM on a marble slab, as I did, I noticed a cramp starting in my right leg. I have now found a cure... Take to it with a steel wool scrubbing mitt... instant relief.

There wasn't an inch of my body that she missed. I could see the dead skin falling off in self defence. It did bother me slightly that it was a darkish colour. I wondered if it was tinged with blood!

Then came the massage... more of a Tiger Grab all over with a wobble of the wobbly bits, followed by some heavy pounding and slapping. After half an hour, BTM pulled my arm so I came to a sitting position; there is no way I would have managed without her assistance. I felt and am sure looked like one of those old sea lions that you see rolling around the rocks before slurping into the water. Well in my case a plastic bucket full of hot water was thrown at me from afar.

I somehow seemed to manage to slip and slide my way to a cubicle to douse myself in case any bits had been missed by BTM. She had done a thorough job. I dried off, paid my $10 and bade her *auvoir* positively floating out in my glowing and gleaming new skin.

Well folks you may think I am a devil for punishment… but I thought I had better try the Moroccan *hammam*, public bath and massage.

This time I came prepared, I purchased a scrubbing mitt and selected the lowest grade of coarseness. I also purchased a new bottle of Sunsilk shampoo with coconut milk. The Moroccan Momma was half the size of the Tunisian one and did a better job. I don't think I will ever need to shave my armpits or legs again, even so. MM must have shares in Sunsilk I feel, because she just about finished the whole bottle. It was difficult to keep my mouth shut when she was tipping buckets of water over me. It is a definite no no to drink the water in Morocco. Then soap and shampoo got in my eyes and I was in such a lather I could not attempt to clear it out. Quite painful. However the massage was very good, done on the washroom floor with soap and water. I almost relaxed.

A French lady and I were the only outsiders there and she and I had a good laugh afterwards.

BUDDHIST PILGRIMAGE

On a local bus from Kathmandu to Lumbini in Nepal, the Buddha's birth place, I sat beside a woman from Australia. Before long, she noticed that her camera was missing. It had been on her lap but somehow disappeared. After a search of the bus a Nepali boy found it under a seat. She foolishly put it back on her lap again and further down the track it went missing again, this time for good. She was most upset, as she had photos of Chitwan National Park where we had both been riding elephants to see the one horned rhinoceros. After wishing her well, we went our separate ways.

At Lumbini, I slept in a stable. Christ was born in a stable; perhaps this completed the circle from my Christian upbringing. With jute mats on the straw covered floor, a blanket and a pillow, I was reasonably comfortable. I went for an early morning walk with the mist curling around the ancient buildings and rising over the distance hills. I sat in meditation under the Bodhi Tree, where the Buddha was born. Pilgrims from all over the world flock here to this sacred place. I paid a visit to the Maha Devi Temple. She was the Buddha's mother and was on her way to her parent's home to have the baby but stopped to bathe in a pool, as the day was so hot. When she got out, the labour pains began, so she held onto the Bodhi Tree and that is where the Buddha was born.

The Buddha Siddhartha Gotama grew up in a palace about twenty-seven kilometres from here at Kapilavastu. He had a very protected and charmed life until he was twenty-nine and went on his search for enlightenment. I jumped at the opportunity to see the ruins at Kapilavastu, with a group of Nepalese. Our first stop was in a small village called Pasha which had without a doubt the filthiest restaurant I have ever been in. I refused to eat or drink there and for me that is saying something.

The rattlie old bus drove us on to the Japanese Monastery, which is part of the Lumbini Development Programme. The Japanese have also built a luxury hotel for their pilgrims in the area. We bounced around on a dirt road until we got to Kapilavastu to see where the Buddha's parents ruled their Kingdom. We saw the eastern gate where the Buddha had left from to lead his ascetic life. There is a small village and museum, where we saw pottery dating back to 800-300BC. We drive on to Bhairawa to eat Dahl baht, the most popular dish in Nepal.

When I finally got back to my 'stable room' I find I am sharing it with a mouse and a Nepali lady. I massage her swollen ankle, caused by a fall. We have no common language but make do with signs. A few days later I find a Thai group in the temple being led by a Thai man I know. He invited me to come on the bus with his group. I hastily got my things together as they are leaving right away. I believed we were heading for Kushinagar, where the Buddha died, but in actual fact we end up in Sravasti where the Buddha spent 25 years. Oh well never mind, everything changes.

We crossed the border from Nepal into India, where I am mauled by an Indian man in the street. I shove him away and walk on. I console myself with the fact that I have travelled a long way for free ... even if it is not where I want to go. I find a single room in the hotel where the group is booked. The only problem being they don't take Travellers Cheques, Australian Dollars, Visa Card, or Nepalese Rupia and I have no Indian Rupees. US Dollars would have been fine but I have used most of them up, I only have enough for food for the next few days. There is no currency exchange to be found. A day later I found an Indian man who exchanged Australian dollars.

At Sravasti we visit the ruins of the temples and stupas where the Buddha gave his teachings for twenty-five years. Five hours later we arrive in Lucknow on our air-conditioned bus to find that India is in the middle of an election. Not the best time to be on the subcontinent. The marauding campaigners are yelling and throwing their arms around in gatherings of hundreds. Some voters arrive on tractors and trailers, some loaded on bullock carts, horse and cart, and bicycles every spare inch is taken up with humanity. Loud speakers screech out non-understandable words, even to the locals I imagine. I get the feeling that something big is brewing up to bursting point.

Most of the Thai group goes by train to Agra. I head east in the bus with six Thai monks, who can't speak a word of English and one Nepali man who can, we have this huge luxurious bus to ourselves all the way overnight to Varanasi. In the middle the night the bus broke down and the driver and his offsider are skilled mechanics, they get us going again. We stopped at a border crossing at which the police are particularly belligerent and make a big deal of checking forms and waving papers around. Finally they came into the bus shining their torches in our faces, not a pleasant experience on a dark and dusty road. At last they lift the boom gate and our driver manages to get us to Varanasi at 5 am. I worked out that he had been driving for twenty-four hours without sleep. How did he do it? I have no idea. He was an excellent driver and I complimented him on it.

Now the next part of the journey should be in the *Guinness Book of Records!* The motorized rickshaws in India are a tight squeeze with a driver and two passengers in the back, but we had two monks, one Nepali man, two Indians and me, plus my backpack and three other bags in the one rickshaw for the twenty minute drive to Sarnath. Sarnath is where the Buddha preached his first sermon after his enlightenment. There are still deer in the park, as there were in the Buddha's day.

My accommodation in the Thai Monastery was really good and much appreciated after the long journey from Nepal. The sheets were clean as was the bathroom. I had a large room with bunks all to myself. A short walk away was the Deer Park where I went to see many important ruins and a large stupa*. Young boys pester me to guide me around, they are cheeky and hard to brush off. One day I took a taxi with the monks to see the river Ganges where devotees are bathing, chanting, praying, doing their washing and bodies are being cremated. It truly is an amazing sight. Not only are there dead dogs in the water but half burned bodies, bloated bodies wrapped in saris and there to add a little lightness is a floated candle with flowers around it.

Back at Sarnath I saw an Indian woman massaging her baby. This is a daily ritual from day one until about the age of two or three years of age, and then it tapers off to three or four times a week until they are about seven. I got friendly with a family of eight children and their mother and father who live in a humpy near the monastery. They invited me to sit with them around a small fire, while they warm the soles of their feet in the early morning. I visit the Chinese Restaurant so often that I am greeted like part of the family. They advertise NUDDEL SOUP and MUSSRUM SOUP and they serve espresso coffee which makes a nice change from chai, the Indian tea made of herbs and served with milk and lots of sugar.

From Varanasi I took a train to Gaya, at the train station I am told to queue at window three or four in the next building. What a sight, hundreds of people pushing, shoving, jostling in many queues. In the midst of all this lie two cows sprawled out and quite oblivious of the chaos around them. I finally get to the window and am told to queue at window five or six. Back to square one, practicing patience, tolerance and flexibility. I waited on platform four for two hours, as the train was late. I saw an empty seat on the platform and was about to squeeze into it when an Indian gentleman appeared and said "Madam you have taken my seat", so I reluctantly stood up and found a box to sit on.

There is a last minute stampede as the train is now coming into platform three. We need not have rushed; it is a further hour before we leave. When I am aboard I find I have a general ticket rather than a reserved seat ticket, which causes some concern for the conductor who I think, is waiting for me to put some rupees in his hand to provide me with a seat. Then a young man took pity on me and offered me space on his bench seat. He is a physiotherapist on his way to Calcutta. He offered me a cigarette and some guava. The cigarette I refused but the guava was very refreshing. I bought some nuts to share with him. The train stops frequently and as it is hot, we have the window down. The usual platform sellers are pressuring us to buy their goods at every stop. At one of the stations for no apparent reason we get a bowl of steaming hot chai thrown at us. My companion cops most of it on his clean white shirt. He leaps up, sticks his head out the window and yells "Bastard" with great vehemence which makes us both feel better.

On the train they serve chai in lovely little pottery bowls and they use them like throw away plastic cups. You see them abandoned up and down the tracks in droves.

I arrive three hours late in Gaya and book in to the Buddha Hotel. The manager did not win any votes for politeness. OK it was nearly midnight but insisted he only had a Deluxe Room, take it or leave it. I filled in the usual forms in triplicate and before I had finished he demanded "Give me eighty-five rupees" I said "Please" in a loud voice. Relations were not looking good. There was no globe in the bathroom, he was most indignant when I asked for one and proceeded to stand on the bed with his grotty bare feet to remove the one and only globe from the bedroom. The room was filled with flying creatures, which had all committed suicide by morning. At 7.30 am a loud buzzer sound filled the room, I ignored it, then it went off again. There was a knock at the door and a terse voice said "Madam, do you want tea or coffee. No, only mineral water was my reply. Did I want a bowl of hot water, no; I just wanted to leave as soon as possible. I walked sullenly to the bus station and was told by a taxi driver that the buses were on strike. It was a ploy to get me to take his taxi. I kept on walking and found a bus going to Bodh Gaya. I intended to try and get some sleep, as I had very little the night before.

On the bus I took pity on a family group standing up and offered to put their son on my lap, only to find out that he suffered from motion sickness, but I managed to get his head out the window in time, where it stayed for the thirteen kilometre journey. I held his forehead while his grandmother wiped his face and mouth with her hand and sari.

I stayed at the Burmese Monastery in cell ten on a wooden slatted bed with a paper thin mattress, sheet, mosquito net and electricity, all for fifty cents. What more could one ask for. There is a sign on the notice board that one of the monks has a bad back and can anyone help. I offer my services only to find out that he is an Australian from Melbourne but has not been back there for twelve years.

I walked to the Mahabodhi Temple where the Buddha attained his enlightenment, under a Bodhi Tree. This too is a very special place, visited by Buddhists from all over the world. There is an ordination of a Taiwanese monk, Tibetans doing full prostrations, lay people doing walking meditation, using prayer beads and prayer wheels, others pouring rice or cracked corn over a bronze bowl, others sitting in meditation or waiting for a Bodhi leaf to fall. I managed to gather some too.

At dusk Hindu women and men walk to the river to worship the sun god for a puja and give offerings, burn incense and light little fires. All this inspires the kids to let off crackers and some sound like bombs going off. The next day an Australian girl and I hired bicycles and rode to the Japanese and Tibetan Temples as well at the Root Institute, we pulled up at a small village and bought some local food. We came across a large group of doctors and nurses removing cataracts for 10,000 patients in three months. What a job.

For my last part of the journey, I took the Doon Express train to Calcutta, which ran the usual two hours late and we went through the change of platform again. I was in a top bunk of three and I slept like the proverbial log.

Every journey I have had to India has been life changing … This one was no exception.

* A round domed building, erected as a Buddhist shrine.

HAZARDS

When you come to the end of your rope, tie a knot in it and hold on. Eleanor Roosevelt

You can only become street wise by getting out on the street. Common sense is a big bonus when travelling. I was ripped off on my first trip to India. I was travelling alone, walking on a crowded street, is there any other in India, when a gentleman approached me and wanted to read my palm. He held my hand, led me to a less populated alley, showed me his international business card and started his hocus pocus. He asked me for quite a large sum of money, we haggled about the price, he got angry and for the sake of my safety I paid up and walked away. I learnt a lesson that day. In Turkey I wanted to photograph a brown bear that a man had on a leash. He was carrying a blue plastic bucket. I took the photo and he turned the bucket over to reveal the sum of money I was meant to pay. It was exorbitant. I was with a young Australian fellow who was very nervous. I said, "Let's leave him some money and walk away." Actually we ran in case he let the bear loose on us.

- I was told in Canada that squirrels put more people in hospital than any other animal in the country. Don't feed them; their bite can cause hepatitis and bubonic plague.

- If you suffer from motion sickness, don't read or write in a car or bus. Eat and drink lightly before the journey. Get fresh air through a window if possible.
- Be aware of pickpockets, especially young girls in Europe, they are extremely cunning and up to all sorts of tricks. They will hold a newspaper out to give you while the other hand is delving into your bum bag.
- Keep your valuables close to your body at all times, if they are not in a safe.
- Keep valuables in a secure safe or even a locker with your own padlock. In overnight trains or buses, sleep with your valuables inside your clothing.
- In Asian countries on trains or buses, use a chain and padlock to tie up your locked bag to a solid place. A dog choker chain is handy for this.
- Drive by bag snatchers, can not only grab your bag, but damage your shoulder as well.
- Don't count your money in public places.
- Don't wear jewellery that can be grabbed from your body.
- If you are bitten by a dog, see a doctor as soon as possible.
- If you lose your passport, contact the nearest consulate or embassy.
- In case of theft contact the police station and get a written record from them for insurance purposes.
- Bed bugs can occasionally bite you; the bites don't start itching till a couple of days later. Calamine lotion works well.
- Biting insects are worse at dawn and dusk, protect yourself as best you can with spray, roll on, coils or nets. Taking B Vitamins help prevent bites.

- If a savage dog is coming towards you, pick up a stick or stone and throw it at him. If no ammunition is available, even the act of pretending to reach for something will buy you time. Yelling loudly helps as well.

THE GORGED TIGER CHINA

We booked into the Gorged Tiger Cafe and Guesthouse at Tiger Leaping Gorge, in China. The name should have alerted us that we were in for something different. We just didn't know how different. Margo the Australian owner was having a cold shower (there was no alternative) when we arrived. Her Chinese offsider showed us to the room on the first floor. Margo flitted past with hardly any clothes on muttering something to herself and waving her arms around. We were under the impression that a fellow country woman would give us clear, understandable information. How wrong we were. The shower was on the rooftop, a nice sunny area complete with Tibetan blue and white tent with the endless knot painted on it. We were only a few hundred kilometres from the Tibetan border. The loo seemed nearly as far. Down the stairs, through the locked front door, past a shop, past the reception/dining area, over a courtyard/car park, up some steps to a trough type pit, beside the road with no light. Trying not to drop your torch down the hole.

The owner eventually appeared in a local head scarf, T shirt, miniskirt and thongs. The more we tried to communicate the more she flipped about leaving sentences half finished and coming back with a new subject. We could not nail her down to get any information about hiking in Tiger Leaping Gorge. I tried a new tack and asked her where I could get a good massage in the town of Qioatou. She pointed to a ten-year-old girl who had also been flitting about and said "Ting Ting will do it for you". Immediately this Chinese child started to thump my back. I tried to question the Aussie lady again but it fell on deaf ears in a flurry of leaping in and out the front door, as she sprang on any unsuspecting prospective customers. Some poor unfortunate backpackers from Europe got caught in the trap, they were so bemused they could hardly speak. My friend, Sue, went into hibernation and couldn't utter a word. In fact she took two hours to stop shaking after we left. We went for a walk to find other accommodation when we could get away from the woman who was driving us to distraction. We left behind another poor unfortunate backpacker from Coffs Harbour to deal with Margo. He had helped her open a bottle of local wine, which she drank noisily between checking the door for passersby.

We found a really nice hotel with clean en suite run by a very friendly and helpful Chinese family with no English. We went back to Margo's and as an excuse told her we could not cope with the loo situation as we both felt squeamish in the stomach.

"What from?" she wanted to know. "Food we ate" I replied, but actually our systems were so churned up from her eccentricity, that we really did have a problem.

"You don't understand," she said "it is quite easy, you just go down the stairs, leaving the front door open (hoping it doesn't slam behind you, as we don't have a key) the toilet doesn't get locked at night (if she remembers) you won't have a problem." What does she take us for, a pair of idiots? We went up stairs dragged our bags down from the room which had three stuffed toy cats on the beds, paid for our cup of tea and walked away with the relief of a prisoner leaving jail, after a short sentence. We sat in our new hotel room in a semi comatose state, not knowing whether to laugh or cry...

We laughed.

FIVE DAYS WITH MADONNA

Hye Won, a monk, Moon Su Ji, his assistant, Dennis, my mate and I set off in Madonna (Hye Wons truck in other words) with Madonna (the singer) blasting out around the cabin, which set the mood for the next five days of adventure. We actually got to know the Madonna tape quite well. You may have gathered by now that Hye Won's favourite singer is Madonna. Rather strange for a Zen Buddhist Monk, but life is full of surprises. With our knees cramped up in the back seat and the road full of valleys and bumps, twists and turns and at times just enough room for one vehicle, we made our first stop... to release the poisonous snake we had caught while crossing a mountain stream, from the black plastic bag, deep into the forest. This certainly made life easier for us to put our hands into the remaining black plastic bags full of fruit and snacks for the journey. The road is so rough that my pedometer which normally counts steps got so confused it started to be activated by the bumps. So just by sitting in the truck I can do 3000 steps!!

We had lunch at a very exclusive restaurant in Yeoungju, a city one and a half hours from Namdaeri, the village of Hye Won's Monastery where we were staying, One of Hye Won's supporters invited us for a meal but the lady owner of the restaurant would not hear of him paying. We had pine tree mushrooms (they had not umbrellaed out yet) with beef in a sauce, tempura mushrooms and many varieties of vegetables. The specialty was fried grasshoppers; well I have always wanted to try them and never been game, so here was my opportunity. Actually they are delicious and I got quite a taste for these crisp and crunchy morsels, even managing to pick up two at a time with chopsticks. We pulled up at a bank to change money and Hye Won parked on the foot path which was cheeky, then to get off he drove ALONG a pedestrian crossing.

On to Andong, another city full of high rise apartment blocks. The sides of the roads are spectacular with different flowers and trees planted for miles on the approaches to towns and cities. We pass fields of rice, so neat and tidy, with vegetables growing on the banks of the canals. Everything is orderly and clean, we seldom see rubbish at the side of the road and all the cars are new and clean. Black and grey are the favoured colours. We have noticed that people are very conscious of recycling. We pass many traditional homes with their gently sloping roofs which tilt at the ends, many hazy mountains in the background to complete the perfect landscape. We call at Hahoe Folk Village which Queen Elizabeth II visited five years ago. There is an exhibition hall with many photos of her meeting local dignitaries and watching a bullock plough a field with a wooden plough. Some of the buildings here were built in the 15th and 16th century. The whole village is built round a bend in the river. Our next stop is Pongsongsa Zen Temple established in 672AD. One temple building is the oldest wooden structure in Korea.

We had dinner in the basic dining room, sitting on the floor and afterwards a tea ceremony with one of the monks… floor sitting again. We were guided to the shrine room for evening chanting, hopping up and down and bowing, which gives the knees some relief. We were shown up some steep rocky steps to an amazing old building of dark timber with timber slatted doors covered with thin white paper. Handmade wall paper for the walls and what looks to be yellow lino on the floor but we find out later it is paper that is why you must take your shoes off. We sleep on mats on the floor. I decided not to go to early morning chanting at 4am as my knee is so painful from sitting cross legged on the floor. After 6am breakfast in the dining room, which has clear plastic gloves filled with water hanging from the ceiling to keep the flies away (doesn't work), we met the abbot who is a good friend of Hye Wons. Another tea ceremony and we heard the story of the Queen visiting his temple and shaking hands with him… something she does not normally do with anyone, so we all had to shake his hand, with much merriment.

We visited an ancient Confucian school, once again very old timber buildings where Confucian scholars learned the philosophy. The crepe myrtle is out and looks superb in the gardens of these beautiful structures. The government is very conscious of keeping their heritage well maintained.

Now we are off at great speed on an Expressway, Madonna sometimes reaching 130 kilometres an hour, we check for speed cameras. Madonna has tyre problems so while they are getting fixed Moon Su Ji and I catch forty winks on the back seat. This travelling is exhausting. We arrive at a small private temple belonging to Ning Won, a professor abbot, where we stay the night sleeping on the floor in the shrine room. Within an hour of our arrival his dog is bitten by a poisonous snake and begins to get paralysed and its face all swollen, it has to be rushed off to the vet for an injection… it survives.

Everywhere we go we are treated like royalty, the food and drink never stops, no wonder we are putting on weight. The other monk here is an artist and presents us with a beautifully hand painted black and white fan. 4am chanting again, no rest for the wicked. Dennis sat meditating with his fingers in his ears as the gong beside him was beaten to a pulp, not a melodious sound at that hour of the morning, or any time for that matter if you are close. Breakfast consists of porridge with pine nuts, pickled garlic, capsicum and potato salad, coleslaw, peas, cabbage in chilli, mushroom soup, bread rolls and other side dishes. That was just the first course, after that came boiled peanuts in the shell, peaches in a bed of ice, smoked slices of cheese, potato chips, grapes, plums and then a tea ceremony of the blackest, strongest tarry tea I have ever seen or tried to drink. It is polite to drink three cups.

Off to Busan, the second largest city in South Korea and we visit Haeundae Beach, there is not a soul in the water and it is a bit grubby, so we decide not to swim. We were taken for a cappuccino by a lady from the temple at the Nongshin Hotel, each cup was AUD$10. We visit a fishing village and fish market, with every manner of fish imaginable.

The next night we stay with a friend of Hye Won's called Mrs Pak, who runs a health retreat for people with life threatening diseases. Part of the treatment is for the clients to sleep on a bed of rocks. You have heard of a bed of nails, well…. these are sharp rocks, with a light plastic mesh to hold them in place, a silver sheet and cane mat underneath and a doona on top. The opportunity was too good to miss. I opted to sleep on the rocks with just shade cloth over our heads and conned Hye Won, Moon Su Ji and Dennis to do the same. The pillow was like a brick, large seeds like hazelnuts, compacted and covered with cloth. Would you believe it, we all slept really well. Before breakfast we were herded in to vehicles and rushed off to the Bath House with Mrs Pak's fasting clients. What bliss, hot and cold baths, icy showers, body scrubs, shampoos and back to Mrs Paks for breakfast, luckily we are not expected to fast. Beautiful soup made from soya sauce, rice flour, mushrooms, tofu and green beans with more side dishes. Sitting on the floor of course.

Off to stay the next two nights in a magnificent house at Goseong, belonging to a very rich disciple of Hye Wons. It is her weekender and has four loos, one of which has more buttons than a jet plane for different purposes it is called a Loo Loo. I wasn't game enough to press any of the buttons. Three large bedrooms, a huge living room, kitchen, balcony room with a fabulous view of the islands, with fishing boats weaving in and out of the red and white buoys in the water, which are used for growing oysters and seaweed. There is a large caretaker's house beside the main house. We did a load of washing in a hi-tech washing machine, the laundry also has a loo. We take a walk down the steep cliffs and to our surprise find two Canadians, one Irishman and one Aussie, who have been picnicking on the rocks. They are all here on a two year contract to teach English. We hardly see any foreigners. They point out the amazing dinosaur footprints in the rocks. We scramble over rocks and oyster shells to get to the water for a swim with our sandals on. It is a bit grotty, so we don't stay in too long. We take a shower back at the mansion with jets of water spraying every inch of our bodies from the wall and if that is not enough, there is a hand nozzle too, even here we sleep on the floor. The living area is like being in a temple or chapel with lights behind the interior windows in the cathedral style ceiling. There is a fully equipped bar in one corner and Hye Won finds a bottle of pine tree wine in a white china bottle the shape of a pine tree. It is pretty strong stuff from all accounts. The owner is not here and told Hye Won to treat it as his home; we are taking her at her word. We had a drive to Geoji Island but couldn't find a nice beach to swim at. We had a short walk through a forest and all had a sleep in a rest area on some tables. We are all pooped. Dennis cooked garlic omelettes and two minute noodles for dinner it was great.

We set off for Masan another large city to get an Express bus to Seoul; we arrived with two minutes to get on the bus, a hasty farewell to Moon Su Ji while Hye Won parked the car, the bus left before he got back. I was very sad not to say a proper good bye and thank you for such a wonderful time. My eyes filled with tears as we left the bus terminal.

BIRDSVILLE RODEO AUSTRALIA

Have you ever seen Mexican Roulette played? OR have you ever been courageous enough to play it?

A few years ago I went on a bus trip to the Birdsville Races in Queensland. What a day in the country that was. A powerful dust storm blew in on race day and we had to buy masks, just so we could breathe. At night when the dust had settled we went to the Rodeo; part of the entertainment was Mexican Roulette.

This consisted of a few brave volunteers, with a belly full of beer, for Dutch courage, clambering over the fence in to the ring where a circle was drawn in the dust; a wild bull was released from the chutes. The last man standing in the circle won $50 and a bottle of rum. The bull came out with head lowered, snorting and scraping the dust with its front feet, fire and brimstone bursting out of each nostril. A few men ran for the rails as it charged across the arena, twisting and turning, ready to attack whatever was in its path. The field quickly got narrowed down to two men standing but one who appeared slightly disorientated, was hit smack bang in the kidneys and didn't move, lying sprawled out on the ground. The crowds cheered but were soon subdued as we realised the severity of the situation.

The bull was herded into a yard, the dust settled and the poor chap was carried out on a stretcher to the waiting ambulance, which was called to retrieve the unconscious body. The show must go on. Later in the proceedings there was an announcement to say the injured man was in hospital but had lost his false teeth. Would volunteers join the search to scour the dusty ground for the missing denture? Loud applause went up when it was found in one piece, albeit with a good coating of dirt.

Roughing it in Burma

Aussies are attracted to Aussies I find overseas. I met up with Jim at the Bangkok airport in 1992 the only way I could get into Myanmar at that time was on a tour. This was part of Jim's three month world trip. In Mandalay we decided to leave the group and take a boat down the Irrawaddy River to Bagan. We were told this was not possible. We thought otherwise, we took a horse and cart to the wharf, I conned the driver into letting me take over the reins much to the amusement of the locals.

The boat captain sent us off to an office in town to see if we could get tickets. It must have been our lucky day because we managed to talk our way into leaving the next morning at 5am. We boarded the boat in the dark, which was just as well, because if we had seen the rust bucket that was to take us overnight on the river, we may not have been so keen. We zigzagged our way across the river, from bank to bank, stopping at small villages on the way. We passed under the Ava Bridge which was engineered by a Burmese man, who is now a monk. I have met him on a few occasions and he is a real character. He speaks several languages, knows everything that is going on in the world. Asked me how Bob Hawke and Kerry Packer were doing.

Some locals boarded the boat with samosas, fried vegetables and hard boiled quail eggs. They were delicious. One man tried to sell us some pepper for motion sickness, we declined. We shared a 'saloon' area with a monk and two other Aussie adventurers. For lunch we bought boiled rice, pilchards and cabbage, cooked on the deck.

We are an obvious attraction to the locals. One man in a golden jacket said to me the only English words he knows "I love you". A feeling of sadness came over me as I gaze towards the river bank. These beautiful people are so warm and friendly, they live so simply and they work so hard, they want what we have in the western world, thinking they will be better off. We want what they have thinking that we will be better off.

The river is majestic; the alluvial soil is planted right to the water's edge. At dusk we stop at a village as the boat cannot navigate at night. Jim wants to go looking for a hotel, as he does not want to sleep on the deck. It is raining and the soil is slippery and muddy, we clamber up the bank, only to find there is no hotel, only a guest house and it is full, or so they say. They fear what the government would do to them if they take in foreigners we feel. We stopped to buy some deep fried vegetables at a roadside stall, where Jim decided he would take over the cooking. We caused a traffic jam as the oxen drawn carts could not get through the forty or fifty people who had come to see these crazy visitors.

We found a café, for want of a better name, where Jim had Chinese beer and Mandalay rum, we slipped and slithered our way back to the boat in the dark. Some locals on board were on their way to the markets with beautiful red and black woven blankets; so we bought one each and settled in for the night on the saloon floor. As soon as I lay down a huge cockroach started heading towards me, Jim was no help; the rum had taken hold of him. What took hold of me was a serious Burmese stomach bug. I got no sleep with my nocturnal visit to the only loo on board, which luckily was close by. I took several pills and potions for diarrhoea to no avail. Jim was fine and had a great sleep. Perhaps I should have taken a dose of rum.

We finally arrived in Bagan and I did survive the night, feeling like a wrung out rag. We got a horse and cart to the Ayeyar Hotel in Bagan to join up with our group again. We went straight off on a tour of the pagodas, which were wonderful but I had trouble staying awake, so in the afternoon I went back to the hotel and slept for four hours.

When we read the fine print of our tour guide it explained that if we left the tour at any stage we would be deported instantly. Phew, luckily we did not get caught. It was a wonderful adventure and when I phoned Jim back in Sydney after his three months travelling around the world, I asked him what the highlight of his trip was; he said "the journey down the Irrawaddy River"

FUNERAL PARLOUR CAFÉ

I arrived in Ho Chi Min City with my friend Sue. We each took a motorbike taxi from the airport to our backpacker accommodation, from memory about seven kilometres. With our backpacks between the driver's legs we climbed on to the pillion seat and took off. The traffic was so horrendous that we did not know which side of the road they drive on. Sue was nervous, I told her to look up at the beautiful French architecture of the buildings, rather than what was happening at ground level. We got to our destination to find it boarded up and closed down. This form of transport is only for the adventurous!!

We asked our motorbike drivers to take us to some cheap accommodation, they took us to a hotel which was much too expensive, so we paid them off (one US dollar) got our trusty Lonely Planet Guide out to check out our next move.

Before long a dozen cyclo drivers where vying for our business. Cyclo's are pedal powered, by humans, similar to rickshaws, except you sit out in front. Things got heated as we slowly made our plan. The cyclo drivers started to squabble over who was taking us to our next destination. Then all hell broke loose, one driver on my right leaned across me and punched another driver in the face who was on my left. Before he hit the ground he was whacked again, by this time there was blood streaming from his nose and all over my backpack, we grabbed our bags and headed off down the street, thinking the Vietnam war was about to start again.

Other cyclo drivers who had been waiting in the wings pedalled beside us along the road seeking our attention. We walked briskly on until only two were in pursuit. We asked them to take us to Chinatown, where we found some cheap beds, settled in and calmed down.

By now it was evening and we felt hungry, we went looking for something to eat. We found a door open into a well lit barn type building, something like a hayshed with bays each side, lots of candles burning, people milling around, chanting, meditating and some eating at tables in the centre of the building.

Thinking it was a café, we were invited in by a man at the door, sat down and food was placed at the table for us. All very nice, we thought. We found a man who could speak a little English and he explained to us that we were in a 'Funeral Parlour", where the families and friends were honouring the dead. When we looked closely we could see coffins with a photo of the deceased on each one. Everyone was so good to us that we went back the second night for more.

MY TIBETAN TWINS

Kalsang and Lhadon were three years old when I first met them. They live with their parents Dorjee and Tsamchoe in northern India at a town called Paonto Sahib. Dorjee is the librarian at the Tibetan Settlement School and Tsamchoe is a teacher's aid for the Kindergarten and first grade children. There are 500 Tibetan children 3-18-year-olds and 30 teachers at the school and all of them are sponsored by overseas benefactors.

I first met Dorjee several years ago before he married. He was the librarian at a monastery at Dharamsala, where HH the Dalai Lama lives and is the spiritual leader for his people in exile. Dorjee was at a memorial service for Princess Diana at the large Anglican Cathedral. It was a cold and wet, miserable day, the church was a few kilometres from town but just about everyone was willing to face the elements and pay their respects to Princess Di.

Dorjee and a couple of others were off to a Tibetan Buddhist nunnery and orphanage, after the service, and invited me to tag along. I did not take much persuading. We caught a local bus and in no time were at our destination. Dorjee knew some of the nuns and introduced us, but as they did not speak English, it was smiles and sign language. We then went on to an interesting monastery built by the Japanese. It was funny to see a Japanese garden right in the heart of India.

On the way home an English girl and I started singing on the bus, poor Dorjee was so embarrassed he didn't know where to look. It did cheer up an otherwise pretty sad day. Some days later my English friend and I took Dorjee to dinner at an Italian Restaurant which was full of Israeli backpackers. Many young Israelis get out of the Army and go travelling. India is one of their favourite destinations, because it is so cheap. They grow dreadlocks, wear hippy clothes and do meditation courses.

Dorjee and I swapped addresses and vowed we would write when I got home. True to our word, the correspondence went on for many years and continues to this day. Dorjee told me how he had been transferred to Paonto Sahib and had met a lovely Tibetan girl, Tsamchoe. They were duly married and produced the twins, a girl Lhadon and a boy Kalsang. Very unusual in Tibetan culture to have twins, so it was quite an event. As the adopted grandmother, I am called Momo.

His father escaped from China with Dorjee, his brother and two younger boys, when Dorjee was thirteen years old. It took them a month to walk over the Himalayan Mountains to Dharamsala. His father got them settled into school and then made the long trek home. His parents are illiterate and even if Dorjee could get a letter or news through to them, there is a chance that they would be thrown in jail and tortured. So Dorjee doesn't dare contact them. A couple of years ago Dorjee got word that his father had got through to Kathmandu. I supported Dorjee to travel to meet his father for a very emotional reunion after twenty years. Two years later his parents and a sister managed a visit to Nepal. They sent me photos of this joyous occasion. Once again it gave me great pleasure to help Dorjee to be able to see them.

Dorjee now speaks three languages, Hindi, English and Tibetan. The school library that he is in charge of is neat and tidy. Everything is listed and filed in order. He has used his imagination to encourage the students to read and learn. It is a credit to him.

I visited them in 2002 year. At first the twins were very shy and only peeped at me from behind their mother's skirt, but after a few days we were the best of mates. Dorjee and I took a rickshaw into the village, so that I could purchase a small table and two chairs for the twins. We also had loads of stationery to bring back for the school, so it was quite a load for the poor fellow pedalling the cycle rickshaw for all his worth. The twins were so excited with their new gift and even took them to bed with them. As they sleep in the bed with their parents, it was quite a squeeze. When I saw them in the morning, they were sitting at the table, which was on top of the bed! The family only has four pieces of furniture, three beds and a table.

Each morning as soon as my eyes are open Tsamchoe would bring to my bed a hot Thermos of sweet milky tea and some chapattis, and then later an omelette or porridge, or noodles. One day we had traditional Beef Momos. These were prepared in a small alcove on a burner and steamer. Dorjee walked miles to get the beef and then had to cut it finely, no mince here. It is wrapped in homemade pastry with garlic, onion and spices and put in the steamer to cook. They have only cold water to shower in, so water has to be heated on this burner for a bucket shower. The toilet is of the squat variety. One night Dorjee took me on his rounds to make sure all the older boys were doing their chanting, sitting on their bunk beds in large dormitories.

The head of the school is a tall upright Tibetan lady. Most of the teachers live in the settlement, which is not far from the school, but Dorjee and his family lived in a school building but have now been able to move to an old house in the settlement. Most of the pupils are boarders; only those few living in the settlement come to school by the day. Kalsang and Lhadon firstly went to a crèche during the day while their parents were at work. Now they attend school full time.

They are gorgeous little kids and get on very well together. They have very few toys but amuse themselves with bits of string and sticks. Dorjee and Tsamchoe are very keen for them to be well educated.

I am now sponsoring Tsamchoe to become a primary school teacher. She has passed her first exams with flying colours. It is heart warming to help these people who are so willing to help themselves and to see the value of further training. Dorjee and I now email each other, as he is allowed to use the school computer. He has virtually taught himself.

The school is set in the middle of a wheat field in a small valley. It is a beautiful area which gets very hot is summer and very cold in winter. I think of my Tibetan family daily and wish I were closer to help with their day to day chores, but they are happy and healthy and never complain. We have so many lessons to learn from them.

My Tibetan Family in India

PEACE AND LOVE PARIS

On the bus from Charles de Gaulle airport I sat beside a distinguished gentleman from Melbourne on his way to his French villa for six months. He was so kind and generous. He gave me a map of Paris and a metro ticket to get me from Opera station to Louis Blanc. His name was John Thistlethwaite or Entwhistle, one of those sorts anyway. I was most grateful for his assistance.

I found the Peace and Love Hostel, which I had booked on line for four nights to find it has an age limit of 35. I clearly did not fit the criteria. I just managed to squeak in after a lot of smooth talking. I was even put in a dorm on the first floor rather than the seventh as planned; NO LIFT. It is very noisy as the main fire station and police station are nearby, the bar on the ground floor goes to 2am but that did not stop me sleeping. I was exhausted from hard travel in Tunisia and Morocco.

The two bunks are so close that two people cannot pass between them at the same time. I was fortunate to get a lower bunk and two fellas took the two upper ones. It is in a fairly grotty part of town but close to the Metro which is good as I am here to have both hands operated on for Dupuytrens Contracture. The specialist doctor lives about an hour out of Paris. A canal off the Seine is just over the road and beside the river are many homeless people living in tents, on mattresses or lounges. It is a sad sight to see in such a historic city.

You are not going to believe this but after my four nights at the hostel, I stayed in a two storey gate house of a friend of a friend outside of Paris in a gorgeous village called Chatou. It has two bedrooms two bathrooms, all mod cons and is separate from the main house which has two rampant lions to greet you. I was invited to a sumptuous lunch in the garden overlooking the Seine. I arrived with two bandaged hands, having just had my second hand operated on. We walked the two dogs along the river bank and saw children riding at a Pony Club. After hearing about my tale of the hostel my friend insisted that I come and stay. I jumped at the idea, and from this luxurious accommodation I managed to visit the Eiffel Tower, Arc de Triumph, Sacra Coeur, Montmarte, Grand Palace and the Louvre, but am really happy to be out of the city into the Peace and Love of Chatou. It had been 18 years since my last visit to this magic city.

LAUGHTER

Laughter attracts joy, releases negativity and leads to miraculous cures. Rhonda Byrne

Laughter is the best medicine. We have been hearing that for years, but now it has actually been proven. Dr Madan Kataria, an Indian medical doctor founded the International Laughter Yoga Club in 1995 in a park in Bombay with five of his friends, after researching the healthy benefits of laughter on the mind and body. There are now 6000 groups around the world and probably the same number in India, he has lost count. Laughter can diffuse a heated situation; it is a great alternative to drugs, alcohol, gambling, and smoking to cope with stress. The mind does not know the difference if laughter is fake or real; the benefits are the same. Laughter is an essential part of life, it's healthy to laugh and recent studies have found that people who laugh are less likely to have heart attacks. Laughter Yoga, as it is called, is a cardio/vascular workout for the body.

- Laugh for no reason.
- Laugh when the bus breaks down.
- Laugh when you miss the train.
- When travelling in a group laugh and sing on the bus.
- Chant Ho Ho Ha Ha Ha and clap your hands in rhythm.

- Chant Very Good, Very Good, slowly clapping your hands together, then Yeah, with hands apart and thumbs up.
- Let go of inhibitions.
- Go to an orphanage and do crazy things to make kids laugh. They don't have to understand English.
- Make light of situations.
- Have a 'pulling funny faces' competition.
- Look in a mirror/shop window and laugh.
- Laughter benefits respiration gets you breathing better. Eases depression, improves circulation, the immune system and aids digestion.
- Laughter helps you to sleep more soundly, builds stamina, gives you a feeling of well being, raises antibody levels, and helps to move mucous.
- Relaxes tight muscles, triggers endorphins, the bodies' natural pain killers.
- Helps you to find your sense of humour. Gives you self confidence.
- You can start with a giggle or a titter and end up snorting with your eyes streaming, your nose running, absolutely paralytic, doubled up with mirth.
- In a group do the Hokey Pokey.
- Laughter exercises your facial muscles to prevent sagging and wrinkles.
- It reduces the levels of cortisol, the stress hormone. Can reduce your blood pressure and drives carbon dioxide out of your body and replaces it with oxygen rich air that refreshes you physically and mentally.
- Read funny books, listen to funny tapes, and see funny movies.

- Take a small bottle of soapy water for blowing bubbles. These can be bought at dollar stores. Then blow bubbles for kids and get them to chase them.

There are some precautions for extended laughter.

- If you are in the late stages of pregnancy.
- Have acute slipped disc problems.
- If you have angina, a hernia, uncontrolled high blood pressure, severe flu or fever, glaucoma or advanced haemorrhoids.

Penang and Langkawi
Malaysia

Batu Feringhii, Penang has a relaxed atmosphere on the beach. I have now braved the ocean and haven't encountered any red jelly fish, which I was warned about, but I did see a huge white sort of opaque monster being washed up with the tide. It must have been a couple of feet across and in the centre a gelatinous body, made up of candle like masses all waxed together. Glad I didn't encounter it round my legs in the water. I would certainly have leaped into outer space!

While I was sitting in a resort cafe on the beach, I spotted an Indian gentleman walking by playing a flute made out of a colourfully decorated gourd. After sipping on my chilled coconut juice in the shell and eating the young tender flesh, I took a walk further down the beach. There was a flute player doing magic tricks, with two English gents getting it all recorded on their home videos. After the conjuring act he started to play the flute and remove the lid from a wicker basket. You guessed it, there inside was a five foot beautiful shiny black Malaysian Tiger snake with splashes of yellow at even distances along its body. He asked did we want to see the snake 'dance', certainly. It reared up out of the basket as he played the gourd and before long was swaying its head from side to side and flashing its forked tongue. Marvellous. Then he asked if I would like to put the snake around my neck, assuring me it does not bite I handed my camera to one of the English gentleman and told him to quick smart press the button.

While walking down the street, I saw a rather mangy dog, I told him how beautiful and gorgeous he was, but he obviously didn't understand English. He came at me bearing his fangs and growling, hair on his back upright. I remained calm and I kid you not, a hair's breadth from my calf, he changed his mind and turned away. Phew!

Tonight I am going to the night markets and eating out. I have found Mario's a great Italian Restaurant with excellent cappuccino and special fruit bread toasted. As I have my own kitchen in my apartment I am able to eat cereal, banana and soy milk for breakfast, salmon and sardines on oatmeal bread and some nice soft cheese. I eat out on local food once a day. It is all very cheap.

When I went into a travel agent in Penang to book my flight to Langkawi, the young girl kept pointing to the stairs and saying "Etiquette, etiquette" I thought. Oh dear what have I done that has broken some cultural law that I don't know about. I asked my question again and got the same reply. Finally the penny dropped, she was saying "Air ticket, air ticket" and pointing to the next floor up. When you run the two words air ticket together with a Malaysian accent you certainly get etiquette! Or you did to my ears anyway. I was lucky enough to get a "promotion deal", meaning discounted if I booked a week ahead. The return "etiquette" cost $37 Australian, normally it is three times that much.

Langkawi is as promised, very quiet and everything is very spread out. The beaches are cleaner and the water cleaner than Penang and no nasties in the water. While in Batu Feringhii I saw a man and his small son going up parasailing. When they got a fair way from the shore, the motor of the boat went kaput and came to a dead halt. The man and his son were luckily wearing life jackets, because they came plummeting down in to the sea. The parachute did not seem to ease them gently as one would expect, just zoom, straight down. A jet ski finally saw their predicament and rescued them from the water.

The many different cultures and religions get on extremely well in Malaysia and there doesn't appear to be one nation that are the employers and one the employee. There are mixes of nations working together in most businesses. The Malaysian man, Zachary who owns the guest house where I had three nights in Langkawi, told me "I am a Muslim… not a good one, because I drink alcohol, but I don't make bombs". Well that was a relief! He owns three dogs called Chivas Regal, Jack Daniels and Baileys. He is very helpful and runs a good show. He was a business man in Penang but retired to the island when he turned 50. He tells me that all domestic air fares are half price when you turn 50. Now wouldn't that be nice if the Australian Government took a leaf out of their book. I am in a fan room with bathroom outside. The Room is clean, bed comfortable with clean sheets and is mosquito proof. I am paying $7 a night and have the use of a fridge and cooking facilities. The one shame is that is quite a hike to the beach, so I have today checked out "chalets" close to the water.

I had two glorious weeks in Langkawi and want to come back for more. It is very quiet, the water is clear and clean, the locals are friendly, the food yummy and the sunsets are 'out of this world'. I would sit in the ocean as the sun was drifting down through the fluffy clouds, the streaks of colour changing by the minute, a different palette every evening, marvelling at creation and thinking how blessed I am to be experiencing this daily natural light show.

My chalet was an A Frame type timber with high ceiling fan, own bathroom, balcony and TV, but best of all 10 metres from the beach. Not bad for $18 a night. A few chalets away were a couple in their 70's from Hawaii. Lucius is a Professor of Education, Communication and Technology, a Fulbright Scholar and part time pastor. Dona is a linguist, they are both counsellors and have lived in such diverse countries at Saudi Arabia, Laos, Japan, Korea, Washington and Samoa. They speak many languages and are interested in learning more about local people, cultures, traditions and religions. Dona and I struck up an immediate friendship and talked and walked for hours. I taught her to do Qi Gong on the beach each morning. We would walk to the north end of the beach and there at one of the 5 star resorts was a Reflexology Walk. Imagine a bed of nails but substitute small individual rocks sticking up, set in concrete. We managed to focus our minds for long enough to get to the end.

For a day's outing I boarded the fast ferry, at 38 knots, from Langkawi, to Thailand. After a pleasant 45 minute journey we landed at Satun, close to the border of mainland Thailand and Malaysia.

I was told that Satun was a sleepy fishing village, but I found it to be much more. It is quite a large town with a Mosque and Buddhist Temple, hotels and businesses and of course the ever present markets. I climbed into the *sangtaew*, the local transport-basically the back of a utility truck, with boards for sitting on both sides and a roof over the top. They can comfortably seat around 10 passengers with their bags from the markets, the odd motorbike tyre, live chickens or whatever. I have been in one near the Burmese border in Thailand and counted 29 people plus all their goods and chattels.

Back to Satun, we stepped out of the *sangtaew* at the 7/11 store. Bought some snacks and wandered up the street to find a hairdresser. There was Simon asleep on the loungy chair that one lies in to have a shampoo, hanging your head back over the basin. There were no customers, so Simon had decided to rest. He was surprised when his neighbour from the shop next door woke him to find *farangs* – foreigners wanting a haircut. We established a price 150 baht, about AUD $5.50, it would take an hour.

I lay back on the loungy chair which Simon had just vacated. He shampooed and massaged my hair, head and scalp with several different potions and lotions. It felt like I had died and gone to heaven. After about 20 minutes of this relaxing treatment, he towel dried my hair. I moved to a chair, where he wrapped me up in a sheet, so as not to get scratchy pieces of chopped hair down my neck. He gave me two glossy magazines to read, well look at the pictures, as they were in Thai, while he proceeded to snip away, very carefully and mindfully, enquiring how I wanted it cut. With his limited English and my limited Thai it was a strange combination of words and sign language.

He told me he had studied hairdressing in Bangkok for a year before opening his own business in his home town Satun. He would very much like to see Australia and enquired as to whether I had a boyfriend. Perhaps he was going to volunteer for the job! After an excellent cutting job he directed me back to the loungy chair again for more shampoo and conditioning until my hair felt light and silky. This time he massaged my head, neck and shoulders, finishing off with the percussion action of a Thai massage. I.e. Hands together in prayer position and gentle but firm blows to the shoulders with just the border of the little fingers hitting the body. That great thwack, thwack, thwack sound it makes as fingers touch the body and the air is compressed out through the palms.

Then back to the cutting chair where he discovered the power was off, so he could not blow dry my hair. He pointed to the light and said "No". I got the message. He dried my hair with a towel as best he could. I came away feeling a million dollars. No smart salon in the world could have done it better and they certainly could not have matched the price.

Did some shopping in the market and on the ferry on the way back to Langkawi I was allowed to sit on the roof and watch the beautiful tropical islands go by. Even saw two of the famous Sea Eagles hovering and weaving in the sky.

The local Malaysian paper had an interesting photo of a Brazilian girl, who got herself into the Guinness Book of Records by having the most body piercings of any in the world. 1093 to be exact. I counted 7 studs in her tongue, 3 nose rings, 12 studs down the bridge of her nose and 33 around her lips. Goodness knows where the others were?

I found some very good Capsicum liniment for my back. The label reads for All Wind Troubles. Sprains, Cramps, Back ache and MUMBNESS. I had a good reflexology session with Joe, on the beach. He has a large corn on the knuckle of his finger from putting pressure on it for so many years.

I was invited to an Open House Party and met a very eccentric local artist. He wore a wide brimmed black hat, a long grey beard. Sports jacket, shirt and tie, shorts, one blue sock and one grey. One brown lace up shoe, one black with no shoe laces. He went round the room shaking hands with everyone and was the life of the party. His photo is in the tourist guide book and his main claim to fame is painting a picture that is over one kilometre long.

One day my new friend Dona and I went into the main city Kuah, with its beautiful parks and government buildings, Langkawi Fair, which is a huge shopping mall. The airport is now international, so I hope that all these thousands of tourists are not going to change the ambience.

Back in Penang for four nights at Batu Feringhii I had some casual clothes made and bought some fake label tennis shoes, which lasted about three games at home.

FIRST TIME IN HAWAII

My six-hour flight from Vancouver to Honolulu had run late and I arrived about midnight. The Hostel International is very good and close to Waikiki beach and shops. I have come to the conclusion that Waikiki is a combination of the Gold Coast in Australia and Phuket in Thailand but with a rock breakwater wall. The beaches are busy, but full of interesting sights. The first time I went to the beach a large Afro American lady called me over and handed me about eight postcards. I asked her how much she wanted for them and she said 'no, they are free, I over bought'. How nice!

I am missing Canadian Tim Horton's coffee; I am afraid Starbucks is too strong for me. I bought a nice sarong and left it sitting on a rock wall where I stopped to drink my coffee. Wandered off and had a swim, realised I had left it behind, went rushing back and there it was, no problem. I have been eating Korean food at the International Market, as well as buying food to eat at the hostel. Today I saw a woman having a water massage. She lay face down in this machine with all her clothes on, they folded the top down and a plastic sheet covered her body before all these jet sprays went up and down her body, firing out water as they went. She said it was good.

There was a big street parade one evening because the local kids had won the Little League Baseball World Series. The mayor, Mufi Hannemann went first. What a handsome Hawaiian he is. Then came dignitaries, one in a white convertible Rolls Royce, many red convertible Mustangs, Chevs, T Model Fords, and hot rods. Marching bands, cheer leaders and then the victorious team, each in his own convertible or in a dickie seat. One Ford was exactly the same as one my mother had with a dickie seat. Boy, if only we had it now.

There are many beautiful banyan trees, covering huge areas. The only bigger one I have seen was in India; it covered a quarter of an acre. This morning I went to the beach early and there on the beach was an abandoned blow up lilo. I washed it off, blew it up and found I could get a good fifteen minutes lilo lolling before a minor detail of a hole caused it, and me to sink. Trying to get onto it was an art in itself. Finally a lady advised me to bring it between my legs, then lie back and get my balance. I told her I was trying to mount it as you would a horse. She got a good laugh out of that. I walked up to the top of Diamondhead Crater. That was a challenge, but worth the view at the top. I circled the island of Maui on a bus, visiting a Japanese Buddhist temple and multicultural cemetery and the big waves of the north shore.

REPAIRS ON THE RUN ALL OVER

Have you ever been in a foreign country and needed some running repairs? Even though you have checked everything before you left home, the inevitable does happen. Wear and tear on clothing and body takes its toll. Take heart, there are countries where you can get prompt and efficient service for items that normally would have be thrown away at home.

For instance, in Nepal whilst waiting in a queue for your trekking permit, it is possible to get your joggers sewn up. It only costs $2 and you can get a lot more mileage out of them.

In Myanmar (Burma) almost anywhere in the capital Yangon, your thongs can be rejuvenated by either having the top strap replaced, the hole that the strap goes into glued up, or even a new sole replacement, all at very little cost. Nothing is thrown away in this country.

You have a favourite pair of sandals that you are very attached to and loathe to get rid of. They have seen you through many miles, carried you through sandy deserts and wet streams, over rocks and boulders, slippery waterfalls and dirty shower blocks. They have been repaired over and over again, but you feel there is still life left in them. In the Banglampoo area of Bangkok, in Thailand, there is a wonderful lady who will sew on buckles, glue on false backing, to strengthen straps, and put thick soles on that will outlast the rest of the sandal, so the whole procedure is self perpetuating.

You have travelled through India and it has been pretty rough going, on and off buses, trains, elephants, rickshaws, motorized and man powered. Your day pack has had a pounding. By the time you get to Darjeeling the zipper as finally given up the ghost! In a small side alley, in a hole in the wall, your zipper will be replaced like new. It is almost worth the trip, just for this purpose.

On the island of Koh Samet in Thailand, you are in a bungalow and the light and fan have ceased to function. Power on the island is from a generator. You report your problems to the owner at the café. She sends a thirteen-year-old boy to fix it. He arrives with a screwdriver and a pair of pliers. Without checking to see if the power is turned off, he pokes the screwdriver in to a spaghetti like tangled mass of wires. At this stage your curiosity is over come by the need for self preservation and you retire outside the bungalow, to safer ground. You see a fireworks display of sparks and hear some snapping noises and wonder if the boy is going to make fourteen. After a short time he emerges triumphant with meagre tools intact, the fan and light functioning and you are left with your mouth wide open in sheer wonderment.

You are in Kuching, the capital of Sarawak, Malaysia and your cigarette lighter has run out of gas. No problem. Just near the main bus station there is a gentleman seated on a stool, with a box for a work bench and in three seconds flat he has your old lighter in several pieces, refilled and back together again for quarter of the price of a new one. He has done it so many times, I am sure he could do it with his eyes closed.

In Pandan a remote village in Sarawak a large crowd has gathered on the footpath. On closer inspection you find a man speaking into a microphone attached to his neck. He has a large cloth laid out in front of him, with a pile of teeth on it. He is a travelling dentist. Even though he is speaking Malaysian you can get his message. He holds up a pair of molar forceps and throws them to the ground. *No good.* Next he holds up a common-a-garden plastic handled screwdriver. This is best for extracting teeth! His patient sits on a stool, the dentist asks him to bite on a wad of cotton wool which has been soaked in something out of a bottle. After a short while the operation takes place. One swift flick of the wrist and the tooth joins the pile on the ground and another wad of cotton wool is put in the jaw to bite on. While the dentist wipes the screwdriver on a rag on his knee, he then lines up the next patient, all this for $6 with some Chinese herbs thrown in. Who is worried about sterilization?

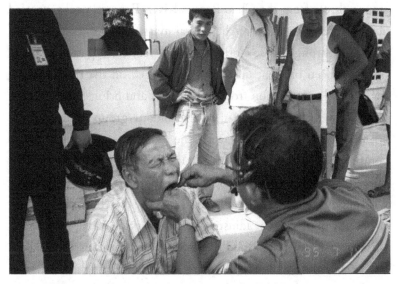

A street dentist in Sarawak, Malaysia

MASSAGE AROUND THE WORLD

In September 1992 I travelled with 28 fellow Australians to Bangkok to learn Traditional Thai Massage. The training took place at Wat Pho Traditional Medical School just near the Grand Palace and a stone's throw from the Chao Phraya River. For two weeks we used acupressure, yoga and stretches. Thai massage is done on a mat on the floor through loose clothing. It was very testing as we Aussies have not been brought up to sit cross legged on the floor and the massage releases tension from the muscles and brings up emotions.

Two years later I joined twelve of our group to do a more advanced course and we learned the technique of using steamed compressed herbs, in a calico bag, on the muscles to relax them. At home I was able to adapt these Thai movements to a massage table with good results and very much easier on my own body. In my early fifties, my body was not adjusting well to working on the floor. After this course I stayed at a Buddhist Forest Monastery west of Bangkok at Kanchanaburi and taught the monks and nuns English. This was my first experience as English teacher and it was challenging to have a class of fifty or so monks, most of them well over school age.

After four weeks I flew to Kathmandu in Nepal and arrived in the middle of a Hindu Festival which lasted for six days. The main focus of the event was sacrificing animals for the Gods and around each corner there was a yak, buffalo, goat, duck or chicken being beheaded and cut up. The blood from these animals was then spattered onto the front and back of car and truck windscreens. I decided it was time for a massage, I found a little Nepalese lady in a side street, whom I bargained with and ended up paying AUD$11.50 for an hour. I was pleased I had not paid more as she pulverised my body to a pulp nearly. She gave me 'Chinese burns' on both arms, rotated my breasts as if trying to unscrew them, grabbed my legs to stop me running away, then walked all over my back! Actually it sounds horrendous, but it felt good afterwards.

I took a bus to Pokhara to trek for five days in the Annapurnas. I found a nice boy called Dharma to act as guide and porter. I never would have made it without him. I said to him one day, 'I should have done this 30 years ago' he said 'but Noni, you would not have met me'. He was right, he wouldn't have been born. Every night he would massage my poor aching legs and knees, and with some guidance from me, he did an excellent job. He had a reference book and I was able to write some inspiring things in it about him. Back in Pokhara I found a barber who also did massage. It was more of a grab rather than smooth flowing strokes or working into the muscles but was quite relaxing. As I had caught a heavy cold in the mountains I am sure it helped my immune system. The next day I tried a Shiatsu massage from a Nepalese man who had learned from a Japanese tourist. I ended up showing him some Thai stretches and Australian movements, so he became quite an international masseur.

While having a banana lassi drink from a roadside stall one day, I looked down to see a very snotty nosed cow drinking the washing up water from a dish on the ground! Luckily I am a seasoned traveller and managed to polish off the rest of the lassi without it coming back up.

My next country was India and I was staying at the Burmese Monastery in Bodh Gaya. This is a very famous sacred place, as the Buddha became enlightened here over 2500 years ago. I can understand why, it is so peaceful and tranquil sitting under the Bodhi tree at the Maha Bodhi Temple. One of the monks at the monastery had a bad back, so I was called upon to see if I could give him some pain relief. In the Burmese tradition monks are allowed to be touched by women, whereas in the Thai tradition it is a no-no. The monk happened to be Australian and had been ordained for twelve years. I ended up giving him a few massages and managed to alleviate most of his pain. As 'payment' he gathered wood to heat the water for my shower. I have been paid in many currencies and objects for massage including an emu egg in a beautiful carved wooden bowl, given to me by an Australian aboriginal. I also massaged an Australian girl staying at the Burmese monastery and received an hour's massage from an Indian man who charged just AUD$2.50 an hour. That was ridiculous so I had three more massages and gave him a good tip.

In Calcutta, I visited Mother Teresa and the Sisters of Mercy, this was an experience never to be forgotten. There I massaged babies who were blind, some children who were five years old but the size of a one-year-old, a nun with a bad shoulder, orphans and street children and many more. In India you see grandmothers sitting on the ground with squirming babies on their legs being massaged with oil from a bowl beside the baby, who is obviously loving it.

A five day Vipassana meditation course in Myanmar (Burma) was my next stop. I pushed myself through the pain barrier to sit crossed legged on a cushion on the floor and when I managed to walk out with both legs intact, I decided it was time to have a massage, Burmese style. Nini came very highly recommended. I took an English speaking Burmese friend along to translate, as Nini can't speak English. I am pleased I had a witness because no one would have believed me. Nini used acupressure points only on the left side of my body, when he got to my neck, he got firmer and firmer and closer and closer to the 'knock out' points, which we were told to avoid in any massage course. I had time to think 'My god, he is getting close to them on both sides of my neck', when bingo, my lights went out, I was totally out of it. I came back with a knee jerk reaction as my body convulsed and I wondered which country I had landed in or whether I had made it to nirvana. My friend refused to let me pay Nini, so I have no idea how much this experience cost. Initially I felt energised and relaxed but the next day I had one hell of a headache. As I never get headaches it was pretty darn scary.

Back in Thailand, I went to Chiang Mai and had a Thai massage, this one made up for all the cheap ones. It ended up costing me AUD$700. While I was being massaged in a room with several others, with my bumbag close by, somehow the money was lifted from my wallet. It could have been worse. I could have lost my passport, visa card and traveller's cheques, the lot. I still love Thailand and have now been going there for twenty years.

My daughter joined me for the last three or four weeks of my journey on the island of Koh Samet. While I was away, she had done a massage course and wanted to practise on me. She was great, the massage was done with love and compassion and she told me she would look after me in my old age. Boy have I got something to look forward to in my 'dotage', as she calls it. For nearly twenty years I have had daily massages on Koh Samet by my friend Sala and his wife Saima. I feel healed, happy and harmonious every time I leave the island and intend to keep going back for many years to come.

Since this trip I have had massages in many countries including Austria, Bhutan, Cambodia, Canada, China, Croatia, Hungary, Indonesia, Malaysia, Morocco, New Zealand, Singapore, South Africa, South Korea, Tunisia, United States and Vietnam.

NONI'S 10 BEST MASSAGES AROUND THE WORLD

1. **South Korea**: A blind man in the Yangsan-ku area of Seoul is possibly the best massage therapist I have encountered. He has no English, but is very intuitive. He knows exactly where all your sore spots are and gently releases the tension.

2. **Thailand**: My friend Sala massages at Pudsa Beach on the island of Koh Samet. Once again he does not speak English, but gives a perfect Thai Traditional Massage with caring mind and hands.

3. **USA**: In Hawaii at Waikiki Beach a South American man gave me a Lomi Lomi massage which was very relaxing and remedial. It was expensive but worth it.

4. **Malaysia**: On the island of Penang at Batu Ferringii, Mr Anthony, a Chinese/Malay pounced on me, as business was slow that day. He used a beautifully carved Buffalo Horn to scrape my back. It sounds ghastly but felt wonderful.

5. **Thailand**: A Herbal Thai Massage at Wat Pho in Bangkok, which is the home of Thai Traditional massage, is sheer bliss. A calico bag

of selected herbs is placed over a steamer to heat and exude the most aromatic odours, before being placed on your muscles to melt the stress and tension away.

6. **India**: In Varanasi, Ashok took to me with what I can only call a rolling pin. Up and down my spine he kneaded and rolled. Then he used a wire brush on the soles of my feet. That was more than I could bear. When he just used his hands, it was fine.

7. **Nepal**: In Kathmandu I found a wiry, wispy lady with heaps of power. She used 'Chinese Burns' on my arms, rotated my breasts as if to unscrew them, then walked all over my back and legs. Funnily enough it felt good afterwards.

8. **China**: In Beijing I tried reflexology on my feet and legs, up to the knees. First a soak in a herb bath, then I was pushed, poked, prodded, pummelled, preened and pampered by an expert. Certainly gets the life force pumping through the body and excellent for the immune system.

9. **Cambodia**: In Siem Reap near Ankor Wat, the sign said Massage by the Blinders! I couldn't resist investigating. These beautiful Cambodian people, who had been through so much, do an excellent job of intuitive massage and it is a great way for them to earn a living.

10. **Myanmar**: In Yangon, Nino came highly recommended. He also had no English, so my Burmese friend came with me to translate. I sat up fully clothed while Nino pressed the points on my neck and shoulders, when BINGO he hit those knock out points, intentionally!! I was unconscious, my friend nearly fainted, by body came back with a knee jerk reaction and next day I had a shocking headache. As I never get headaches it was pretty scary. This is one to avoid.

Rannati a Child of India

When I first arrived in Bodh Gaya I saw a beggar girl asleep on the footpath, up against the wall. She had such a beautiful face and looked so serene. Beside her were a stainless steel bowl and a stick. A few days later I saw her walking, navigating her way through the other beggars, street sellers and myriad of people with her stick. She was blind. I put a few rupees in her bowl each day. Today I asked her if she would like a banana lassi (milk, yoghurt and banana drink).

Through an interpreter, she said she would. We sat down under a tree. I ordered the lassi. She waited patiently with a genuine look of anticipation on her face. I found out she is 12 years old and her name is Ranrati, the youngest of five children and the only one that is blind. She comes from a very poor family. Her skin is black, but brown with dirt. She wears no shoes, tattered clothes and some simple earrings made from wire hooked through her ears threaded with a bead. I passed her the lassi, guiding her hands onto the glass. She held it ever so gently, as though it was a cherished baby bird, so as not to harm it. She took small sips, savouring every mouthful. The look of delight on her face was a joy to behold. She slowly passed me the glass when she had finished and put her hands together by way of thanking me.

No Ranrati it is me who should thank you. You made my heart sing, from such a simple gesture. You made my heart cry to know the life ahead of you as a beggar on the streets of India...

Travelling Without the Language

Some people are afraid to travel because they don't know the language. The thought of not being understood or not being able to understand is too daunting for them. Call it foolhardiness, intrepid, adventurous, or what you will; this has never stopped me from leaping into foreign countries with no advanced accommodation bookings, no contacts and quite often no knowledge of the city or area I have leapt into.

I have no knowledge of any other language, except English. This is not taken from an arrogant point of view that I believe everyone should speak English, but I find it a fun challenge to get around and make myself understood with sign language, drawings in the dirt or sand, mud maps or no maps. I do make it a must to learn the 'greeting' and 'thank you' for every country I am about to visit.

You would be amazed at the nice people you meet when you look (and probably are) lost. Amazing too at the interesting places you end up when not knowing where you are going. You may even miss some of the better known sites, but they are more likely to be crowded and you stand a bigger chance of being 'ripped off' by vendors or pickpockets. Take the plunge and go anyway. I guarantee you will have the experience of your life, one that you will never get sitting at home pondering.

A friend and I landed in Ho Chi Minh City a couple of years ago, of course having no knowledge of the Vietnamese language. We did however have a Lonely Planet Guide – every traveller's bible.

The taxi driver at the airport offered us a cab to the city. Being a seasoned traveller, I said 'Let's find a cheaper way'. My friend and I opted for a motorbike taxi. With a bit of hand signs and our guide book, we got the ride for US$1. Cheap enough, as it was about 5 or 6 kilometres to the hotel we found in the Lonely Planet. After a few kilometres we still had no idea which side of the road they drive on in Vietnam. There appeared to be four or five lanes of traffic going in four or five different directions. When we came to an intersection, we closed our eyes and prayed hard. I told my friend to ignore the traffic and look up at the beautiful French architecture, as she was feeling rather nervous.

We got to the hotel to find it boarded up and well and truly closed down. We managed to get our motorbike drivers to take us to another hotel, but it was way beyond our budget so we paid them off. While we were studying our guide book on the footpath, for our next move, several cyclo (rickshaw) drivers materialised to try to get our business. They were all talking over the top of us, our backpacks were safely between our legs, when out of the blue, one of the cyclo drivers punched another in the face, his arm extended right across our faces. Before his opponent hit the ground, he issued another whack in the guys face. By this time we were in fear of our packs getting bloodied, so we grabbed them and made a hasty retreat, running up the road with cyclo drivers pedalling beside us, pleading for our custom. Finally when all had quietened down, we hailed a peaceful cyclo driver and got him to take us to Chinatown, to a cheap hotel.

We travelled for three weeks in Vietnam without the language, no advanced bookings for rail, bus or accommodation. It really was not a problem. We travelled by local transport from Ho Chi Minh to Hanoi and Halong Bay, stopping off along the way to hire bicycles at Na Trang, we managed to find our way around.

Keep in mind that in Asia, the locals will give you directions even if they don't know what you are asking, rather than say they don't know and lose face.

BUS TO WAT TAM WUA

I climbed into the rather dilapidated, aged bus and managed to position myself under one of three fans as the weather is hot and extremely sticky. I prepared myself for the drive to Wat Tam Wua, a Thai Buddhist Forest Monastery, an hour and a half from Mae Hong Son in northern Thailand.

The driver chats away on his mobile phone as we cross major roads with motorbikes, kids, dogs and vehicles all vying for a place on the busy road. Then he adjusts the rear vision mirror, not as you would think so that he can see what is coming up behind him BUT so he can see himself in the mirror and run the fingers of both hands through his hair at the same time!

We pass a shrine and he takes both hands off the wheel to pay his respects to the Buddha with a 'wai' in the prayer position. As the road is steep and windy, we need all the divine help we can get!

In fact at one stage I looked to see if he was reading a book perched on the steering wheel, because his head was bowed down for such a long time. He then looks in the mirror to give his offsider (conductor would be a bit grand for the lad) at the back of the bus some hand signals, both hands of course.

I had thought that maybe I was mistaken and this ancient bus actually had auto pilot installed. Occasionally he ventured to watch the road but on a particularly sharp bend he decided to take it on the wrong side of the road. As he could not possibly see what was approaching I wondered what was going on, until I saw three motorbikes overtaking us on the *inside*. From the Buddhist concept that was very likely a compassionate act, but as he put all of our lives in danger, I hoped his bad karma would not come back to him right at that moment. All was well, we made it.

There are a number of small plastic bags tied to the hand rail above the seats for those that could be feeling a bit squeamish with motion sickness from the never ending sharp bends. Luckily no one had to use them.

After half an hour my body was feeling a bit strained as I had to sit 'skewiff' because the seats are jammed together so closely that there is no way I can sit facing forward. They are obviously made for petit Thais not large 'farangs' (foreigners) like yours truly.

It seems that when the driver gets bored he devises a new trick to keep himself occupied and amuse the 'farangs' sitting 'skewiff'. This is the 'piece de resistance'... he breaks off a few sheets of toilet paper from the roll sitting on the dash board, forms it into something like a corkscrew and rotates it up his nose, twisting and turning it to remove any blockages. I kid you not. I have trouble restraining myself and am pleased I am not travelling with any one, for fear I would lose the plot totally.

I had a two kilometre walk into the monastery from the road to regain my composure.

LOCAL TRANSPORT

Life is either a daring adventure or nothing. Helen Keller

Where possible use unusual local transport. The experience is fun, you will get to meet the locals and see the sights at a slower pace, or even at very much faster pace! Here are some of my best experiences.

- Austria. Horse drawn carriage, Vienna.
- Botswana. Okavanga Delta by mokoro (dug out canoe)
- Botswana. River cruise Chobe River
- Bhutan. Riding a mule to Tigers Nest Mountain.
- Cambodia. Motor bike taxi or pedal rickshaw in Phnom Penh.
- Cambodia. Fast boat from Phnom Penh to Siem Reap.
- Canada. Trail ride on a horse at Whistler.
- Canada. Bus from Whitehorse, Yukon to Edmonton, Alberta on to Calgary..
- Canada. Local ferry up the Inside Passage from Vancouver to Skagway, Alaska.
- Canada. Driving a snowmobile from Birch Lake to Webbwood, Ontario.
- Canada. Paddling a canoe on Birch Lake, Ontario and Vancouver Island.

- Canada. Bicycle in Stanley Park, Vancouver, cycle along the St Lawrence River in Montreal and Laval in Quebec.
- Canada. Float plane over Birch Lake, Ontario.
- Canada. House boat on Lake Temagami, Ontario.
- Canada. Train from Vancouver BC to Sudbury, Ontario.
- Canada. Cruise on Maligne Lake to see Spirit Island.
- China. A mule ride at Tiger Leaping Gorge.
- China. A sheep drawn sulky in the Gobi Desert.
- China. A Bactrian camel in Inner Mongolia (two humps).
- China. Mongolian pony in Inner Mongolia.
- China. Very fast train from Shanghai to the airport 432 km/h.
- Croatia. A show jumper in Sinj.
- Denmark. Ferry from Frederickshaven to Gotenberg, Sweden.
- England. Riding an Irish hunter horse in Surrey, jumping ditches.
- Germany. A boat down the Rhine.
- Germany. Bus down the Romantic Road.
- Greece. Ferry to 20 different Islands.
- Greece. Train from Athens to Istanbul, Turkey.
- Holland. Train which goes onto a ferry to Copenhagen, Denmark.
- Hungary. A boat ride on a river in a cave at Tapolca.
- Hungary. Horse drawn carriage at Hortabagy National Park.
- Hungary. Boat on the Danube from Budapest to Vienna, Austria.
- Indonesia. Outrigger canoe from Lombok to Gili Air.
- Indonesia. Horse and cart in Lombok and Bali.
- Indonesia. Open 4WD around Bali.

- Indonesia. Ferry from Lombok to Perama Island, Satonda, Sambawa, Komodo, Rinca, Flores and Moyo Islands.
- India. Row boat on the Ganges.
- India. Ride ex racehorses in Darjeeling and Chennai.
- India. Bus from Sikkim to Kathmandu in Nepal.
- India. 2nd class sleeper train from Goa to Delhi.
- India. Taxi truck in Darjeeling at 3am to see the sunrise on Mt Everest.
- Ireland. Bus from Killarney to Dublin.
- Italy. Train from Rome to Brindisi.
- Laos. Boat down the Mekong, Luang Prabang.
- Malaysia. Ferry from Langkawi to Satun, Thailand.
- Morocco. A Dromedary camel in Essoauira (one hump).
- Myanmar. Boat down the Irrawaddy River from Mandalay to Bagan.
- Myanmar. Row boat on the Irrawaddy River at Yangon.
- Nepal. Ride an elephant to see the one horned rhinoceros at Chitwan National Park. The next day walk with the rhinos.
- Nepal. Bus from Kathmandu to Lhasa in Tibet.
- New Zealand. Train from Christchurch to Wellington.
- Norway. Mailboat on a fiord Flam to Voss.
- Norway. Train from Bergen to Oslo.
- Scotland. Ferry to the Orkney Islands.
- South Africa. Paddle a canoe Orange River.
- South Africa. Topless bus in Capetown.
- South Korea. Bus from Masan to Seoul.
- Spain. Train from Barcelona to Avignon, France.
- Switzerland. Train from Lucerne to Barcelona, Spain.
- Thailand. Sangtaew (utility truck) from Kanchanaburi to Three Pagoda Pass, Myanmar with 29 others.

- Thailand. A motorbike taxi or tuk tuk in Bangkok are pretty hair raising.
- Thailand. Disco bus from Ban Phe to Buriram.
- Thailand. Ferry on the Chao Praya River.
- Thailand. Trekking on elephants at Chiang Mai.
- Uganda. Horse riding at Jinja.
- Uganda. Motorbike taxi or bicycle taxi.
- USA. Train San Diego to Tijuana, Mexico.
- USA. Train on the Klondike Railway from Skagway, Alaska to Fraser on the Canadian border.
- USA. Bus Portland to Seattle.
- Vietnam. Boat in Halong Bay.
- Vietnam. A Motorbike taxi or cyclo in Ho Chi Min.
- Zambia. River cruise on Zambezi River to see hippos.

YUNNAN CHINA

We are travelling well, despite the lack of Mandarin. We, my friend Sue and I, really enjoyed the Xishaungbanna region, staying in the capital Jinghong, the nicest city I have been to in China so far. We have been to markets, seen minority groups in their national dress and taken heaps of photos. I experienced the hot springs and wallowed in the warm water with the locals. Had a great massage by a blind man and also had my hair washed and cut and a head, neck and shoulder massage for $3.50. Can't beat that can you? We travelled for sixteen hours in a 'sleeping' bus that was a first. The double-decker bunks are three across. I happened to be in the middle row up top and spent all night grasping the metal rail to keep myself in the bunk. Most of the road was a goat track and at one stage we went through a creek with boulders tossing us around and nearly out of bed. We passed a loaded truck coming the other way and narrowly escaped being hit by it when it teetered on the brink of toppling over on us. It was better not to look what was happening ahead of us. We also went on a brilliant new freeway. There is much development taking place in China and everything is done on a big scale and manual labour. The farmers work so hard in steep terraced country. We came through rice paddies, vegetable gardens, tea and rubber plantations, nature reserves, forests, mountains of unbelievably spectacular scenery, delightful villages.

We met up in Kunming with a friend of a friend, an Australian named Peter, who is teaching at a university. He has been so helpful, with local advice and knowledge. We wandered around Green Lake watching the locals flying kites, blind people performing skits, orchestras playing local instruments, people singing and dancing, flocks of seagulls taking off on the lake. This is amazing, as we are so far from the sea. We walked around the main university with 20,000 odd students, with magnificent buildings and tranquil grounds with squirrels playing and leaping in the trees. The weather has been very good to us, warm sunny days, and cooler at night but not too cold. As we get further North West, this will change.

We read in our guide book about horse riding in Dali up Jade Green Mountain, sounded exciting. We left Kunming on the overnight train headed for Dali in a soft sleeper, arriving at 6am and shared a taxi with two western guys to the Old Town. Found Jim's Tibetan Guesthouse and thought we had landed in heaven. A huge, squeaky clean room, modern bathroom with western loo, twenty four hour hot water, three quarter comfortable beds with doonas. Electric blankets were just the thing for the chilly nights. The Tibetan furniture of dark carved wood with gold paint picking out the design, was most unusual, a power board for recharging batteries – not ours – the video and mobile phone completed the luxury and all this for $17 for the room with free breakfast and internet. We fell onto the beds and slept for a few hours before venturing out into the narrow streets of Dali, packed with cafes, shops, souvenir sellers, magnificent old buildings and temples, red lanterns, three wheeled bicycles with trailers hauling heavy loads of everything from building material to fruit and veg. Old ladies carrying heavy baskets with a band of webbing around their heads and under the baskets

Tiger Leaping Gorge got its name from a legendary tiger who was supposed to have leapt onto a rock in the Yangtze River to the other

side of the gorge. Now there is a concrete statue of the tiger poised
to leap. The Gorge is awesome with steep sides sloping down sharply
from the 3900m peaks of Yulong or Jade Dragon Snow Mountain.

On our first day we decided to walk the lower path along the road
for nine kilometres. The river is full of surprises, sometimes dead
calm at others treacherous rapids, running into narrow channels or
islands of small rocks, other times widening out to a vast expanse
of water. We are lucky to see it now as there are plans to build
eight dams along the upper reaches. These dams will flood 13,000
hectares of fertile farmland forcing hundreds of thousands of people
to relocate. In its path local culture, history, plants and animal life
will be lost forever.

We got a minibus back to Qioatou, the small town at the start
of the gorge where we stayed in a very nice modern hotel. For two
days we wondered why we couldn't get hot water, so we managed
with a thermos of hot water, meant for our tea, from the basin in the
bathroom. I even washed my hair this way. The third night an English
speaking Chinese man asked one of the friendly staff why we didn't
have hot water. Simple, the hot tap was cold and the cold tap hot and
it took five or ten minutes to come through. We both immediately
had a nice hot bath. It was wonderful. After walking along the north
side of the river we got a minibus to take us to the south side and
walked along a flat stone paved walkway for three kilometres to the
same spot in the river. It was amazing how different the aspect was.
We were able to get really close to the rapids and hear the roar of the
water gushing and swirling. It inspired me to do my Qi Gong in the
energy coming off the waves. We decided to walk back along the path
rather than take a colourful rickshaw, pulled by a young Chinese lad.

The next day we hired a driver and car and went to the middle
rapids at Walnut Gardens. Our driver kept saying 'very danger'.
The road was rough and at one stage we had to stop as there was a

rock slide and rocks the size of tennis balls were ricocheting down the mountain slopes on to the road in front of us. We also saw large chunks taken out of the road where sharp boulders had gouged out holes where they had landed. Some of these boulders were larger than tea chests and just left lying where they fell or pushed to the side of the road.

We went to a village called Youkuo where hundreds of houses are being built. We wonder why as it is in a very remote, inaccessible area. We enjoyed lunch basking in the hot sun at a guesthouse. Unfortunately Sue left her camera lens here and didn't notice until we got back to Qioatou twenty thee kilometres away. Back we went again to pick it up, another hour's journey avoiding the rock fall.

The next day we hired horses, actually mine was a mule and as stubborn as... Sue's was a small pony. We followed the hiking trail on the high path for eight kilometres.

This time we were led, in places the path slipped away into the valley below and the horses insisted on walking on the outside of the path, close to the edge. The only thing to do was look at the spectacular view of the Yangtze below and the snow capped mountains above. The stirrups were too short and tied under the girth, which meant that our feet were dragged inwards and our ankles ached from this obscure position. Our knees were permanently bent at right angles on these most uncomfortable wooden framed saddles and inadequate blankets for padding. We climbed up and ever upwards over rough steep rocks. Some Chinese riders ahead of us where too scared to ride the tough area and dismounted to walk. The steel bars on the saddle nearly gave us blisters on our hands from hanging on for grim life. At one spot which was more level I was allowed to ride by myself without being led but as there was no bit and only the lead rein on one side of the headstall, I had little control. My mule did not understand leg aids, funny that.

We got to a Naxi (minority group) run guesthouse and had lunch sitting in the sun. We couldn't help but notice the dried liver hanging above our heads complete with dried maggots in abundance. We didn't order lamb's fry. As I was mounting to head home the stirrup webbing broke. Our leaders laughed and said 'very danger' and tied yet another knot in the webbing and off we set. Riding through family's back yards observing life and work in this beautiful gorge. It was a great way to see the country.

We bussed it to Zhongdian, or Shangri La, as it is now known. It is close to the Tibetan border, with many Tibetans living and working the land here. We were invited on to a farm to meet the family, who live in a fairly newly built two storey timber house with little furniture or home comforts. A large wood burning contraption heats the house and acts as stove and oven. We were offered yak cheese that was so tough we could not get our teeth into it. Butter tea which I find always difficult to swallow, but the warmth and hospitality of the Tibetans is always generous.

At night we joined the locals in the Market Square for street dancing. It appeared that all citizens and visitors enjoys this nightly exercise. We were welcomed with open arms and managed to pick up some of the dance routines with much laughter and joy. By the sides of the road there are stalls selling fly switches-cum-feather dusters made of fluffy yak tail hair. I wished we could have brought them back to Australia.

Our trip to Pita, a frozen lake was exhilarating to say the least. On the way up the mountain it began to snow, there were huts along the way which supplied oxygen. Luckily we managed without. Getting off the bus we saw piles of ex-army great coats for hire. We immediately pounced on these as it was freezing. I put my umbrella up to protect us from the snow but it was pushed inside out very rapidly. It was a long precarious walk to the lake over wooden slatted walk ways. We saw one Chinese lady negotiating it in high heeled shoes. On one of the local buses there was no heating, so we wrapped ourselves in all the clothing we possessed, especially as we had to have a window slightly open, as the locals chain smoke. We could hardly breathe, what with the cold air outside and the cigarette smoke inside. One Chinese man's mobile phone rang to the tune of Click Go the Shears. We were amazed.

Our journey in Yunnan was special and very different from other countries. China is such a vast land with stunning scenery, friendly people but see it now, before it all changes.

IN A FOUR BERTHER ON THE PACIFIC OCEAN

My friend Rhondda rang to see if I wanted to make up a fourth in a cabin on a Pacific island cruise for ten nights. My response was, give me five seconds to think about it. OK only if I can have a lower berth. Fine...done deal

The very first night I was woken by a loud thud on the floor, it was Suzanne falling while getting down the ladder at 2am from the upper berth. She cut her head, banged her knee and later we found out from the ship's doctor, she had broken some ribs, otherwise she was fine! With the help of painkillers she soldiered on and didn't complain.

After that I volunteered to take the top berth. We participated in nearly everything ranging from the Single Mingle, to Rock 'n Roll lessons, yoga, we swished around in the spa on a rough sea, listened to a great Country and Western singer and a pianist in the bar. We disembarked at Noumea and took a local bus to Anse Wata Beach where we swam and lazed in the sun. That night Sandra, our other fellow cabin mate performed as a squaw in the Country and Western Show. She was great. We all joined in the line dancing and games.

At the island of Lifou we looked around a local craft market and watched the locals performing traditional songs and dances. They were so colourful and bright. We snorkelled and walked through the beautiful rain forest; on a local bus we visited a village with a marvellous pig farm.

Our next port was Vila, we hired a car and driver for three hours to take us to see the cascades, went on the punt across to Erakor Island from Le Lagon. I had been there twenty years before, it had not changed much. I bought my two granddaughters some 'grass' skirts, leis, bracelets and head bands in vibrant colours. They love them.

The final port was Wala, a very unspoilt island where we had a swim and a guided walk. Along the way we saw local children playing conke shells, men making fire from a coconut shell and a stick and then a large snake with a bulge in its belly, it had just eaten a rat. I ate some yam and beef in coconut milk that was cooked in the ground. That night we watched the floor show on the ship which was always high class professional entertainment. We played Canasta a lot and none of us could make much headway with Rhondda a constant winner.

One night I won $200 at Bingo, what a bonus. Sandra ended up with an infection in her leg and had to see the ship's doctor for antibiotics. Rhondda suffered bad headaches and a very painful knee. Luckily I remained healthy. We had a ball.

CRUISING

Slow down and enjoy life. It's not only the scenery you miss by going too fast – you also miss the sense of where you are going and why. Eddie Cantor

Cruising is a great way to get started on a travel adventure. I have been with family and friends several times to such diverse locations as Pacific islands, Hawaii, Hobart and the Melbourne Cup. You are transported to your next destination, sometimes while you sleep. You don't have to repack your bags each night. There are swimming pools, spa, saunas, beauty salons, hair dresses, massage therapists, classes to attend, competitions to enter. Something for everyone. You have the same comfortable bed each night, room service, about six meals a day, nightly entertainment and see wonderful tropical islands and cities along the way. What more could you ask for? I have been on small sail boats around the Croatian and Indonesian islands

- Cruises are good value; travel with three friends and share a four berth cabin.
- Even sharing a cabin with three strangers can be fun.
- Keep alert to discount fares and special deals.
- Ask for an upgrade closer to your departure. This can happen.

- The beauty of a cruise is you can do as little or as much as you like. If you want to sit in a deck chair and read that's fine. If you want to participate in activities there is always plenty to do.
- Some people get really dressed up for dinner, others are pretty casual.
- There is a small hospital on board with doctors and nurses in attendance.
- There are organised tours at the ports or you can do your own thing.
- There is a great deal of flexibility on cruises.
- Great photo opportunities.
- There are email facilities on board, quiet areas to read or write, play cards, go to movies, phone home, attend educational lectures, keep fit, dance, sing, do yoga, play bingo, gamble, perform in the nights entertainment and much more.
- If you want to take your children or grandchildren, there are child minding facilities for younger ones and entertainment for teenagers.
- At the ports, you get a taste of the country and may inspire you to go back and see more.
- Cruising is stress free travel. Enjoy.

HORSES RACES SAIGON

The young boy beside me was plucked from the top rail of the fence at the track by a security guard. It reminded me of a suction pump being pulled from a blocked drain. His sister got the same treatment. Their mother said nothing; she was too intent on viewing the strangers in her midst. You see the Saigon Races are not a huge tourist attraction and foreigners are not allowed to bet. The track is within the city limits, so the crowds are full on every Saturday and Sunday. They rush to the saddling enclosure to view the equines before each race and then there is a mad dash to the rails, while the horses get led to the starting barrier, which seems to be miles away. As the programmes are not in English, we have no idea about the distance these poor little ponies have to gallop, with the help of a fine whip, carried between the jockey's teeth, when not in use. Some of the ponies are led to the track from a motorbike or pushbike. Imagine the winner of the Melbourne Cup arriving this way! The mind boggles.

We had just eaten a delicious salad roll filled with pressed meat, chilli, sliced carrots, liver paste and goodness knows what at the food stalls below the concrete seated grandstand. The stalls are glass fronted wheelable barrows that have a sign in red Saigon Horse Racing. Just in case you happen to forget where you are. We are definitely in the minority. We have only seen four other westerners.

We had walked most of the way to the track in high humidity and with the temperature rising, the foot path was melting our feet, so we hailed a couple of motorbike taxis to finish the journey. Our drivers were careful, the traffic chaotic but everyone seems to know the unwritten rules. Red lights are ignored but taken slowly, they can be negotiated. We weaved in and out of pedestrians, cyclos, bicycles, trucks, buses, other motorbikes and all manner of pedalled machines.

Our first stop at the track was to view the horses, ponies really. Most were skinny and under fed. We saw small bags of paspalum grass that was their only nourishment. Some of the stalls were empty. Empty of horses, that is. In a couple of stalls there were men urinating on the back wall. Just as well the mud floors could cope with it. The track itself is well maintained, the dirt raked and the railing strong. In the centre there are several soccer fields on green grass.

One small and weedy chestnut was being hosed down and not enjoying the experience at all. It took three men to do the job. Two holding onto ropes and one using the hose. It was fractious and kept jerking its head in the air trying to escape the strong pressure of the water. We noticed it had one eye missing. Had it met with foul play in the past I wondered. A few of the others had a cloudy damaged eye. It doesn't bear thinking about.

Some were fully shod, others no shoes at all, while others were only shod on their front feet. The minimum age for jockeys is 14 but I fear the rules have been stretched as some of them look about eight.

As they came out onto the track I gave a running commentary, seeing as we didn't understand a word that came over the loud speakers. No 1 looked quite perky and alive, No 2 was very doughy, both horse and rider, No 3 was well up on the bit, No 4 was way too thin to last the distance, No 5 the jockey looked very nervous, No 6 looked somewhat crossed with a mule, No 7 was itching to go with hind quarters doing a merry dance, No 8 had blinkers on and had tripped a couple of times getting to the starting barrier, No 9 had two crooked front legs, No 10 was a likely looking black pony with a cropped mane, but No 11 was my pick, a handsome bay with a confident jockey. What a shame we couldn't put a bet on…it romped home, first past the winning post.

CHASING HOBBIES

I am willing to create. Julia Cameron

If you have a hobby at home you more than likely are interested in including your hobby as part of your overseas experience. There are specific group tours for music, art, culture, textiles, ecology, massage, Tai Chi Qi Gong etc, if you want to focus on your interest. You can also do your own research and plan your own experience.

I have done two courses in Bangkok of Thai Traditional Medical Massage, a Qi Gong Study tour in China, the Nadaam Festival in Inner Mongolia, a retreat in an ashram in India, all with groups of Australians. I have done retreats in Thailand and Myanmar and led groups to Nepal, India and Thailand, cruised to the Pacific Islands, Hawaii, Tasmania and the Melbourne Cup with friends and family. I went alone on a Buddhist Pilgrimage to Nepal and India. These are some of the best trips I have experienced. I have seen young people lugging large guitars around the world, for their own and others enjoyment. I decided a guitar is too big, so taught myself to play the harmonica. It has brought me a lot of joyful moments and I hope to others also. I was brought up with animals and have a special love for dogs and horses. Canada's Wild West Calgary Stampede was spectacular; I went every day for six days. The performing dogs were amazing; I saw them also in Edmonton at the Klondike Festival. In Ottawa I visited the training centre for the Royal Canadian Mounted Police. Polo at Smiths Lawn in England was special. Prince Charles, Prince of Wales was playing in an International Tournament and his parents, the Queen and Prince Phillip were there to watch. Show jumping at Spruce Meadows in Canada was excellent. The Spanish Riding School in Vienna and performing horses in Hungary were something I will never forget.

- Small instruments such as a harmonica, Jews Harp, penny whistle, recorder, ukulele, spoons even a comb with some tissue paper can be fun.
- Textiles in Vietnam, quilting by the Mennonites in Canada, knitting and weaving in the Himalayas are wonderful.
- Museums, art galleries, concerts, photography all over the world are a great way to learn about the history and culture of a country.
- Sports such as football, tennis, baseball, basketball, equestrian events, Dragon Boat Races, skiing are wonderful to watch or participate.
- Swimming, surfing, snorkelling, diving, windsailing or even bungee jumping if you are crazy enough.
- Hiking, biking, canoeing or white water rafting can get the adrenalin pumping.
- If your interest is a certain breed of dogs, horses, cats, birds or even bird watching is fascinating.
- Whale or dolphin watching, zoo or game park animals, komodo dragons, fish, research where the best areas in the world are.
- Maybe postcard, stamp or coin collecting is your thing. Even key rings, fridge magnets, shells interest you.

- Do you paint or sketch? These are really precious personal memories to bring home.
- Collect funny signs, sayings, and incorrect spelling on menus.
- Pursue your hobbies; you won't be disappointed.

KOH SAMET CAPERS

While sitting on the beach watching Jeffery, a local Thai friend trying to start his boat with the anchor rope twisted around the blue hose of the water boat, I raised my head from the Sudoku to see what would happen next. The water boat delivers fresh water to each of the bungalows, as Koh Samet is a *dry* island and fresh water has to be brought from the mainland daily. Over the horizon came a huge grey Navy vessel rather like a troop ship carrier, with at least 20 men on board, all with a life vest round their necks.

The lady, who brings the blue hose from her water boat, on a life raft ring, hastily detached the hose, flaps her arms at her husband on the boat to move quickly, out of a collision course. She swims out to the boat with the blue hose trailing in the water.

Jeffery finally gets untangled from the hose and his motor springs into life as he takes off at a speedy rate. The carrier blows its horn, tables, chairs and umbrellas are swiftly moved back on the beach, with all hands helping. Small children were guided away from the ropes and swimmers waved aside in the water, sunbathers were moved further a field in their deck chairs. One of the uniformed official gentlemen on the vessel recorded every move with a camera. It was very important stuff. Sand bags are filled to form a ramp as the slip way is lowered on the water's edge.

Two lots of men run with ropes from the ship to fasten them to sturdy trees. The only problem being that the men from the right side of the Navy carrier rushed to the tree on the left side and the men on the left side of the ship made a dash for the tree on the right, cleverly forming a crossing of the ropes and successfully preventing the vehicles from leaving the carrier. When the mistake was realised, a loud cheer and much laughter went up from the now large crowd of onlookers.

First down the slipway came a fully loaded truck with among other things, 44 gallon drums, planks of wood, tables and chairs and such like, this was followed by a D6 Caterpillar bulldozer with a blade up front. It came creaking and groaning and clanging down amid much yelling and shouting of instructions from the crew. Next another large truck, loaded to the hilt with an odd assortment of goods and there perched right on top is a long necked rooster, straining to see what the hell is going on. I presume its legs are tied, as it does not leave its lofty position. It had good cause to look aghast because what happened next was just as I predicted, the truck got bogged in the loose sand. Much rocking back and forth and spinning of wheels only managed to dig itself into a deeper sandy and gritty grave.

The bulldozer by now had demolished a rock wall, which the driver either did not see or could care less about. He was called back and a tow rope was attached to the truck and out it came, to live another day. There were as many men on the beach as there were on the Navy vessel. They included Police, National Park Rangers, waiters from nearby restaurants; all the customers had left their dining to join the fray. After the truck, came a larger than life roller down the slipway. It flattened the sand that the truck had dug out and scattered from the bogging episode.

It was quite the event of the day. One never knows what will happen next on Koh Samet.

Perhaps in several days time the sandy track that is actually called a road will resemble a highway...then again maybe not.

CALGARY STAMPEDE CANADA

'The greatest outdoor show on earth!' the banners scream. The parade lasts for two hours and there is standing room only along the city streets. The parade is marred for me by what happened to the most beautiful pair of black Clydesdale horses after they proudly trotted past me pulling a wagon. They came down hard on their knees on the bitumen road. As they hobbled off to the side with bone, flesh and blood vividly evident, I put my hands to my face and the tears flowed.

The morning dawned bright, the sun glistened on the bunting and colourful decorations. There was an air of excitement in the crowd, who had just finished the traditional breakfast of pancakes and maple syrup. Everyone was dressed for the occasion in cowboy hats, shirt fringes flapping and stitched cowboy boots.

Greetings of 'Howdy' and 'Yahoo' were exchanged. At last the first marching band appeared, keeping their rhythm as they formed lines, blew trumpets and beat drums. We were surprised to see an all-girls band from Marion College, Goulburn, NSW. They had come all the way from Australia and only a short distance from our home town.

Two bands from Thailand about thirty strong, one all girls from Chiang Mai, in the north. Another surprise, the Calgary Polocrosse Team. As Polocrosse originated in Australia, we gave them a loud

cheer. Also a Polo Team, another ancient horse sport. Red Indian
tribes on paint horses, with full headdress of feathers, bow and
arrows. A Scotsman in full kilt instructing his two Border Collies
to herd four sheep along the street, an amazing skill of man and
animals. Heavy horses pulling floats and wagons representing other
nations, community groups, charity organisations. Presidents and
committees, officials and mayors. Rodeo queens and princesses, past
and present, riding and waving to the crowd.

Then along came Dennis Weaver, the well known actor who
played Macleod for many years on TV. His famous line when the
telephone rang 'your phones runnin' over'. Marching girls with
wands and banners swirling, a myriad of colours. Oldest inhabitants
of Calgary, descendents of early settlers. Past Rodeo Champions,
sporting heroes, notable citizens in long flashy cars, clowns, jugglers,
roller bladers, line dancers and two step dancers. Army tanks
doing spin turns, churning up the tar on the road, military bands.
Beautiful Tennessee Walking Horses in their shiny black coats, tiny
miniature horses, smaller than a dog, acting like spoilt children.
Trail riding clubs, Park Rangers, Royal Canadian Mounted Police,
whose headquarters are in Ottawa, Ontario. Heavy horses from a
special Canadian breed.

After every few exhibits a street sweeping vehicle came along
to keep the road clean and free from droppings. Commercial floats
of all shapes and sizes, bullock drays, mules, donkeys, foals. Trick
riders carefully balanced astride two horses, with a rider on their
shoulders. Scottish Pipe Bands, Chinese Dragons weaving in and
out, up and down. Appaloosa horses, stage coaches, early fur traders,
people on high stilts, Royal Mail riders. Miniature aeroplanes doing
circles on the tarmac. Four in hand chuck wagons, preparing for
one of the highlights of the nine days to come. It certainly whetted
our appetites.

The organizing of so many people, vehicles and animals was a credit to those dedicated committee members of the Calgary Stampede. **YEE HA!**

Mang Madly British Thailand

In the past I have owned and loved British Bulldogs. Therefore I was delighted to find Mang, A British Bulldog in Rayong, a large industrial city in Thailand.

Mang was snoring happily in the doorway of a shop. I started to admire him and asked his name. As he heard my English voice, he leapt up with great enthusiasm. The more I patted him the more he spun around in avid excitement, knocking goods off the shelves and wreaking havoc.

Shop assistants came running to rescue the flying pencils, paper, clips, erasers etc. Mang is totally oblivious of the destruction he is causing. His focus was on his new found friend, huffing and puffing and snuffling, asking for more attention.

When I wanted to take a photo of him, there was no way to calm him down to sit still.

When I went to leave he followed me out of the shop and his owner had to come running out to drag him back from the street. A week later I went back to see him again, this time he was asleep behind the counter, exhausted from the heat. On hearing my voice he again sprang to all fours and promptly piddled all over the floor.

My apologies were met by the owner with a grin and *mai pen lai* ...never mind.

It really is getting too embarrassing to visit Mang again. The mind boggles at what would happen a third time.

TEARAWAY MULE TIGERS NEST BHUTAN

There was one more mountain to climb, The Tigers Nest Monastery clinging to the side of a sheer cliff overlooking Paro in Bhutan. I very nearly chickened out because an old injury in a knee was stirred up in a massage a few days ago, the altitude had caused a few headaches and sleep deprivation. However I could not leave Bhutan without seeing the most famous site.

The taxi driver from Paro to the base of the mountain could not accept that I was on my own, no guide, no tour group, female and no spring chicken.

I arrived early at the starting point to be told there were no horses available to ride up the mountain, as they were all booked by tour groups. I could wait till they came down, riderless, as it is too steep to ride down, or the other option was to hike up. That meant a three hour wait or climb, huff and puff my way up. An hour later an Austrian group turned up, mounted and took off, that left three horses and one mule. With that the mule escaped galloping and pigrooting trying to throw off the saddle, into the distance, closely followed by two Bhutanese horse handlers yelling obscenities to no avail. They disappeared over the horizon and after ten minutes reappeared with handlers still in hot pursuit. As the mule was heading in my direction I spread my arms out and made 'woo' noises. Obviously it did not understand English as it speared past me as if I did not exist. Finally he came to a halt with the three horses and it took two men five minutes to put a headstall on it. Then came the 'good news', I could ride *it* up the mountain! I said 'he is a bit wild', 'no problem' was the reply.

I mounted him from a large rock and Sonam led me away with a rope attached to the headstall. I did not even have the luxury of a bridle with reins. My mule immediately started to buck and pigroot, while being tugged by Sonam on the other end of the rope and me yelling '*hold up*'. I can't remember when I have felt so powerless. Finally he was subdued and resigned to the fact he was going to have to climb that mountain for an hour or so. With Sonam pulling and me kicking, we caught up with the Austrians. My mule friend wanted to be in the lead, as we passed some of the other horses, they would lash out with white gnashing teeth at us, narrowly missing my leg!

One of the Austrian ladies whose bottom overflowed the saddle by some inches, in fact the saddle could not even be seen, started to slide off to the right on a tight bend. She screamed and miraculously one of the helpers was able to leap under her and slide her back into the saddle before she toppled over into the ravine. All this viewed from the rear was quite a spectacle and kept my mind from the hazards of the journey on the edge of the cliff. At this stage Sonam decided that the mule had calmed down and proceeded to tie the lead rope to my saddle. It was a great lesson in trust on my part, having ridden horses all my life and mostly with a bit more control over them.

After a cup of tea at the cafeteria I decided to let my mule have a well earned rest, while I climbed on for one and a half hours to the Tigers Nest. It is truly magnificent but at the entrance, I discovered I had left my permit at the bottom of the mountain, safely locked

in my hotel room. What to do? I asked the friendly guide of the
Austrians if I could sneak in with his group. He very kindly said that
one of his group had backed out, so I could take her place. Phew! I
wandered through several shrine rooms, up and down more stairs,
in absolute awe of the centuries of Tibetan Buddhist history, then a
trek back to the cafeteria for a delicious lunch before the walk down
the mountain. When I got to the base in the afternoon, I shared a
taxi with an Indian tourist, visiting more dzongs and monasteries
on the way back to Paro.

What a way to spend my last day in Bhutan before I flew out
the next day for Bangkok. The whole Bhutan experience had been
fantastic, a very memorable journey of loving kindness, generosity,
steep majestic mountains, ancient monasteries, friendly, beautiful
people, interesting animals, good food, safe drivers and days of
strenuous exercise.

Noni having ridden a mule and hiked up to
Tiger's Nest Monastery, Bhutan

FLOODS AND FUN IN SOUTHERN THAILAND

We started off in a taxi from Surathani to Nakhon Si Thammarat in Thailand. There were four of us, all Westerners, jammed in the back seat and three Thais in front, for the two and a half hour journey. The rain pelted down and the driver insisted he couldn't go any further and dumped us on the outskirts of the city. We are determined to keep going, as we are following a famous Thai Buddhist Monk on a pilgrimage.

After much negotiation we find another driver who is willing to take us on the next leg of our trip which will take us to Pak Panang, a further twenty-eight kilometres. We scramble into his dilapidated vehicle only to find the steering does not seem to connect to the steering wheel, the windscreen wiper only hits the windscreen intermittently, then flips off the side of the car before a slow return to do another swipe at the windscreen. The brakes of course are affected by the water on the road, if in fact they worked in the first place. Visibility is just about zero and I have my umbrella up in the back seat, as the windows are stuck in the down position.

Finally this driver refuses to go any further; I can't blame him as the tyres are now ploughing through a couple of feet of water and the engine is coughing and spluttering in protest. With our backpacks on our heads we start walking along on what we believe to be the road. We cannot see it because it is covered in a couple of feet of water. We are beyond caring about trying to keep dry.

A brave Thai man pedalled towards me on a rickshaw and I managed to climb aboard, keeping my backpack at shoulder height through lack of space to put it anywhere else. With great strength he pushed the pedals for about 500 metres till we reach the edge of the swollen river. A police launch picked us up and ferried us across to the other side, which is also under water. Here we climb into the back of a utility truck, where we are driven through the flooded streets of Pak Panang to Wat Rampradit, a Buddhist Monastery whose ground floor is under water also.

We are greeted warmly by a monk who tells us to make ourselves at home up stairs. Many other people have the same idea. The famous monk and our teacher arrived by police launch as well and he pays us a visit to make sure everyone is safe. He is worried that I have not got any dry clothes, but somehow I manage. There is a group of about ten farangs *foreigners* and we find ourselves some space in a corner of this large area above the shrine room and we are given some mats to sleep on. We try to air our clothes as best we can but space is limited. Everyone is in a joyful mood, despite the fact our sleeping bags and clothes are damp and some soaking wet. We are invited to the kitchen and provided with delicious traditional Thai food. Nothing is a trouble to these wonderful, generous people.

More rain falls in the night, people are coming and going, the floor is hard, my body aches and I end up sitting against the wall with my wet pack as a cushion. By now I and cold and wet, but morning comes despite the lack of sleep. The rain has eased and the water has receded a little, so we venture to take a walk down the street, sloshing through the mud. We are caught in a downpour of rain and run for shelter under a verandah, the tide rises again and we dodge the flotsam and jetsam that floats along the street.

After a couple of days the flood waters diminish and the poor local farmers and shopkeepers are devastated. The monks go on their alms round* and everything is donated to the flood victims who have lost their livelihood and had their fields and homes destroyed. Trucks follow the monks to pick up bags of rice, bottled water, buckets, shovels, cooking utensils etc from the disciples, some of whom have travelled long distances from all over Thailand to hear their teacher.

The Thai lady, who takes me to the bus for the overnight trip to Bangkok, insists on paying for my fare. I have never met her before, nor have I ever travelled on a Deluxe VIP bus with dinner included. The generosity of these people overwhelms me. I have learnt many lessons on this journey.

* Lay people donate food and supplies to the monks as they walk in the streets with their bowls.

HEKOU CHINA

In Hekou we met a most unique character. His name is Tom, he is a chain smoking, 34-year-old Chinese man, who speaks good English and has ADHD big time. He told me I had excellent English, which sent us into hysterics.

Hekou is just across the border of China from Vietnam. My friend Sue and I had arrived on a comfortable overnight train from Hanoi to the border town of Lao Cai on the Vietnam side. We had passed through customs, even without a word of any Chinese language and the green uniformed authorities without a word of English. Not an easy task. Not another foreigner in sight and in fact not for the next three days.

We were wheeling our bags, with day packs on our backs down the street, when Tom rushed at us, chased after us and took us to the bus station, which we had passed because all the signs are in Chinese and there was no sign of a bus. Tom told us he was the Assistant Manager of the Bus Company and would be delighted to arrange tickets for us. We realised before too long that Tom had a concentration span of about two seconds. While begging our pardon, excusing himself, apologising and smoking forty cigarettes, he shuffled the ashtray round his empty desk, pulling his chair close to mine, shaking our hands, pushing the chair back again, lurching out of his office to climb a ladder to put a new DVD in the TV for the waiting passengers, while holding the used DVD between his teeth. He showed them to us on his return and then we got back to the discussion of bus tickets. He would have to ask the manager. Out he rushed again and came back with a time and price. We agreed. Out he raced again to get the tickets and have another ciggie. By this time we were getting tired and drained just by being in his presence. He meant well, but was exhausting us. We noticed that the tickets had attached to them a bill for Life Insurance. I said we were fully insured and did not need it. He assured me the Chinese Government made the rules and with that took me out to a wall with several posters of fatal bus accidents, showing dead bodies lined up on the road, mangled and twisted buses and vehicles, blood spattered everywhere. Not very auspicious for our forth coming bus ride. I am pleased to say we did not need the insurance.

Tom was like one of those moths that fly around a light, in fact if he had wings, he could certainly be mistaken for a large one, his face even looked like one, with a mixture of flying fox thrown in, with all due respects. He told us he has a sister and two brothers in uniform, army that is.

In self defence we said we needed something to eat. Tom said it would not be a problem; he would take us to a restaurant where all the local policemen ate, so it must be good. We walked a couple of blocks and were ushered into a private room by Tom who said he would like a beer. We said we were not beer drinkers and either should he be. In fact we took the opportunity to tell him that smoking was bad for him and his second hand smoke was killing us too. He obviously had a problem with mucous, as he hoicked and spat nonstop, including into the glass at the table. This was really too much. Put us right off our meal.

He was like a buzz fly in and out of the room to order tea, then vegetables, then rice. He sat and ate with us and when it came time to pay they had charged us an exorbitant price and we got into a heated discussion, finally saying we would call the police. Tom, to his credit said he would pay half. We would not allow it. We finally turned on our heels, having leant a big lesson.

Tom went back to the office, where we had chained our wheelie bags to a bench for safety. I always carry a dog chocker chain and strong padlock for such occasions. Tom greeted us like old friends and had a cup of tea with us at the station cafe. Here we met a two-year-old called Oo La La, who ran around smashing cups of tea onto the floor while her family were so engrossed with their card game, that they did not notice, even when she walked out of the cafe into the bus station. Finally after 15 minutes the grandmother decided to go and look for her.

We decided it was time to board the bus, said our farewell to Tom who asked first for Vietnam paper money, then Australian paper money. We settled on a coin. He looked at it and said how much he loved Queen Elizabeth and kissed the twenty cents. We collapsed into our seats for the five hour ride to Mengzi.

MYSTERY TOUR CANADA

The Mystery Tour that my family gave me for my birthday was just brilliant.

We set off for Temagami, a huge lake nearly three hours north east of Sudbury. Here we boarded the Party Girl II, a 10 ton, 40 foot long, 10 foot wide luxury pontoon house boat, it was to be our floating, cruising home for three days and nights. It can accommodate ten people, so with just five of us on board, we had plenty of space to cook, eat and sleep. The girls, Molly and Olivia, had the loft, my son Will and his wife Coline the stateroom and I had my own space at the front of the boat on a comfortable sofa bed. There was a water slide at the back of the boat and a swimming platform. At the front a BBQ and space for chairs. The boat is steered either from the bottom on top sun deck.

The lake is beautiful and full of small and some large islands. The 'camps' are only allowed to be built on the islands, no waterfront buildings on the mainland. The camps range from palatial log homes with little bridges to other islands, docks to tie up their float planes, hot tubs, pontoon and speed boats, fishing runabouts, canoes, kayaks and jet skis, to humble timber shacks and everything in between. The native trees have been left undisturbed and it is very picturesque. There are also areas were the houseboats can dock and go ashore to build fires and explore the woods. We found one of these one night and lit a bonfire. The girls had a wonderful time roasting marshmallows and stoking the bonfire, putting on pine needles and dried bracken fern to watch it sizzle. We also found a 'dunny' in the woods, over a 'long drop' made from a timber base and loo seat, even loo paper in a plastic bag to keep the rain out. This came in very handy the next morning as I woke early and the water had not been turned on in the boat. I decided I would even face the threat of a bear! Luckily none visited me but the mosquitoes bit me in places unmentionable!

On the second night we encountered a huge storm the rain came bucketing down, the thunder roared, the lightning flashed, and the boat rock and rolled, the girls were terrified and the adults were hoping it would all go somewhere else. We found a sheltered cove, but still the wind was buffeting us around. We anchored about 30 feet from shore but the jolly anchor would not grip. We tossed and turned and finally got two anchors taking hold...or that is what we thought. I woke early the next morning to find us up against a log, with the overhanging trees hitting the top deck and the back of the boat only feet from crashing into shore. I woke Will and he pulled on one of the anchor ropes to try to move us out but the anchor had lost its grip, then he tried the other and got us to a safer spot away from being grounded. He proceeded to cook us all bacon and eggs for breakfast but half way through, the other anchor gave way and he had to madly try starting the motor. It took a long time to kick in but finally we took off into the rain. The visibility was bad, it was hard to see the red and green shoal markers and the cabin had all fogged up with our breath. As we were about to pull into one bay, some young men came running into the water naked. We got the message. Their strategy worked and we moved on.

The one day we had of sunshine was magnificent. We sunbaked on the top deck listened to CD's, Coline and the girls went down the water slide, Will and I were in the water waiting to catch them. The water was chilly but it did not stop us all having great fun.

One night Molly made a deck of cards from scrap paper, using a pen and my Swiss Army knife. She is a very clever kid. She, Will and I played pontoon, Will was the banker and as I had forgotten a lot of the rules, we got hysterical. This is a common occurrence when he and I get together and has been going on since he was a little boy. Of course we set the others off laughing too.

Despite the weather and the bugs, a wonderful time was had by all. Coline had packed tasty food including some delicious salmon done in dill, Will found his navigation skills, the girls played happily most of the time and I had a ball.

THAI MASSAGE COURSE THAILAND

I have a saying-in fact I have many – 'if it feels good, do it'.

I had been a Remedial Massage Therapist for four years and was attending a workshop/meeting of our Association in Sydney in 1992, when an acquaintance mentioned that she was going with a group of fellow therapists to do a Traditional Thai Massage Course in Thailand. A light clicked on in my head and I instantly thought what a wonderful experience that would be. The challenge of travelling with a group of twenty eight Aussies, the steamy heat and frenetic traffic of Bangkok, the experience of learning a new massage technique, it all sounded and felt right.

One of my other sayings is 'never miss an opportunity'. Here was one too good to pass up. I had been in Thailand four years before for about eleven days on my way back from backpacking around the world for six months. My immune system in those days of overseas travel had not kicked in and as a consequence I spent the first four days in Bangkok travelling back and forth, but only to my hotel bathroom. Thank heavens I survived those traumatic detoxes and these days it is very rare for my digestive system to give me any trouble at all. I feel I have become immune to most foreign bugs.

The added incentive was that I had become involved with the Thai Buddhist Monks at Bundanoon, in the Southern Highlands of

NSW and they encouraged me to do the course and invited me to spend time afterwards at their forest monastery near Kanchanaburi, west of Bangkok. Everything fell rapidly into place, as it does for me, when I listen to my intuition. I found a qualified massage therapist to work and live in my home clinic, she would feed the dog, mow the lawns, water the garden, keep the clients happy and baby sit the house. Her mother, a friend of mine, just happened to ring and ask if I had any work for her daughter who had been living in America but was coming home. It all worked out perfectly.

As so often happens, I find myself many times in situations of 'coincidence'. I only knew one person out of the twenty eight heading to Thailand, the one who alerted me to the course. I found myself sitting in the plane out of Sydney beside a woman named Trish, part of our group, who had been a pupil of the local convent in Moss Vale, where I lived. She told me the highlight of her week was getting away from boarding school to learn horse riding at Throsby Park each Saturday and her instructor was my sister Del. She amazed me with the names of a lot of the horses she loved and rode.

The massage course was hard going in the heat. The group went every day for two weeks to Wat Pho, the home of the reclining Buddha and The Traditional Thai Medicine School in Bangkok. There was one teacher to two students. I teamed up with Trish, my new found friend from the plane trip. The teachers spoke no English and we had no Thai language, so it was all done with 'show and do'. The teacher would show the two students the acupressure points and lines and we would work on each other, trying to remember the sequence and copy her movements, getting the right pressure, while remembering to guard our backs and thumbs from strain or injury.

At night we would practice working on each other back at the hotel and compare notes. As in all deep massage, emotions are released along with tension in the muscles. The whole group was feeling fragile and exhausted from this and the sultry heat. Lifelong friends and bonding took place that we did not expect. In the group we had two people in wheel chairs suffering from MS. Anyone who has been to Bangkok will know that that city is not geared for people with a physical disability. It tested us all on many levels, physically, emotionally, mentally and spiritually.

One night for a complete change of pace we went to a Sex Show. We were guided by the hotel staff who organized limo's for us which took us to a reputable establishment that would only charge us an entry fee, rather than some of the more sleazy joints that would not let customers leave without paying an exit fee as well. We heard that some tourists had ended up in a police station because they refused to pay the latter and came to blows with the security guards. The Sex Show was a real eye opener, best you see for yourself.

We all gained our certificates and some like me managed to adapt some of the Thai methods to a massage table. The Traditional Thai Massage is done on a mat on the floor with the client fully clothed in loose fitting Thai pants and top.

When the course finished sad farewells had been said, hugs and tears wiped away from many faces, I headed off on my own to the Sunnataram Forest Monastery at Krong Kra Wia at Kanchanaburi, thereby furthering my journey of the Buddhist philosophy through dharma talks, meditation and retreats. But that's another story.

ANECDOTES 2005 CHINA

In Lijiang we met two nice Chinese Travel Agents on holidays. They were travelling in a group of nine. We asked them was it difficult organising so many people all wanting to go different ways. One of them replied "It is like trying to herd cats".

In Kunming we were watching guests coming to a wedding. The bride and her bridesmaids were handing out peanuts in the shell, wrapped sweets and individual cigarettes. The band was playing *Jingle Bells* and *Auld Lang Syne*.

On a bus in Zhondian a fellow passenger's mobile phone rang to the tune of *Click Go the Shears*.

In a WC beside the road on a bus trip, I was squatting in a waist high cubicle when a man came and urinated in the same trough.

In a WC private cubicle in Lijiang I noticed a beautiful blue and white ceramic pot on a window sill with a Bonsai tree in it. Beside the door on the wall was an ashtray, automatic flush loo and – wait for it – a colour television complete with singing and dancing show.

In Kunming we drank chrysanthemum tea out of a cup, which a young Chinese man poured from a watering can with a metre long spout, while bending over backwards.

In Dali I was photographed in a sheep drawn cart. The poor thing had a plastic drink bottle attached to it, so it could pee and a nappy type bag to catch its droppings.

A menu in Lijiang:

- Spicey lobstey
- Todays special drinds
- Chines
- Eswargot
- Sweet pofato
- Pot stew fiwh
- Leman dali beek
- First lover ice cream
- Deep fried bamboo worm
- 100-year-old gathering
- Ants climbing the tree
- Hot water pork
- Spring Rall

Two excellent books I bought and read in China by Xinran. *The Good Women of China* and *Sky Burial*.

We lugged our bags out of the Old Town in Dali, found a taxi, loaded our bags in the boot and asked the driver to take us to the bus station. He pointed to a building not twenty metres away. We all got a laugh as we took our bags out again.

In Zhongdian we joined in with the 200 locals to dance in the street. It warmed us up as it snowed the next day.

At Bita Lake outside of Zhongdian we hired Army Great Coats to do a two kilometre walk in the snow to see the lake. They were wonderful. The lake and the coats.

In Kunming we saw a woman eating breakfast, smoking and knitting, all at the same time. She was a westerner.

In Kunming we met a ninety one-year-old Danish painter woman travelling on her own.

In Zhongdian during our walk in the snow, we saw a Chinese lady walking the two kilometres … in socks and high heeled shoes!

QUICK PROMOTION

The Canadian Rocky Mountains bring out the spiritual side of everyone who passes through them. You couldn't help but feel moved by their awesome beauty. Just when you think you have seen the best, there around the next corner is one better. It is breathtaking in its stunning reality.

A few years ago on my second visit, I decided to stop over at Athabasca Falls for a few days to enjoy the rich scenery of water, rivers and lakes, forests and mountains, vegetation and animals, so unfamiliar to us in Australia. The bus from Jasper in Alberta dropped me off on a bright clear morning at the Youth Hostel. As I entered the communal area, I spotted a sign saying that if you were prepared to work for two hours that you could stay the night for free. As I am always looking for ways to save money when travelling, so I can stay longer and travel further, I enquired as to what sort of work was required. I had just turned 60 a few days before and I was on my way to my son's wedding in Ontario, Canada.

The manager told me that the two large fridges badly needed defrosting. I could see that she was telling the truth. If I was prepared to defrost them my accommodation was *on the house*. Having dropped off my backpack in one of the six bed cabins and taken a lower bunk, I set to work. It was an icy task and took me a couple of hours to finally rid those monsters of their arctic coats. I had made quite a mess of the floor, so decided to clean that as well. The communal area consisted of dining tables and benches, lounge chairs and couches, stoves, sinks, fridges, cupboards with pots and pans, crockery and cutlery, table tennis tables and numerous other odd bits of furniture. It was a large room and I made the decision to mop the whole floor space, to do the job properly.

After that I walked to the Athabasca Falls to see the plummeting water cascade in a dog leg into the swift flowing river, the noise of the thundering water drowning out all other sounds of nature. I decided not to go for a swim as the river was flowing too rapidly. I knew I had made the right decision when I saw some adventurous white water rafters go rushing by. I lay in the warm sun on a large boulder near the falls, with one eye open in case a bear decided to pay me a visit.

I spent a comfortable, warm night in the cabin but the loo was of the 'long drop' variety about 50 metres away over a rough track. After breakfast, the manager asked me if I could please take on the role of manager for the day, as she had to go and do something some miles away. I accepted the challenge. She assured me it would not be difficult. All I had to do was book newcomers in and tell them the manager would be home later in the day. I took my sketch pad out and drew and painted the wood shed, with the beautiful forest trees and Mount Kerkesin in the back ground. A few car loads of travellers called in to ask instructions about the local area and amazingly enough I was able to help point them in the right direction. I had a really peaceful day, exploring the nearby surrounds, playing my harmonica and meditating.

I had been promoted from cleaner to manager over night. Who would have guessed it possible?

The next day the manager took me in her car to nearby Horseshoe Lake. It was a cold quick dip in the icy blue green water, so once again I took out my sketch pad and amused myself by painting the scene of the lake with its steep sided walls with trees hanging on to the rocky terrain. After sweeping out the cabins, I got my second free night.

What a peaceful few days, breathing the crisp mountain air, absorbing the beauty of nature in the Canadian Rocky Mountains.

MIGHTY MICE INDIA

In Bodh Gaya, a sacred Buddhist site in India, where the Buddha became enlightened. I stayed at a Thai monastery. I was not the only occupant of my humble room. Mice were swarming everywhere. In the forty two degree heat I decided to sit in a plastic tub of water to cool off, as there were no showers or baths in this establishment. This tub was normally used for washing clothes, but I sat in it and dipped water over myself. Then I soaked my sarong in water, wrung it out, lay on the bed with the fan on until the sarong dried out, and then went through the whole process again. It was the only way to cope with the heat and get any sleep.

There was a bucket of water in the bathroom to flush the loo. In the middle of the night, nature called and in the dark I went to dipper the water out of the bucket and felt something moving, it was a tiny mouse swimming around in circles. I took pity on it and tipped the water and swimming mouse out into the garden.

At breakfast time we ate at tables just outside the kitchen, unfortunately I had a very good view through the door and window into the kitchen. Mice were running over everything and into bags of rice, flour etc, using the cups and saucers like big dippers in the fair ground.

I saw some kids in the street with a length of string and a mouse tied to the other end. They would let the mouse go and when it was about to take off up some ladies leg or run over her foot, they would yank the string and go into fits of laughter. Great fun for the kids... not so sure about the mouse.

I went to visit a monk at another monastery and was very kindly offered tea and biscuits. It arrived on a tray complete with mouse droppings. It was very difficult to concentrate on the conversation and not keep looking at the mouse's calling card.

Luckily my immune system has become accustomed to foreign lands and there were no ill effects.

TRAIL RIDING WHISTLER

The ranch was a short walk from the camp ground. The corral was full of saddled horses, the last ride of the day was about to leave. I was the only taker.

A part Percheron steel grey, three-year-old mare named Pepper was chosen for me. Obviously for her weight carrying capacity. She was placid, despite her overbearing size. She was so tall a mounting block was the only way to climb aboard. Luckily one was provided. Unluckily the western saddle was very foreign to my backside and comfort zone, but I managed to wriggle into position to last the one and a half hour journey up into the mountainous country, zigzagging all the way, avoiding our knees being scraped off on forest trees.

It took a while to acclimatize to the loose rein, especially as Pepper decided to trip going down a steep rocky bank. The wild flowers were scattered along the trail in gay profusion. My trail leader decided to pick some for her 'mom'. In a moment of inattention on my part, Pepper took a large chomp at the flowers in the leader's saddle bag and down the hatch they went, making a colourful and tasty afternoon tea for my trusty stead.

The trail followed cross country ski routes, we saw bikers, hikers and dog exercisers, plus a large mound of fresh bear droppings. No sign of the bear, thank the lord. Two weeks later I read in the newspaper of a mother and two children out riding in bear country, when a Grizzly attacked them. The mother protected her children by hitting their horses on the rump to gallop away, but the bear attacked and killed her.

The views from the top of the mountain were breathtaking and the experience a memorable one. Back at the corral (stables to us Aussies) there was an Australian girl working. She could not get comfortable riding boots in Canada, so had her mum send over some good old Australian Blundstones.

We found later whilst shopping in Whistler that half the population serving us were Australians. I can understand why they gravitate there, it's a skier's paradise, the most popular in Canada.

TREKKING IN NEPAL

I booked my flight in Thailand; it is much cheaper that way. My destination is Nepal, where I will be trekking in the Annapurna Mountains, among other things. On the plane I sat beside someone named Chris Cosmos, what a wonderful name. We flew above the clouds but there in its triangular splendour is the peak of Everest. What an awesome sight. The highest peak in the world and we could almost reach out and touch it. When I arrive at the airport in Kathmandu I am told the Dasain Festival is on and the banks won't open for six days. Not having any Nepalese currency for that time is going to be fun! I book into a guest house for AUD $6 a night. Can I afford it, I ask? I finally managed to change some money on the street, found a cheaper hotel, The Sugat for $1 a night, can't do much better than that.

While waiting for two hours in a queue at the Immigration Office for a Trekking permit for the Annapurnas, I get my Reeboks repaired, by an enterprising young man who knows he has captive customers. I wait another hour for a bus ticket to Pokara, where the trek will start.

After six days of acclimatizing, the Post Office is open and I can send some postcards. I go back to the office to pick up my Permit and Park ticket, leave my larger backpack at the hotel, only taking a smaller one with me. On the bus to Pokara we stopped for brake fluid, rather essential in this mountainous country. The 7-hour ride was bumpy, windy, rough and hair raising, over taking trucks and buses on blind corners was common place.

In Pokara I booked a porter named Dharma, a good omen, for $9.50 per day. I paid for his food and lodging on the trek. He will carry my bag and steer me on the right path. I have a sore throat and runny nose, not a good start for five days in the Himalayas, but I head off anyway. After one night in Pokara at the Riz Hotel for $12 a night, I walked to a café called The Garlic Garden, garlic being good for colds, I thought this one is for me, but a blackout hit the town and everything was in darkness, so I walked back to the Riz, where the owner gave me a candle. I sat in semi darkness contemplating my big adventure the next day, setting out with young Dharma to goodness knows what. He is wonderful and he was born near Dhampus, our first stop and knows the mountains well. He is very considerate of my age (55) and ability.

We start our ascent with high steep steps, heat and exhaustion setting in quite soon but the views are stunning and the locals friendly, the hot lemon drinks just what the doctor ordered. My cold inhibits my breathing and the high altitude restricts the air flow, but I press on. You know how high you are when you are looking down on the eagles. A group of Japanese descends and greets us wearing gloves and walking with poles. I had bought a wooden trekking stick from a local, to help lever my tired body up and down for the four hours of the first day.

In the guest house Dharma massages my sore leg muscles, he is good. He wants to visit his family an hour away, overnight. That's fine by me. I gave him some gifts for his many brothers and sisters and wish him a safe journey and return in the morning. I trust him to show up. True to his word, he returns, with thanks from his family. The crisp morning air is fresh and unpolluted, we stop off at Pothana for a hot lemon drink, descend through beautiful forest and on to Bichok, where I play my mouth organ for the local kids. It is a good excuse for a rest.

The Modi Khola Valley is spectacular but once again, what appear to be quite close are actually hours away because of steep sided valleys and peaks. Then it is down, down to Tolka. As Dharma massages my shoulders, I say 'I wish I had done this when I was twenty five'. He says 'But Noni then you wouldn't meet me, I am not born then I think'. He is quite right. Today was easier going but took us eight and a half hours of hard slog to get to Langdrung. At the guest house they heat water for me so I can wash my hair and body. Over dinner Dharma says to me in the nicest possible way 'It is like trekking with my mother'!

After a restless night I wake early to see the sun come up on Annapurna South. I look out on to the picturesque valley with tiered plots of rice going to what appears to be inaccessible places. Just opposite is a waterfall coming down from Ghandrung. We descend to a suspension bridge where monkeys are frolicking. The bridge has lost a few planks that have been replaced with flat slate slabs, which is bit dodgy, but we make it to the other side. There is no turning back. We start the ascent, my leg muscles are 'jellified' from the descent, now I am asking them to go in the opposite direction.

We take a rest lying under a shady tree as it is warm as we look up at the snow capped mountains, like frosting on a cup cake, without the sprinkles. We lean on my pack and Dharma is not puffed at all. He is so at ease and comfortable to be with, forever thoughtful and non intrusive. He lets me go at my own pace, is so patient and polite and always asking if I am OK.

We arrive at Ghandrung having administered first aid to many locals. A severely cut finger, sores and blisters are healed with Tea Tree Oil and Band aids, they always come in handy. At the Trekkers

Inn there is a western style loo, which actually works and a tiled bathroom, such luxury. The bed is comfortable but sleep eludes me, must be the high altitude. Electricity here is water powered. The next day is all downhill, mostly steep with uneven loose rocks, very hard on the ankles, supportive hiking boots are a must. At one bridge a landslide has wiped it out, so we cross the slippery, rocky, icy stream and clamber up the other side. Built over the water is a water driven corn grinder, the hot chocolate that we drink is made from buffalo milk, many donkeys pass by carrying supplies up to Ghandrung. At a waterfall at Birethanti I soaked my feet, ah, that feels better. At one stage I thought I wasn't going to make it but Dharma's encouraging words kept me focused on the path ahead. The trek was extremely challenging and required a moderate level of fitness but the elation on succeeding was all worth it. I gave Dharma my trekking stick, so he can sell it to the next middle aged lady who comes along.

Dharma carrying my backpack in Nepal

ATTITUDE AND DREAMS

Enthusiasm is at the bottom of all progress. With it, there is accomplishment. Without it there are only alibis. *Henry Ford*

Your attitude will see you achieving your dreams. *Noni Gove*

- Make a wish list or collage of places and countries you want to go. Pick out the main priorities; be as adventurous as you can. Dreams do come true.
- It is important while travelling, particularly in Asia that your hosts do not lose face. Respect local customs; you are a guest in their country.
- Be positive and look for the good in all situations.
- Don't allow others to dampen your ideas and plans.
- Keep calm in stressful situations by focusing on your breathing, take a few deep breaths.
- Give yourself time to think and act in an appropriate way.
- Let go of angry thoughts until your mind is calm.
- Become a good listener.
- Never miss an opportunity to take the road less travelled.
- Think of a win win solution in tricky situations.
- Become less judgmental of yourself and others.
- Don't put unreasonable demands on yourself.

- Replace "should" with "could".
- Replace "hate" with "I really don't like".
- Start being creative. Do something you would not dream of.
- Learn tolerance, patience, flexibility, acceptance and trust.
- Replace thoughts of "never" and "no way" with "could be" and "maybe".
- Become more spontaneous.
- Start with small changes and take it a step at a time.
- Take yourself out of your comfort zone. (More on this later)
- Practice saying hello to strangers. Ask them about their travel experiences.
- If a negative thought comes into your mind, replace it with a positive one.
- Writing down what you are angry about, will help dissipate the anger.
- When you wake up in the morning, write down how you want your day to be.
- At night write a list of all the things you are grateful for in your day. You will find the days flow more freely.
- Show compassion in Third World or poorer countries, but don't take their problems on board. Try as you might, unfortunately, you can't save the world.
- Volunteer in an orphanage, or soup kitchen.
- Don't be afraid to say "I'm sorry. Please forgive me".

TROJAN HORSES DALI CHINA

In a cafe, we saw the sign Horse Riding.

I insisted that we see the horses and gear first. They were like Trojan horses and lived up to their image. Manes and forelocks where hogged, their sturdy bodies and legs made for mountains. They were lightly shod, that is, very thin shoes. The bridles, stirrup leathers and girths were made of green hide, there was no bit for the horse's mouth and the reins were made of rope. One red and one grey, there were a few knots where old breakage's had been repaired. The saddles were wooden framed with colourful blankets of red, green, yellow and orange for padding. Not enough, in our case. There was a steel bar on the pommel and at the back of the saddle which was its one redeeming feature as we found out on the steep climb and perilous descent. I was pleased to see a breast plate of webbing and a crupper of chain, covered with plastic hose to go under the horses' tail, to stop the whole thing sliding backwards or forwards. The stirrup 'leathers' were one size fits all, way too short for us but the buckles were embedded in the green hide and the holes a foot apart, so we decided not to alter the status quo.

We set off from Dali with our guide, an old man, part mountain goat, I think, who ran behind us with a lash on the end of a stick for a whip and every time the horses looked like slowing down he wheeled his whip and said "Cha Cha", they positively sprang into action. We took a cobbled stone track out of town up a lane way until we found ourselves behind a very slow moving truck loaded high with bags of tea spilling over the edges and tied with fine rope. It swayed precariously and at one stage hit some over head low hanging power lines above us. We decided to overtake it; it was one of those trucks that have an exposed motor that looks like it runs on two fan belts. After a few Cha Chas we managed to pass it on a steep incline.

We took to a forested area on a dirt path through a cemetery with hundreds of graves. Plain and simple ones made of rocks from the mountain, for the poor, up to elaborate marble headstones with domed arches for the wealthy, all above ground.

It was tough going on the horses and even tougher on our guide, who had no English but smiled a toothy grin. We twisted and climbed over loose rocks, tree roots and slippery dried pine needles until after an hour or so we came to a flat paved walkway, clinging to the mountain like resin to a tree. It had a railing which made us feel a bit safer. We dismounted and tied the horses to trees. Then we walked for 3kms to see the Seven Dragon Waterfall. It was a welcome rest for our backsides and I am sure the horses were pretty happy too. We climbed some steps to see the waterfall but there was not much water about. What there was was glistening in the sun over the smooth rocks. The view of Erhai Lake at Dali with the mountains in the background was spectacular. We could see the eagles soaring below us; we were up at 3000m on Jade Green Mountain, a series of 19 snow capped peaks.

The ride back was a test of faith in our Trojans; we let them have their heads and trusted their excellent judgement. They were wise, intelligent beings and you could see them thinking and looking at which was the safest path. We branched off on the way down and crossed a ravine with loose boulders and rocks laid loosely on top of each other to get through to flatter, lighter country. We saw rhododendrons, azaleas, birch, eucalypts and pines on our journey, many others we could not identify. Our five hour ride and walk had cost us $8 each. We were pleased to see our trusty horses being given some fodder after we dismounted. They richly deserved it. We gave our guide a small gift and he grinned from ear to ear.

Noni and her friend Sue riding mountain ponies at Green Mountain, Dali China

SACRED STUBBORN BOVINE INDIA

The World Health Fair is held in open grounds just out of Dharamsala in Northern India. Numerous tents are set up for the day with games of chance, health checks and the like.

My blood pressure was fine then I had a Tibetan pulse diagnosis, had my tongue checked and my face looked at for a face reading. I ended up with some Tibetan Herbal Medicine for a couple of weeks. It cost me $1.50 and that included the consultation. You can't get much cheaper than that.

I had a go at the hoopla with no success, but when it came to bursting balloons with a BB rifle I was like Annie Oakley with her gun. I scored ten out of ten. The crowd all clapped, I was the only foreigner there and the only female to take up a rifle. To prove it was not a fluke, I did it again, bulls eye.

After that a large stray cow found its way into the area and would not budge. Of course in India the cow is sacred and has right of way on the roads and footpaths. It was causing a traffic jam and no one was doing anything about it, so I took it by the horns and pointed it in the outwards direction, slapped it on the rump and after eyeing me with a disdainful look it decided I meant business and took off. By this time I had caused quite a spectacle and had become the hero of the day. I was hoping I had not offended the bovine gods in any way.

By the way the herbs worked well, they gave me enough energy to carry on backpacking to Varanasi where I found a room right on the Ganges beside the second largest burning ghat. My view was of the bodies being cremated, well those that could afford the timber, those that couldn't just get thrown in the sacred river, as I saw on an early morning boat ride with a young man who allowed me to have a go at rowing the small boat.

I decided to have a massage. Asok came highly recommended and he took to my back with what I can only describe as a rolling pin. Up and down my spine he went. He did the soles of my feet with a wire brush I drew the line at that.

WILD LIFE IN CANADA

It is so wonderful to wake up to the sound of loons on the lake. Reminds me of that marvellous movie On Golden Ponds with Henry Fonda and Kathryn Hepburn. Last night on our way home from a delicious meal at Sudbury's first Thai restaurant, we saw two foxes romping in a paddock. I have heard a woodpecker busy drilling away making a hole in a tree. I saw a dear little robin pulling worms out of the garden. The hummingbirds are amazing the way they hover with their little wings going twenty to the dozen. We saw dragon flies landing on the water in the lake with their iridescent wings glowing with rainbow colours when caught in the sun.

The only porcupines I have seen are dead on the side of the road. They are just not quick enough for the cars. Some years ago on one of my visits I witnessed my daughter in law Coline's parents dog Abbey being 'quilled' by a porcupine. Not a pretty sight and very painful too. Abbey had been hunting the poor thing and in self defence it had released its quills into the dog's muzzle, face, lips, just everywhere. Coline had the job of extracting them with pliers as they get well and truly embedded in the poor dog. First the points must be cut off, to release the poison; it is a three 'man' task. Coline's father holds the agitated and squirming Abbey and I collect the quills, twenty four in all!! It is an expensive exercise if the vet has to do it.

There is a plague of caterpillars at the moment; you see them squished on the road. Lots survive though and turn into white moths that eat everything in sight, and then of course it is the tail end of the 'bug season'. You won't read about this in the travel magazines. Not just mosquitoes and flies but large horse or deer flies, we would call March flies. They have a penetrating bite and the itch lasts for days, they drive the horses mad.

Will, my son, took us on a tour of Long Lake a nearby heavily populated area with magnificent homes on the water front, complete with float planes, every manner of water vessel and snow mobiles for the winter. There are many Finnish families settled here and of course they all have saunas and in winter, go out and roll in the snow and beat themselves up with birch leaves. Very healthy... if you survive it.

Molly and Olivia, my granddaughters, catch butterflies, frogs and turtles and Tilly their dog caught a dear little field mouse. After it got over the initial shock of being in a dog's jaws it came good and was let go in the bush. Will is building the girls a tree house in the birch trees near the house. They will have some fun in there. Many people are out picking wild blueberries and selling them by the road. They are only small but delicious. There are also wild strawberries, no wonder the bears are doing so well.

The family had a pet goat named Golly, it was living in a shed that Will had bought for its home. One morning there was much sadness as Golly was found dead outside her shed. A cougar had killed her.

Coline had shot an ailing bear that was marauding round the house. Unfortunately it was only injured and went up a tree. A neighbour came over with a larger gun and killed it. Coline dug a hole and buried it but the wolves dug it up. The joys of living in the wilderness!

Moose can play havoc if they come in contact with a vehicle on the road, sometimes causing deaths.

The guide on the boat on Lake Maligne, out of Jasper, was full of interesting information. It was the dangers in Canada that I found most attracted the attention of the passengers. He told us that the Elk are the most vicious animals and they have been removed from the parks and streets of the outer areas of Jasper, because they were becoming a nuisance. 'You can end up on their horns being thrown through the air like a rag doll', he said. I had visions of a new sport, instead of Bull Fighting, how about Elk Fighting.

Then there are the bears. If you meet a Grizzly you roll up in a ball and play dead. They may scratch some dirt over you and leave. They don't like fresh meat, but they will come back in two days when you have matured, at which time you had better hot foot it out of there.

On the other hand, if you come face to face with a Black Bear, flap your arms, scream, and wave your jacket above your head, to make you look taller and more formidable. The trick is to know which bear is which in the heat of the moment that could be a problem. The Grizzly has a hump on his upper back and is browner, but if he is standing up looking at you, would you notice?

Now by far the most dangerous is the smallest one of all. Who would have guessed that the squirrel puts more people into hospital than any other animal? If you feed it and get bitten, two days later you can find yourself in a strange hospital bed, rather than one in your comfortable hotel. You could end up with Hepatitis B or C or Bubonic Plague. Not a happy end to your holiday.

The moral of the story is, don't feed the squirrels, and hike with your best glasses on so that you can see the colour and or hump of the bear that has become too friendly.

HELLO DOGS THAILAND

Normally dogs are very friendly towards me, not on this occasion though. Mr. Aggressive came at me as a moving target and scored a bull's eye.

The year when I was teaching English in a temple school in Thailand, I walked every morning on the beach before the school day started. On the way to the beach I passed some exclusive holiday bungalows.

The caretakers had three dogs. Two were very friendly and fluffy, with bells around their necks. Their companion however was younger and more aggressive. I christened the two older ones "Hello Dogs", because they came out to greet me each morning and enjoyed a pat and the attention

In the first week I hired a bicycle and one afternoon was riding by the bungalows, when out came Mr. Aggressive and made a dash for my leg. I just felt his snout on my calf. It was a near miss. I rode past on numerous occasions with no further problems.

The following year I hired the same bike and was riding by the bungalows again and Mr. Aggressive came out to greet me...I thought... instead of which, he came to EAT me!. He lunged at my leg and this time took a large chunk out of my calf, near the knee. Ripped my new pants and left four or five deep bleeding furrows.

The caretakers came rushing out and applied ointment and apologies. Scolded the dog and sent him packing. I rode on to the Youth Hostel, where I was staying and received more attention from the owners there.

Next day I was due to leave early for Koh Samet Island. The hostel owners kindly took me to the pier on the back of a motor bike, to save me numerous modes of transport which was the only other option.

The next day while lying on the beach, a dog snarled at me. Was I giving off some terrible odour that was offensive to dogs? This had never happened to me before in all the years I had been coming to Thailand.

A few days later I walked along the beach to a tranquil spot where I normally meditate just on dusk. After the meditation I got up to walk back to my bungalow, when a pack of dogs came at me, bearing their teeth and growling! I quickly picked up a stick, which was a rather short one and made threatening signs of attack towards them. At the same time yelling at them to get lost, get out and go away. One brave black dog snapped at the stick, we had a tug-o'-war. At this stage a Thai boy came to my rescue and chased them away. Wow! The adrenalin was pumping through my body, like you wouldn't believe.

I just couldn't figure out how this could happen, as I love dogs and up till now had never feared them. Two weeks later, I went to the same spot to meditate and when I opened my eyes, there was the vicious black dog, lying passively at my feet. I felt he was asking for my forgiveness. I had a talk with him, he looked into my eyes and we both knew all was forgiven.

HAWAIIAN FISH TAIL USA

Fish *tail* with a difference.

On my early morning swim, whilst walking in the water, I spied what I thought was a leaf floating around in front of me. On closer inspection I realised it was a small green, yellow and black striped fish, about four inches long. It swam in and out my legs as I walked and when I went into sunlit areas of the water it sheltered in my shadow. It was spooky. This kept up for several laps of the calm water at Waikiki Beach. I showed other swimmers who were just as in awe as I was. One man said to me this is the sort of thing that only happens once in a lifetime, right?

When I came to a school of larger fish my little friend stayed closer, brushing its tail against my leg. The other fish did not want to part and let us through, I practically had to shoo them away. The next school of fish we encountered were shaped like silver pencils; they too hung about and were in no hurry to leave. We enjoyed our walk and I think by now my little fish friend thought I was its mother! I felt a responsibility to it. I kept walking much longer than I intended with my 'personal trainer'. Finally without so much as a 'goodbye' it disappeared.

FAMILY TRAVEL

My eldest sister and I went to Vanuatu many years ago with a friend and stayed at a very nice resort called La Lagon. One day we rented a car and drove round the island. In negotiating the rental deal I asked the agent for a rental car. He kept saying 'I will give you a pony' I said 'no, I don't want a pony to ride round the island, I want a car' same answer 'I will give you a pony'. This went on for quite some time before he took my hand led me out of his office and into the street. There he pointed to a car called a Pony. We both had a good laugh.

I went back to Vanuatu with my daughter, Bindi and her godmother years later. We had a holiday with a difference. Cyclone Uma struck and blew for ten hours. We were without power, running water or transport for several days. There was a foot of water in the unit and the only way we could flush the toilet was to get a bucket of water from the swimming pool. The roof blew off the bathroom, but we were far better off than a lot of local people who lost their homes and their lives.

My husband and I plus our two kids Will and Bindi went on a cruise of the Pacific islands when the kids where in their teens, they were well catered for. Will even won the Talent Quest and got a standing ovation for his act of making rude noises under his arm pit to the tune of Tea for Two Cha Cha. It was a great holiday.

In 1990 I went with the kids and a friend of my sons to Bali. We rented an open 4WD Suzuki and we hooned around the island, we swam and rented motorbikes. I had an encounter with a coral wall on the motorbike and ended up with a few stitches in my arm but even so we had a wonderful time.

Bindi joined me in Thailand for a holiday which was excellent. I really enjoyed taking her to all my favourite places in my favourite country outside Australia. We walked in to Myanmar over the border from Thailand at Three Pagoda Pass and we were entertained in a monastery with refreshments and cigars. Something different.

In 1996 I spent three months living with my kids in Montreal; we explored New York, Quebec, Ottawa, Niagara Falls and Sudbury. We had a couple of marvellous nights, one at Rudi's Pub in New York and one at Solid Gold in Sudbury, a night club were my son had a close call with a Siberian Tiger and there was also a twenty foot python on stage. My kids keep me young.

My Get Up and Go Award as Australia's Most Adventurous Senior was a trip to Vietnam, which I shared with Bindi. We really got on well and had many laughs. Sitting in a small boat on a muddy canal off the Mekong River is an experience not to be missed. A young girl is perched on the bow with a paddle and propels us along the palm-covered waterway with ease. Best to wear flat comfortable walking shoes or sandals that don't mind a bit of moisture.

We tried the local grilled eel on an island in the Mekong. It came with its head intact and had to be eaten with chopsticks. A really tricky performance. The Elephant Ear fish came sitting up between four wooden sticks, as if it was swimming.

The climate in Ho Chi Minh in February is warm to hot and humid, with the odd tropical down pour. In Hanoi in the north it is cooler and tends to be overcast with some misty rain. An umbrella is handy or a light jacket. Plastic raincoats tend to act like a sauna.

Bindi and I stayed in a great hotel with a swimming pool in the smallish town of Hoi An in Vietnam, we found our way round easily. We even walked five km to the beach and had a ginger tea at a cafe called Karma Waters. It was very peaceful sitting in a serene setting by the river. We photographed each other feeding a water buffalo by the road, and then hired a motorbike. I trusted Bind with my life on the back of it and we had a safe landing back at our hotel. She was very good and remembered to keep on the 'wrong' side of the road.

The hour's flight to Hanoi was great and we booked into the Fortuan Hotel for US$12 for the room with free internet and free breakfast. The room was clean, hot water plentiful and the bath was like a tub with a seat in it. Quite fascinating. The only other one I have encountered like it was on a Greek Island. We had pay TV, a phone and a fridge. For Bind's birthday I gave her a night out in Vietnam. We went by cyclo* to Brothers, a superb restaurant set in the courtyard of an old temple. The ambiance, food and service were exceptional. The red wine came from Chili and went down very nicely. It was a birthday to remember.

We took a day tour to Halong Bay, a three hour drive from Hanoi, then a four hour boat ride round the amazing stone cliffs, jutting straight out of the water. We went in a small boat in through a hole in one of the rocks to reveal a circular lagoon. Then we got off the boat to walk through two caves. They were majestic, huge caverns, but all dry, virtually no growth in the stalactites and stalagmites.

With Bindi and a friend of hers we travelled from San Francisco to Portland in USA, in a rented car, then a bus to Seattle a ferry to Vancouver and Vancouver Island. We rented another car and drove to Whistler, camping out when we could. We drove down through the Canadian Rockies from Jasper to Lake Louise, Banff and on to Calgary to the Stampede. What a blast that was. We also enjoyed

Head Smashed in Buffalo Jump. An interesting museum is set in the side of the hill where the Canadian natives would herd the buffalo to the edge of the cliff and force them to leap over. One man decided to stand under the ledge to see them fall over. He got his head smashed in, hence the name. They slaughtered the buffalo and dried it for their meat supply for many months.

Bindi and I also spent time in a Thai Buddhist Monastery in Escondido, California where she stayed on and drove the monks around and helped them on the computer.

Travelling with my family for me is great, we laugh, we cry, we reminisce, and we do things together or go off in different directions. It is a great time for bonding with adult children. I am truly blessed.

* The Vietnamese version of a rickshaw, with the driver pedalling from behind.

Travelling With Disabilities

Set small and gentle goals and meet them.
Julia Cameron

Before travelling to Asia or Third World countries or even to the UK or Europe find information on the state of the streets and footpaths. Some can be dangerous even for able bodied travellers. Remember cobblestones are not easy to walk on and even more difficult to push a wheelchair on. Having said that, I have seen young men in wheelchairs travelling around the world on their own and managing quite well. I admire them tremendously. Wheel chair athletes and others with disabilities travel the world to competitions.

- When booking accommodation be sure to let them know your needs.
- Most major airports provide a wheelchair for those who can't walk long distances to and from the plane.
- Walking with a stick, even if it is not totally necessary can keep you balanced and stable. It also alerts other people that you may be a bit wobbly.
- Major hotels and motels have wheelchair access and rooms for the disabled.

- Many restaurants have wheelchair access to the washrooms in developed countries.
- Some restaurants have tables and chairs so tightly packed in that it makes it difficult to manoeuvre wheelchairs or use a walking stick.
- Battery operated wheelchairs are not good on cobblestones if they are set too low.
- Hiring a car and driver is a good option for being independent.
- Some countries have rental cars with hand controls.
- If you are on medication be sure to take a doctors letter for verification.
- Take copies of any prescription medicines.
- In some countries the national parks have boardwalks and accessible interactive centres.
- Via Rail in Canada has wheelchair access on their trains but you must book ahead well in advance. Most bus lines in Northern America and Canada have wheelchair access.
- Europe has some train and bus lines with disabled facilities.
- New modern buildings in Europe are more likely to have disabled access than the older ones.
- Some countries have wheelchair cabs.
- Unfortunately the Greek Islands are not conducive to wheelchairs.
- Check out your destinations on the internet for disabled facilities.

T-SHIRT SELLER'S
HOME INDONESIA

I met Supiandi on the island of Gili Air in Indonesia. He was selling t-shirts. I ended up buying twelve. I was on a three week holiday, having spent time in Bali, then Lombok when I heard about the beautiful Gili Air, with no motorized vehicles great snorkelling and white sandy beaches.

I thought *this is for me.* I swam, snorkelled and walked each day. It took two hours to walk around the island. I sat each morning on the beach doing my meditation. Supiandi (Andi) would sit patiently on the grass behind me and when I was finished would join me for a chat. We sat and talked for hours, I found he had a wife and son in a village on Lombok the closest island. He supported them by selling t-shirts and souvenirs from his bicycle.

I decided after a week to visit the island of Lombok. 'Andi' was going home for a visit to his family at the same time. He offered to carry my backpack to the boat; he was so small that the backpack enveloped him. He invited me to visit his family. I jumped at the idea. On Lombok we got a horse and cart (the local transport) and visited a Buddhist temple, then a bemo (local taxi) to his village. His extended family of mother, sisters, brothers, nieces and nephews all live in a small cottage. They have no furniture, so they put a cane mat on the floor for me to sit on. I met Sabidi, Andi's wife and Lutfi his gorgeous eight month old son. I went through my backpack and handed out anything I thought would be useful for the now growing crowd of relations and neighbours. Reluctantly Andi took me to the local market, so I could buy some food for the family and toys for Lutfi. We took a big basket which I got him to fill up. He kept saying 'enough' and I kept saying 'more'.

When we got back to his home, word had spread about the fairy godmother from Australia. The room was bulging at the seams I shared out the goodies, Lutfi loved his new aeroplane. I sat with this beautiful family and friends. They brought out some bananas for me, I find the poorer the family the more pleasure it gives them to share what they have. I had to get on my way; Andi came out to put me in a bemo for my next destination. He held my hand, he cried, I cried. No one in the bemo said a word. All was silent. My tears of joy and sadness at leaving were acknowledged.

I wrote to Andi for a couple of years and sent presents for Lutfi… but then the correspondence dwindled off.

All this happened ten years ago. This Christmas I went back to Indonesia and thought I would surprise the family by just appearing. As I walked up to the house, someone called out my name. Who got the biggest surprise?

Andi was working in Malaysia and had been for eighteen months, sending money home to his family. Subidi was so full of joy to see me that I thought she would have a seizure.

Eleven-year-old Lutfi was brought out of school, as was Umi his eight-year-old sister. She took my hand and kissed it, the gesture was so sweet; it nearly brought me to tears. I had come prepared with gifts from Australia. At first the children were reluctant to play with the toys, but after a short time they started to enjoy them. Subidi brought out some warm milk and bananas. Once again the room was filled with relations and neighbours. Mothers breast feeding babies, people hanging out windows and others trying to get in for a look at this friend from Australia.

I took lots of photos and got Andi's address in Malaysia to send him copies. A few weeks later I got a lovely letter from him, saying he thought I had forgotten them. I certainly haven't. They remain in a special place in my heart, I will not leave it another ten years.

Andy, the T-Shirt Seller on Gili Air Indonesia

FOREST MONASTERY MAE HONG SON

I walked the 2 kilometre, from the main road, into Wat Tam Wua forest monastery in northern Thailand. I had not been there for some years and as I strolled between the huge limestone cliffs, covered with tropical growth on either side of the now concrete road, I was in awe of the improvements that had been made. The abbot, Luang Ta, has been a friend of mine for nearly twenty years. His big genuine smile when he saw me was infectious. "Noni" he said "how good to see you come in and have a glass of water and I will get someone to show you to your kuti". A kuti is a small timber bungalow where members of the sangha (monastery community) live. Luang Ta has built many new kuti's since I was here last. The grounds are discreetly landscaped with palm trees, shade trees, shrubs, bougainvillea, frangipani and other tropical plants. There is a large productive fruit and vegetable garden. The grounds also house two large meditation halls, kitchens to cater for large groups doing vipassana meditation and numerous other buildings. A gentle stream runs through the property complete with waterfalls and a wooden bridge. On the other side is a charming lake with shady huts, overlooking the water, to sit and reflect in. A short walk up the steep steps brings you to a large cave. There are now life size statues of two horses pulling a chariot complete with two charioteers, people, dogs and Buddhas, how they got them there is quite mind blowing.

The morning starts at 5am with meditation in your kuti. These new buildings are equipped with a bathroom complete with flush toilet and in my case hot water. A cane mat on the floor with a one inch mattress, hard pillow, light blanket and mosquito net forms the 'bed' A fan, lights and small porch with resident large frog, who posed for my camera, complete the thatched roof kuti. The geckos all say their name, over and over and I have found that if you answer back, they will keep going and outlast you.

At 7am we offer rice to the monks in the new large meditation hall. It has shiny tiles on the floor and no walls, so we can look out on the exotic tropical grounds. At one end of the hall sits the Buddha and other deities on a podium which also acts as a stage for the monks to sit on and have their main meal for the day.

7.30am: breakfast is served for the lay people, a milky rice, a selection of vegetables from the garden, pickles and chillies, eaten in silence.

8am: an hour and a half meditation of walking, standing, sitting and lying. As I have damaged my knee it is quite a challenge to sit cross legged on a hard surface, by the second day I am sitting in a chair, which Luang Ta offers. I am much happier and thank him for his kindness.

10.30am: we offer food into the monks' bowls. This has been cooked by the people who help at the monastery, all vegetarian. We will all eat before 12 noon and nothing there after for the rest of the day, lay people also take this precept. It is not that arduous in the circumstances.

1pm: again walking, standing, sitting and lying meditation for one and a half hours.

3pm: I lead the monks and lay people in Qi Gong, a form of Tai Chi. One girl from Korea is so enthused that she films me, so she can learn the routine.

4pm: a yoga class lead by a Korean teacher, there are many countries represented during my stay including USA, Mexico, France. Korea, Holland and Thailand of course.

Free time to 6pm: the gong is rung, so we walk over the bridge to the other meditation hall for Evening Chanting and meditation for another hour and a half.

8pm: meditation in your own kuti and so to bed.

The four days at Wat Tam Wua have given me much insight and calmness. I am driven by a Thai ex-army man, who is doing a retreat for two months, back to Mae Hong Son, thus avoiding the local bus. In true Thai style we take a detour to a Mud Spa, where I have a black mud face mask. One never knows what will happen next the way I travel.

Then back to the island of Koh Samet, my second home and so relaxed and happy, I may be at risk of becoming a total slob.